364.15

50

Books are to be returned on or before
the last date below.

A

MARIHUANA USERS AND DRUG SUBCULTURES

Marihuana Users and Drug Subcultures

BRUCE D. JOHNSON

A WILEY-INTERSCIENCE PUBLICATION

JOHN WILEY & SONS, New York ● London ● Sydney ● Toronto

Copyright © 1973, by John Wiley & Sons, Inc.

Library of Congress Cataloging in Publication Data

Johnson, Bruce D.   1943-
    Marihuana users and drug subcultures.

    Based on the author's thesis, Columbia University,
presented under title: Social determinants of the use
of dangerous drugs by college students.
    1. Drugs and youth—United States. 2. Marihuana.
3. Heroin. 4. Drugs—Laws and legislation—United
States. I. Title. [DNLM: 1. Cannabis. 2. Drug
and narcotic control. 3. Drug abuse. WM 276 T65m
1973]

HV5825.J62   362.2′93′0973   72-8786
ISBN 0-471-44623-8

Printed in the United States of America

10-9 8 7 6 5 4 3 2 1

Dedicated to my wife Theresa
and daughter Amanda

Preface

Any research in the field of drug use faces the snakepit of public controversy. The present book should add a new snake to the pit of public debate about marihuana and other drugs. The central theme of the book is that involvement in *drug selling*, and not the *use* of marihuana, is the basic factor leading to increased participation in subcultures of drug use. It is participation in drug subcultures, and not the use of drugs, which links marihuana use to various unconventional activities such as hard-drug use, crime, political militancy, and certain patterns of sexual behavior.

But the data demonstrate that almost all drug sellers sell marihuana and that marihuana selling emerges from marihuana use. Since marihuana users have no legal way to obtain the supplies they need, many regular users become involved in selling. Thus, marihuana selling provides the "stepping stone" to hard-drug-using friends, hard-drug use and sale, and deep involvement in the drug subculture. If there is a causal link between marihuana use and sale, and if this link is the crucial factor in hard-drug use and unconventional behavior, perhaps a fundamental change in drug control laws, including governmental distribution of marihuana, may be warranted.

But, regardless of the policy conclusions which might be drawn from the analysis presented, this book should be useful to a wide variety of readers. It contributes to understanding the epidemiology or "why" of soft- and hard-drug use. The book explores major controversies about drug use: Why do students use marihuana? Why do people sell drugs? Does marihuana use "lead to" heroin use? To crime? To delinquency? To poor school performance? Are drug laws efficiently and fairly enforced? Empirical evidence is used to test various theories. After analyzing several controversies, the subculture theory appears to provide the best understanding of the data.

Subculture theory has been utilized to explain deviance and crime, but has not been carefully applied to drug use. The first chapter of this book attempts to further clarify the concept of a "subculture," while the concluding chapter links empirical evidence about drug use to subculture theory. Hence, drug use among college students, and increasingly among high school students, appears to be somewhat similar to processes by which persons are recruited into deviant careers, but with the difference that drug use is becoming legitimated within adolescent culture and hence is not defined as "bad" by other young people.

Since this book is addressed to students, teachers, school administrators, public officials, and laymen interested in the "why" of drug use, as well as to drug researchers and sociologists, I have tried to simplify the presentation of difficult data. Although simplifying complexity is never easy, I hope that the presentation of graphs will help the reader visualize the important findings which are also summarized in the caption of each graph. For interested researchers, the detailed data is presented in Appendix A. Also included is the survey questionnaire which contains many ideas and hypotheses that have not been explored in this book.

The basic thrust of the book is to urge the liberalization of drug laws. Since one technique used by opponents of change is to cast doubt upon the moral character of the researcher, and since almost no one can be completely "value free" in analyzing a controversial topic such as drugs, a few comments about myself are in order. In general, I consider myself, and my friends consider me, to be relatively conventional in terms of life style and values. The choice of indices and topics to be analyzed probably represent my sociological conservatism.

My experience with drugs is severely limited. I have no use for, and perhaps an allergy to, tobacco. I abstained from alcohol until age 22. A doctor administered cocaine and Demerol to me while on the operating table, and provided me with a sleeping pill during recovery. I have a permanent scar incurred from striking a bedpost while passing out during a "bad trip"—on two No Doz tablets. I have never used marihuana or other illicit drugs, partly because I expected that I might be arguing for a fundamental change in drug laws, and that my use of drugs could be used as an excuse by opponents of marihuana use to ignore the validity of my findings. Despite my moral convictions against and lack of experience with drugs, the data and logic developed in the book convince me that fundamental changes in marihuana laws are needed.

This book builds upon my Ph.D. thesis which is separately published. I acknowledge with appreciation the guidance of Bernard Barber and assistance in data collection provided by Robert Falisey. When I was swamped in a morass of data, Daniel Sullivan suggested the additive model of marihuana use which is presently Chapter 4. I am indebted to critical comments provided by Erich

Goode and Denise Kandel, and the typing talents of Valarie Idlett, Karen Wallen, Bambi Gross, Ann Sullivan, Sara Nicoll and Gladys Burkhart.

The study would not have been possible without the financial help given, directly and indirectly, by Columbia University. This help included small research grants provided by the Department of Sociology, the use of an Optical Scanning Machine at Teachers College Computer Center, and the many free hours of computer time provided by the Columbia University Computer Center. In addition, the Computer Center at Psychiatric Institute and Rockland State Hospital were also utilized.

The largest debt, which can never be repaid, is to the 3500 students and friends of students who completed the questionnaire voluntarily. Furthermore, the 21 colleges and more than 100 instructors who permitted the questionnaire to be administered during regular class hours must be acknowledged.

Most importantly, the patience and cooperation of my wife Theresa was central to this book. Not only did she carefully edit the multitude of "final" drafts, but she "liberated" me from the traditional male role of supporting the family while I collected the data, wrote my thesis, and then provided moral support while I wrote the present manuscript.

Bruce D. Johnson

New York, N.Y., 1972

Foreword

Scurrying about the country giving speeches here and there on drug "abuse," serving as consultants to commissions, boards of inquiry, official agencies, and rehabilitation centers, cited by the mass media whenever some sort of proclamation is needed on the subject, is a hardy band of men and women designated and known as "drug experts." It happens that very few of them have done any actual research on the subject of drug use, and most are, in fact, remarkably ignorant of the research that has been done by others. This does not seem to distress anyone a great deal, for these are sane and reasonable men and women—which means that they say the right things to the right people—and consequently everyone is happy in the charade. Thus do we get the irony of the expert who is an illiterate.

It is possible, once in a while, to come across someone who has some idea of what is going on in this area. Even rarer still, we might encounter someone who has actually conducted a study on the subject—although such a person will rarely be officially designated as an "expert." And the rarest bird of them all is the researcher who has made an original contribution to the literature. Bruce Johnson is such a researcher, and this book is the culmination of his efforts. Like any good observer of the real world, Johnson has built on the work of his predecessors, but he has also pushed back the borders of our ignorance a bit, which is, I would think, what anyone engaged in intellectual craftsmanship (or craftswomanship) should be doing.

Three major questions have been taunting drug researchers for decades: (1) Why do young people experiment with illegal drugs in the first place? (2) What accounts for drug "escalation"—that is, the greater likelihood of marihuana smokers using more dangerous drugs? (3) Does the use of marihuana, per se, cause or potentiate "antisocial" behavior? Johnson has managed not only to answer all three questions systematically and empirically but also to weave his answers into a coherent and consistent single story line. Following the law of parsimony, he explains a lot with a little; simple sociological and subcultural factors appear to play the decisive role in the drug equation.

Psychiatrists have claimed for some time that unconventional behavior is causally linked with personality inadequacies. But what do we make of the fact that, as Johnson demonstrates, it is possible to predict—with almost 100 percent accuracy—who will turn on to the use of marihuana and who won't, using such simple social variables as gender, cigarette smoking, political persuasion, religious participation, and friendships? It seems to me that we either have to give up the notion that deviant behavior is powerfully linked to "abnormal" personalities—and, instead, begin looking at it as an outgrowth of certain life-styles of essentially "normal" communities in society—or accept the idea that marihuana use is simply no longer a form of unconventional behavior.

Interest has centered around the "causes" of marihuana use, but even more around the "effects" of marihuana. The literature is replete with studies documenting a correlation of some kind between marihuana use and various outcomes: dangerous drug use, sexual permissiveness, delinquency and crime, difficulties in school, including poor academic performance, political leftism, what have you. Some of these correlations (such as the one between marihuana use and sexual unconventionality) seem to be sustained by all researchers, while others (low grades, for instance) are more inconsistent, varying from one study to another. No matter; in any case, the basic issue can be posed plainly: Do the *effects* of marihuana significantly precipitate, potentiate, or cause certain outcomes, principally certain forms of behavior? Or do these correlations exist because of factors *external to* the effects of the drug? Does marihuana "cause" criminal and aggressive behavior? Does it "potentiate" the use of more dangerous drugs? Do users "go on" from marihuana to increasingly "antisocial" activities? Is a causal mechanism at work here? *Or is the relationship a spurious one?* Does the correlation hold up because of more basic factors related to both marihuana use and unconventional behavior? The "causal" school has had numerous and powerful adherents, and still does. And the "spurious" school, although less legion and certainly less influential, has set forth its argument in recent years. But until now, these fundamental questions have never really been answered with anything even remotely like hard empirical data. Johnson's study convincingly supports the view that the relationship between marihuana use, per se, and unconventional behavior is basically a spurious one; it is a relationship which substantially disappears when certain key factors are accounted for, or "held constant."

Johnson's central thesis is that subcultural involvement is the central causal mechanism impelling young marihuana users into forms of behavior our society has decided are deviant. Having friends who use more dangerous drugs, and buying and especially selling a variety of drugs—in other words, being involved in the criminal drug-using subculture—appear to be far more tightly related to taking part in behavior more unconventional than the use of marihuana itself. The independent contribution of marihuana is relatively insignificant, while the independent contribution of being among others who use a wide range of drugs is formidable.

Johnson's data have not only theoretical, but practical implications. If his analysis is correct, we have to ask ourselves what contributes to the coherence of the dangerous drug-using community—and what can be done to weaken it. It would be difficult to deny that law enforcement plays a significant role in maintaining drug subcultures. As Johnson cogently states, "our evidence indicts the present drug laws, and not marihuana use, as a major cause of heroin use." Could the present legal system be a mad Frankenstein scientist, tediously piecing together a monster offspring, a vigorous criminal drug-using subculture, with high rates of truly dangerous behavior, without realizing it? This pattern is a hoary one of course. Organized crime got a big boost with Prohibition. Junkies victimize their brothers and sisters—and themselves—not because of the effects of the drug, but because of our Byzantine laws. And the lions didn't seem to dim the ardor of the early Christians very much. No one would claim that because a few laws haven't worked, therefore no law can ever work. But if we don't have the courage to see the monstrous effects of the past and current legal efforts, this society is doomed to a self-imposed avalanche of suffering. Let us hope that Johnson's study will help us in formulating a more sane and less destructive drug policy for the future.

Erich Goode

Department of Sociology
State University of New York at Stony Brook

Contents

MARIHUANA USERS AND
DRUG SUBCULTURES

CHAPTER 1
Theoretical Overview

The late 1960s and early 1970s have seen an enormous and well-documented increase in the use of marihuana and hallucinogens such as lysergic acid diethylamide (LSD) among college students and in middle-class circles. Gallup surveys show that the following proportions of the college student population had ever used marihuana: in spring 1967, 5%; in spring 1969, 22%; in December 1970, 42%; and in December 1971, 51%. Similar increases in hallucinogen use occurred: in spring 1967, 1%; in spring 1969, 4%; in December 1970, 14%; and in December 1971, 18%.[1] Studies of the U.S. adult population have found that while 4% of the population had tried marihuana by Oct. 1969, 11% had tried it by March 1972.[2] Here is evidence of one of the most striking social changes to occur in America in the 1960s.

Perhaps the most noteworthy aspect of the phenomenon is that the possession and use of marihuana was completely illegal during these years. Furthermore, it occurred among a basically law-abiding white middle-class population. Thus, an increasingly large minority of the college population decided to disobey laws that had the support of more than two-thirds of the adult U.S. population.[3]

That the increasing use of drugs has been a growing concern to the American public is obvious: laws against drug users are popular and pass through Congress with minimal opposition. Gallup finds that "few proposals have been so overwhelmingly unpopular as the proposal to legalize the use of marihuana."[4] But public concern apparently extends only to drugs such as marihuana, hashish, hallucinogens, cocaine, heroin, amphetamines, barbiturates, and tranquilizers. Many psychoactive substances that are used to excess by society are not seen as part of the drug problem. Alcohol, tobacco, coffee, tea, caffeine, aspirin, and No-Doz are rarely considered drugs by the average American. True, alcohol and

1

tobacco are seen as problems in America, but only as distinct from the drug problem.[5]

Implicit in the definition of the "drug problem" are social assumptions, which are seldom recognized. In reality, certain drugs are defined as problems because certain values that society considers important are disobeyed or ignored; yet the same drugs may be beneficial when other values are referred to. Barber indicates that many psychoactive drugs have been developed and utilized in ways that seem beneficial when judged by values of health; they cure disease or restore physical or psychological health.[6] But many psychoactive substances, including amphetamines, barbiturates, tranquilizers, and aspirin, while possibly beneficial in low doses, can be quite harmful to physical and mental health when used in high dosages.[7]

Indeed, the history of drugs that have become problems demonstrates that many substances originally promoted as harmless or even beneficial, such as heroin and cocaine and more recently amphetamines and barbiturates, have come to be regarded as more harmful than beneficial.[8] Even the highly stigmatized drugs, cocaine and heroin, would probably not be particularly harmful if used only as directed by a doctor. But drugs are not always used in the way doctors direct nor by the persons to whom drugs have been prescribed. In many cases of drug consumption the line between prescribed usage and unwitting misuse is exceedingly thin; questionable, too, are the casual prescriptive practices of some doctors.[9]

Federal and state governments have not remained neutral on the issue of drug consumption. They have passed laws designed to restrict drug consumption to medical use. Although these laws are not particularly clear about what constitutes "medical" use, most prescriptions made by doctors are considered legal or medical. Almost all other kinds of drug consumption are considered abuse. The American Medical Association (AMA) states that "drug abuse [is] taking drugs without professional advice or direction."[10] A recent federal law has the term "abuse" in its title (the Comprehensive Drug Abuse Prevention and Control Act of 1970) and regulates substances according to their "potential for abuse."[11]

The concept of abuse as used by the AMA and federal law carries connotations of excessive and harmful consumption of drugs, which is not explicitly part of the definition. Thus, the isolated use of one or two amphetamines and the consumption of ten tablets per day for a year are both branded abuse if taken without a doctor's advice; yet both are "medical" if obtained with a prescription. Surely, such a polemical and value-laden term as "abuse" is too inclusive to be scientifically useful in trying to understand various degrees of drug use.

A. DEFINITION OF TERMS: NONMEDICAL AND ILLICIT

What is needed is more-neutral terminology and careful definitions. The terms
"nonmedical" and "illicit" better suggest what is "wrong" with certain kinds of
drug use. Nonmedical drug use is undesirable because both individual doctors
and the AMA classify certain kinds of drug use as wrong or not, according to
accepted medical practice.[12] The term "illicit" implies that certain kinds of drug
use are wrong because federal and state laws define certain drug-related acts as
part of our criminal law. In addition, these laws are supported by a large
majority of the nation's population,[13] so in some respects, we can say that drug
use is illicit because it is disapproved of by society. Thus, the use of the terms
"nonmedical" or "illicit" does not imply that there is anything naturally wrong
with such drug consumption. Rather, medical and political elites, with the
support of the public, have defined particular kinds of drug consumption as
undesirable or criminal.

It is important to distinguish "legal" from "illicit" drug use in order to
develop scientifically useful indicators of illicit drug use, the major focus of this
book. The following five criteria, obtained from federal drug legislation and the
opinions of important medical experts, will permit us scientifically to define
"illicit" drug use:

(1) Using substances defined as illegal by federal or state laws, including
cannabis (marihuana or hashish), heroin, cocaine, and hallucinogens.[14] While
most laws, because of constitutional restrictions,[15] do not prevent the use of
these substances, the laws against possession are clearly intended to prevent use.

(2) Using a drug, with or without a prescription, with the specific intention
of gaining euphoria, or getting "high." Jerome Jaffe, in a widely cited medical
textbook, states that "the use of medically prescribed barbiturates to induce
sleep is permissible, but the self-administration of the same amount of
barbiturate to induce euphoria in a social situation would be abuse" in the
United States.[16]

(3) Using such prescription drugs as amphetamines, barbiturates, and
tranquilizers in a manner inconsistent with medical directions (e.g., in larger
doses or more frequently than recommended by a physician).[17]

(4) Possessing an illegal or prescription drug obtained from a nonmedical or
nonpharmaceutical source.[18] Thus, drugs obtained free or purchased from
friends or drug dealers are definitely against federal law.

(5) Giving and especially selling an illegal or prescribed drug to another
layman are clearly against the law and subject the offender to severe penalties.[19]

By applying these five criteria to drug-related acts, one can classify persons as
engaging in illicit drug use, purchase, or sale according to information that
respondents voluntarily provide in questionnaires.

An important point in understanding illicit use, although not taken into consideration by the law, is the degree of involvement with various drugs. The seriousness of a user's involvement is generally held to be in direct proportion to (1) frequency of use, (2) proximity in time of most recent use, (3) the use of highly stigmatized drugs (cocaine and heroin), and (4) the number of different drugs used.[20] All of these factors are essential to differentiating between regular and less-regular use of any or all illicitly used drugs. Once information on patterns of illicit drug has been obtained, an examination of why certain persons use drugs and use them heavily is possible.

Central to this book is a demonstration that the present laws governing drug-using behavior in America have an important impact upon patterns of drug use. In particular the laws that make the possession and sale of cannabis illegal play an important role in recruiting people into and maintaining "drug subcultures." The evidence will demonstrate that involvement in these sub-cultures rather than the use of drugs should be the focus of public concern. Yet, because of present drug laws the use of drugs and subculture involvement are highly correlated, both in fact and in the public mind. Thus, drug *use* is mistakenly blamed for certain outcomes that subculture involvement and present drug laws probably cause. If drug laws governing cannabis were altered to legalize marihuana on a restricted basis, fewer people might become highly involved in drug subcultures than do so at present.

Why drug laws, especially marihuana laws, exist in their present form is controversial,[21] but it is clear that such laws have gained considerable public support since enactment in the 1930s. Thus, an attempt must be made to know more about the rationale and theories behind present drug laws.

B. THE OFFICIAL POSITION

There is a definite reason for stressing the importance of drug laws and the definitions used by medical elites in regulating various drugs. These laws and medical opinions provide some insight into the theories implicit in present drug laws.

Unfortunately, examination of the drug literature demonstrates that it is difficult to find a coherent set of concepts that provide a theoretical understanding of drug use. The clearest attempt to formulate basic concepts is found in "Drug Dependence."[22] This essay contains a series of definitions of dependence on different kinds of drugs, an unannotated review of the literature, and some allusions to psychological and social factors that may affect or be altered by drug use. Other short articles in a wide variety of journals constitute attempts at some kind of theory.[23] However, trying to connect the anecdotes, a few statistics, the growing experimental evidence, and the many assertions about what drugs do to a person's physique, psychology, and involvement in society to some kind of meaningful theory is an almost impossible task. The best summaries of such theories are by authors opposed to the present laws.[24] Nevertheless, for purposes of identification and comparison, reference will be made to authors and books as proponents of the *official position* if they arrive at conclusions that support or might be used to support the present drug laws.

Although each chapter of this book details theories held by the supporters of the official position, two of the main theoretical assumptions of this position will be noted at the outset. One is that passing laws that prohibit the possession or sale of various substances and the efficient enforcement of such laws will control or prevent persons from using or abusing drugs. There is contained faith in the ability of legislators to provide the laws and funds necessary to allow police to cope efficiently with illicit drug use. The one serious attempt to stop marihuana smuggling, Operation Intercept, was eventually called off because of the large economic and political costs. It may have caused a minor shortage of marihuana, but it appears to have had no influence upon the increasing marihuana use by college students.[25]

The second basic assumption is that the use of drugs is responsible for a large number of negative outcomes. Thus, the official position holds that the more frequent the use of marihuana or other drugs, the greater becomes the use of other dangerous drugs; the involvement in criminal, sexual, and aggressive behavior; and the inability to perform well in school. While the Bureau of Narcotics and Dangerous Drugs (BNDD) is willing to admit that social and psychological factors may influence the link between the use of marihuana and unfavorable outcomes, it maintains that such social and psychological factors cannot fully explain the association.[26] This assumption is most amenable to empirical testing. In almost every substantive chapter in this book the assumption that the use of marihuana or other drugs is a cause of bad outcomes will be tested and found deficient.

C. PARENT CULTURE AND PEER CULTURE

This book will attempt to prove empirically a sociological theory of drug use. Specifically, it is a theory of socialization into progressively more unconventional groups. It is basically directed toward understanding illicit drug use among middle-class American adolescents. However, since the data is limited to a sample of college students, the theory cannot be generalized to all adolescents in the United States.

A reading of the literature on deviant or delinquent behavior suggests that there are three theoretically important cultural or subcultural standards to which middle-class and perhaps lower-class youth may orient themselves: the parent culture, the peer culture, and drug subcultures. These concepts are related to, and overlap, each other; differences between the three cultures are not absolute. A demonstration of the theory entails statistically analyzing empirical measures of these concepts. While there may be many other subcultures in both adult and adolescent societies, these three cultures are central to an understanding of illicit drug use in America. To anticipate the basic theoretical argument, we suggest that students who are deeply committed to the parent culture are very unlikely to use drugs, while those who are committed to the drug subculture are likely to use a wide variety of drugs. Involvement in the peer culture provides a transition between the parent culture and drug subculture for many students.

The starting point in our study is the parent culture. This culture defines what middle-class American adults want children and college students to do in various spheres of life.[27] Of course, there may be many different subcultures in the adult population that have conflicting views of what youth should do.[28] Despite diversity in the adult population, it is probable that the vast majority of middle- and perhaps lower-class adults would agree with many of the following expectations. The parent culture thinks that high school and college students should try to go on to the next higher educational level; do well in school; attend classes; respect teachers, authorities, and laws; abstain from sex before marriage; avoid tobacco, alcohol, and the nonmedical use of drugs; avoid involvement in crime and violent behavior; attend religious services; and respect the property of others.[29] This abbreviated list of expectations outlines some of the types of behavior that this book will try to measure empirically.

There is continuing pressure on adolescents from parents, teachers, and other adults to conform to these standards. Although the sanctions applied to violations of these expectations differ widely, it is probable that all American youth experience considerable pressure toward conformity to adult values. It is not surprising that large proportions of the youth population do conform to these expectations.

One may refer to students who abide by such parental cultural standards as "conventional," in a relatively value-neutral sense. The term "conventional" does not mean that students have never broken a law or done something against adult wishes. Rather, conventionality is a matter of degree. Conventional students are less likely to violate adult expectations than "unconventional" students.

Unconventional students are those who frequently ignore or violate parental cultural standards: they use alcohol or cigarettes at an early age, engage in premarital sex, avoid religious services, and use drugs. The term "unconventional" is used in place of "deviant," "immoral," "delinquent," and other terms generally equated with "being bad." Similarly, the term "unconventional behavior" will here be used in precisely the same manner as Robert Merton's definition of deviance: conduct that departs significantly from norms.[30] In the present context the norms are those that the parent culture has set for the adolescent, teenager, or college student.

Yet the parent culture does not completely dominate all adolescents. Indeed, it structures the social world of the average teenager into highly age-graded institutions known as schools. Except for his parents and teachers, the average American youth has minimal contact with adults.

This segregation of youth has produced the peer culture.[31] Its essential characteristic is that an adolescent spends large amounts of time interacting with peers of his own sex, age, and grade in school. The peer culture has developed and emphasizes several crucial norms: (1) A person must be loyal to his friends and attempt to maintain his group association. (2) Social interaction with the peer group should be conducted in locations where adult social controls are relatively absent. Thus, the peer culture is found among youth who "hang out" on a street corner or a drive-in, who "drive around" with friends, who visit with each other between classes, etc. (3) Within each peer group, there exists a veiled competition for status and prestige within the group.[32]

The concepts of peer culture and peer group are closely related. A particular adolescent may belong to a group of relatively close friends, which can be considered his peer group. However, such peer groups do not exist in isolation; they are part of a wider phenomenon, the peer culture. Individuals experience the peer culture through involvement in a particular peer group.

The general norms and values prescribed by the peer culture will produce similar behavioral outcomes among widely different peer groups. Thus, persons who are highly committed to peer groups in a small town, an upper-class suburb, a black ghetto, or a working-class urban area are more likely to exhibit certain kinds of unconventional behavior (such as theft, drug use, and speeding) than other adolescents in their own community who are less, or not at all, involved in such peer groups.

An adolescent may belong to a peer group that is not strongly affected by peer cultural norms and values: a peer group that spends most of its time in a parent's home or going to school-sponsored activities may be unlikely to be involved in unconventional behaviors.[33] Such a peer group is committed to, or controlled by, parental cultural influences rather than peer cultural.

The concept of peer culture is continuous. A person can be classified as highly, somewhat, or little involved in the peer culture according to the amount of time, emotional investment, and commitment he makes to his peer group. Basic to the argument of this book is the hypothesis that students who spend a great deal of time with their peer group in relative isolation from adult controls are likely to engage in a wide variety of unconventional behaviors. In other words, the greater the peer cultural involvement, the greater the involvement in unconventional behavior.

Unconventional behavior will emerge from peer group participation because of the norm of *veiled competition*.[34] To the individual, a crucial measure of success lies in what his friends (peers) think of him. Yet, there is continued competition for prestige within each peer group. Despite a democratic ethos maintaining that the peer group has and wants no leader, the competition for prestige in the group is concealed "under a veneer of non-competitive good-fellowship and fun."[35] This competitiveness leads individuals in the group to experiment with new forms of behavior. Such "operating innovations"[36] frequently depart from what adults want adolescents to do but are an important way by which an individual can claim a higher status within the group. If a particular innovation, such as the smoking of marihuana, is done by one person in a peer group and no negative consequences such as arrest or poor health occur, the person can claim a higher status within the group. Such activities are likely to be repeated, with others in the group participating. Once patterns of activity develop, "they generate their own morality, norms, standards and rewards."[37] Patterns of action that may not have been permitted at an earlier time become tolerated, then accepted, and perhaps even demanded of those participating in the peer group.

Behavioral innovations like marihuana use almost never originate with the innovator; they are copied from role models observed in the mass media or some group outside the individual's own peer group.[38] Role models may appeal to individuals in a wide variety of different peer groups. Because peer cultural norms support innovations and defiance of adult authority, new forms of unconventional behavior are quickly copied by other peer group members and may become a common activity of the group. If this activity becomes acceptable to a wide variety of peer groups, it may be said to have become institutionalized in the peer culture. Thus, peer culture norms and values operating through many different peer groups can and do provide a mechanism by which technological innovations such as portable phonographs, transistor radios, and powerful cars are desired by youth and by which rock music and drugs become acceptable to discrete segments of the population. More important for our purposes, the peer culture provides a means by which behavioral innovations become institutionalized activity. (Chapter 3 will show how marihuana use has become one of the activities common in the peer culture.) Further, persons highly involved in the peer culture are more likely than the less involved to engage in such institutionalized activities as drag races, minor theft, parental disobedience, party-going, frequent dating, and sexual intercourse.

The peer culture also provides the basic norms and values supporting several distinctive adolescent subcultures such as those centered around gang delinquency, violence, or theft.[39] The peer culture norms and values and the recruitment of highly peer-oriented youth provide the basis for the organization of such subcultures. Detailed examination of such subcultures must here be restricted to the drug subculture.

D. DRUG SUBCULTURE

An understanding of drug use requires a narrower concept than the peer culture, but one that is related. The concept of drug subculture satisfies this requirement. This concept emerges from the intellectual development of the subculture tradition in delinquency research[40] and from those who have attempted to apply the subculture concept to drug use.[41] Although there is no clear and concise definition of a subculture, an elaboration upon Wolfgang's definition will suffice. He states that a subculture "is composed of values, conduct norms, social situations, role definitions and performances, sharing, transmission, and learning of values."[42] The term "drug subculture" will herein refer to those conduct norms, social situations, role definitions and performances, and values that govern the use of illegal drugs and the intentional nonmedical use of prescription drugs. Excluded from, although related to, this concept of a drug subculture are norms and values governing the medical use of drugs, the use of drugs for dieting and sleeping, and the consumption of cigarettes, alcohol, coffee, and tea.

The most important elements of a subculture are the values and conduct norms. Values are here understood to be shared ideas about what the subgroup believes to be true or what it wants (desires) or ought to want.[43] For example, some of the values used to justify the illicit use of drugs include the belief that drugs increase creativity and self-understanding, and makes a person more sociable or relaxed. Even though a majority of drug users may not endorse such values, those involved in drug-using groups are more likely to believe such ideas than the noninvolved.

Conduct norms are even more crucial to understanding a subculture. *Conduct norms are those expectations of behavior in a particular social situation that are attached to a status within the group.*[44] There is one conduct norm central to participation in the drug subculture: Thou shalt smoke marihuana. Data in Chapter 4 demonstrate that a person all of whose friends smoke marihuana is very unlikely to abstain from marihuana. Other, less strongly held conduct norms are that a member should share (or sell at cost) his drugs with friends and be willing to experiment with certain hard drugs. But, for present purposes, the most important conduct norm separating noninvolvement from marginal involvement in the drug subculture is the expectation that a person will use marihuana. Thus, if a person regularly uses pills but will not try marihuana, he is probably not participating in the drug subculture.

An attempt will be made to show empirically that two similar, but separate, drug subcultures exist in colleges in the New York metropolitan area, and perhaps in American society, and that they share the marihuana conduct norm as an indicator of beginning participation. However, the hard drugs that increasingly regular participants begin using after marihuana are different in each subculture. To anticipate our argument in Chapter 7, marihuana users in the white drug subculture will be turned on to hallucinogens, amphetamines, sedatives, and methedrine, while those in the black drug subculture will take up cocaine and heroin.

Until it is demonstrated empirically that these two drug subcultures exist, reference will be made to "drug subculture" in the singular. Since many of the inferences made about social processes are probably similar in each subculture, use of the singular term is justified. It should be kept clearly in mind, however, that most inferences about the drug subculture apply mainly to the white drug subculture because of the nature of the sample obtained for analysis in this study (see Chapter 2).

An individual experiences the drug subculture through participation in a specific social group. For example, if a person is, or wishes to become, a member of a group that smokes marihuana, the person will be expected to use marihuana. The status of "participant" in the group means that when the particular social situation of marihuana smoking arises, the person will be expected to abide by the group norm; his role performance is actually to use marihuana. This conduct norm does not apply when the group is not smoking marihuana. Behaving in accordance with the norm does not necessarily mean that the person agrees with all the beliefs and values of the group or subculture. Thus, the person may smoke marihuana primarily because he wants to remain an in-group participant even though he may not agree that marihuana is beneficial or that it increases sexual pleasure, creativity, relaxation, self-understanding, or sociability. However, repeated participation in this group and in marihuana smoking will increase the probability of his agreeing with such values.[45]

But a subculture is more than just the behavior of a few persons in an isolated group. The basic idea of subculture extends beyond individuals or particular social groups to a wide variety of social groups. Different groups may have very little or no contact with each other, but they may behave in a similar fashion because they abide by the same conduct norms and share similar values. Thus, groups as diverse as Hell's Angels, college sororities, Haight-Ashbury hippies, midwestern high school students, Manhattan professionals, and black street-corner youths are participants in the drug subculture when each group is involved in the activity of smoking marihuana. The only thing that such diverse groups may have in common is the marihuana conduct norm and perhaps values or beliefs about marihuana. If for some strange reason a midwestern high school student who smokes marihuana found himself with a Harlem street-corner group in which a "joint" was being passed around, the student would know what to do without being told. He could recognize the joint as a marihuana cigarette, realize that he is expected to smoke it, know how to inhale, recognize the effects, comment on quality of the drug, and espouse beliefs that would be familiar to the blacks.

The concept of drug subculture is independent of interaction within a particular group or even many different groups. The subculture refers to conduct norms, values, and customary patterns of behavior that are widespread in certain segments of society. These conduct norms and values are available to anyone or any group who wishes to abide by them. Attempts to follow these conduct norms and values will lead to similar behavior (e.g., smoking marihuana) in widely different groups in widely different locations (assuming that marihuana can be obtained). Even though the drug subculture is conceptually independent of particular persons and groups, the conduct norms and values would soon disappear if no one or no group interacted in accordance with such norms and values.

How then, does the drug subculture relate to the parent culture and peer culture? The drug subculture is both different from and dependent upon the norms and values governing the use of drugs in the other two cultures.[46] The parent culture uses prescription drugs in a semimystical belief that taking a drug will provide the solution to almost any ordinary everyday problem.[47] Drugs are used to loose weight, get to sleep, pep one up, and ease depression when the obvious solutions of reducing food intake, getting proper amounts of sleep, and relaxing are rejected by adults for various reasons.

In addition, both the parent and peer cultures stress the consumption of cigarettes and alcohol for reasons virtually indistinguishable from the values in the drug subculture governing the use of marihuana. Thus, alcohol is consumed to "feel good," "get drunk," "increase sociability," and "loosen restraints." Cigarettes help a person "relax," "enjoy life," and "gain prestige" (this is the message of cigarette ads). It is doubtful that the present drug subculture could have emerged in a culture in which certain substances were not used in a manner similar to that of alcohol and cigarettes in America.

Likewise, the drug subculture is an outgrowth of the peer culture. The drug subculture is highly dependent upon the conduct norms of the peer culture that regulate the loyalty of an individual to his peer group, stress that peer group activities be kept semisecret from adults, and permit a person to gain status in the peer group by being the first or the best at doing something that might be disapproved of by adults. Many individuals highly involved in the peer culture appear to be likely candidates for participation in the drug subculture.

Like the peer culture concept, the concept of the drug subculture is continuous; individuals may be viewed as not involved, somewhat involved, or very involved in the subculture.[48] It will be demonstrated that it is the depth of involvement in the drug subculture and not the frequency with which a person uses marihuana or drugs that is basically responsible for the undesirable outcomes attributed by the official position to use of marihuana.

This study will attempt to use the concepts of peer culture and drug subculture in both a theoretical and empirical, or statistical, sense. A good theory must be empirically testable. The criteria of testability allow the theory to be challenged by the data and thus be exposed to the risk of failure.[49] Throughout the book, operational definitions of the major theoretical concepts will be developed. As an indicator of what the official position means by marihuana use and drug use, the Frequency of Cannabis Use Index and the Multiple Drug Use Index will be employed. An indicator of peer culture participation will be the Peer Culture Index, and of drug subculture participation, the Illicit Marketing Index. Relating these various indices to each other in predicting some dependent variable will enable us to test various theories.

Developing an empirical measure of the drug subculture concept encounters two basic problems. First, students are likely to confuse what they are *expected* to do in a specific situation (the conduct norm) with general beliefs and values about what they *should* do. Thus, respondents are not likely to agree with the conduct norm that they should use marihuana when among marihuana-using friends. Students will confuse this norm with the value that no one, including close friends, can dictate what the individual will do. Yet many respondents who deny that friends have anything to do with their use of drugs are probably affected by their peer's use of marihuana. Hence, it is generally more rewarding to infer what the conduct norms might be by measuring the respondent's behavior rather than by developing questions that attempt to tap attitudes about what students think should be done in certain situations.

Second, it is virtually impossible to measure the respondent's actual drug-using behavior without violating the student's privacy and anonymity. As a result, the present study depends heavily upon the respondent's self-report of drug use. But this reported behavior, although accurate in a majority of cases, may be untruthful in some cases. A basic problem of such self-reported data is pressure toward conformity to various cultural and subcultural conduct norms. Thus, heavy drug users may be likely to underreport drug use due to parent culture pressure against drug use. But the same person may respond to conduct norms within the drug subculture by overreporting his use of drugs. In the literature on deviant behavior, both kinds of untruth have been noted. Blum, studying drug sellers, found that about half of the respondents felt that other drug dealers would brag about or exaggerate their income from drug sales;[50] unfortunately, Blum could not validate the respondent's earnings. Gold, studying delinquent behavior among juveniles, compared information given by the respondent's friends with the respondent's self-report. He found that about 17% of the respondents concealed a crime to which a friend was an eyewitness.[51] Everything considered, the underreporting of drug use by respondents in the present survey is probably more common than overreporting, especially when the subculture's suspicions of survey research is considered. Several ways of dealing with the problems of underreporting, overreporting, and sample biases are discussed thoroughly in Chapter 3.

E. PLAN OF THE BOOK

Having briefly outlined the theory this book will attempt to prove, it is necessary to impose some organization upon the following chapters, which may not seem closely connected at first reading. Chapter 2 discusses why and how a sample of 3500 college students in the New York metropolitan area was obtained. Although the sample is biased in the direction of heavy drug use, Chapter 3 shows that other drug surveys using more representative student samples obtain results parallel to the findings of the present sample. It also develops indicators of illicit drug use. The Frequency of Cannabis Use Index and the Multiple Drug Use Index are operational indicators of what the official position refers to as marihuana use and drug use. This chapter also develops the Peer Culture Index and shows that there has been a dramatic increase in the use of marihuana among those who were highly peer-oriented in high school, thus demonstrating that marihuana use has entered the peer culture.

Chapter 4 attempts to answer the question, Why do students use marihuana? It suggests that a large number of background factors are significantly related to the use of marihuana. But these background factors are highly correlated with, and increase the probability of, gaining friends who use marihuana. It is marihuana use among one's friends that primarily determines the respondent's use and regularity of marihuana use.

Chapter 5 demonstrates that the more frequent the use of marihuana, the greater the probability that the respondent will sell cannabis; no other factor strongly affects this relationship. Information on drug buying and selling yields the Illicit Marketing Index, which measures the degree of participation in drug dealing. In addition, it is suggested that this index is a more powerful indicator of participation in the drug subculture than measures of drug use.

Chapter 6 deals with several possible explanations of whether and why marihuana use leads to heroin use. Several theories held by the official position are shown to be either wrong or misleading. It is concluded that it is not marihuana use but involvement in drug selling by which students gain intimate friends using heroin and other hard drugs and hence begin themselves to use hard drugs.

Chapter 7 attempts to extend subculture theory; it sets forth the hypothesis, and provides empirical evidence, that there may be two different subcultures of drug use on college campuses in the New York metropolitan area. These subcultures appear to be structured along racial lines, as previously noted. The processes by which college students are recruited into, and become increasingly involved in, their respective subcultures are virtually identical for both races, as are the processes by which students become involved in drugs of the racially opposite subculture.

Chapter 8 demonstrates that the official position's concern about marihuana use and drug use as an important factor in explaining juvenile delinquency, crime, militancy, and sexual behavior is misleading. When drug dealing is held constant, the regularity of marihuana use appears to be an almost unimportant factor in explaining these activities, although the use of three or more hard drugs appears to have some effect upon these outcomes.

Chapter 9 shows that measures of drug use are significantly, if weakly, related to low grades and difficulties in college. However, when participation in drug dealing is held constant, the relationship is negligible.

Chapter 10 demonstrates that the police are fair, but not very efficient, in apprehending drug offenders. Police are "fair" in the sense that they stop or arrest persons who are heavy drug sellers and not simply heavy drug users.

Chapter 11 attempts to specify more clearly the concept of drug subcultures and indicate how the data provide evidence of various conduct norms and values in the subculture. In addition, it tries to bring into focus the effect of laws making marihuana possession and sale a criminal act.

The book concludes that if public officials wish to regulate drug consumption and drug subcultures effectively, there must be serious discussion of making marihuana legally available, although on a restricted basis. But before arriving at such important conclusions, the evidence must be presented. We turn first to a description of the sample selected for analysis.

REFERENCES

1. For a summary of the first three Gallup surveys, see "Latest Findings on Marijuana," *U.S. News and World Report,* Feb. 1, 1971; for the 1971 survey, "Gallup Finds a Continued Rise in the Use of Marijuana and LSD on Campuses," *New York Times,* Feb. 10, 1972.
2. Gallup Poll, "One Young Adult in Eight Has Tried Pot," Princeton, N.J.: American Institute of Public Opinion, Oct. 25, 1969. "Poll Finds Surge in Marijuana Use," *New York Times,* March 26, 1972. National Commission on Marihuana and Drug Abuse, *Marihuana: A Signal of Misunderstanding,* New York: New American Library, 1972, p. 38, indicates that 15% of those eighteen and older had tried marihuana by August 1971. We will henceforth refer to this National Commission report as the Shafer (the Commission chairman's name) Report.
3. Shafer Report, Ref. 2, p. 155. Also Gallup, "One Young Adult in Eight." Ref. 2.
4. Gallup Poll, "Public Opposed to Legalizing Marijuana," Princeton, N.J., American Institute of Public Opinion, Oct. 23, 1969.
5. Joel Fort, "Social Problems of Drug Use and Drug Policy," *International Journal of the Addictions,* 5 (June 1970), 322.
6. Bernard Barber, *Drugs and Society,* New York: Russell Sage Foundation, 1967, pp. 166-169.
7. Henry Lennard et al., *Mystification and Drug Misuse,* San Francisco: Jossey-Bass, Inc., 1971, p. 9; Nathan B. Eddy et al., "Drug Dependence: Its Significance and

Characteristics," *Bulletin of the World Health Organization,* vol. 32, 1965, pp. 724-730; and Julius Wenger and Stanley Einstein, "The Use and Misuse of Aspirin: A Contemporary Problem," *International Journal of the Addictions,* 5 (Dec. 1970), 757-775, show many dangers from excessive aspirin consumption. Monroe Lerner and David Nurco, "Drug Abuse Deaths in Baltimore, 1951-1966," *International Journal of the Addictions,* 5 (Dec. 1970), 707, show that between 1951 and 1966, 12% of all drug-related deaths were caused by narcotics, 7% by aspirin (salicylates), and 76% by barbiturates and other sedatives.

8. Charles Terry and Mildred Pellens, *The Opium Problem,* New York: Bureau of Social Hygiene, 1928, pp. 75-85. Sigmund Freud used and recommended cocaine during his early career: Lennard, Ref. 7, pp. 3-5. For analysis of the harms of amphetamines and barbiturates, especially in Scandinavia, see Nils Bejerot, *Addiction and Society,* Springfield, Ill.: Charles Thomas, 1970, pp. 28-82.

9. Lennard, Ref. 7, pp. 24-37.

10. American Medical Association (AMA) Committee on Alcoholism and Drug Dependence, Council on Mental Health, "The Crutch that Cripples: Drug Dependence" (pamphlet), Chicago: AMA, 1968, p. 2.

11. Comprehensive Drug Abuse Prevention and Control Act of 1970, Public Law 91-513, Oct. 27, 1970, signed by President Nixon on Nov. 2, 1970.

12. AMA, Ref. 10.

13. Shafer Report, Ref. 2, p. 155.

14. Comprehensive Drug Abuse Prevention and Control Act, Ref. 11, Section 202.

15. Although laws against the use of drugs still exist in some states, a Supreme Court decision, *Robinson* v. *California,* 370 U.S. 660 (1962), held that laws criminalizing the use of or addiction to narcotics are a "cruel and unusual punishment" and hence unconstitutional. Thus, laws regulating the possession and sale of drugs have become the major means of controlling drug use.

16. Jerome Jaffee, "Drug Addiction and Drug Abuse," in Louis S. Goodman and Alfred Gilman, eds., *The Pharmacological Basis of Therapeutics,* 2nd ed., New York: Macmillan, 1958, p. 285.

17. Ibid.

18. Comprehensive Drug Abuse Prevention and Control Act, Ref. 11, Section 404(a).

19. Ibid., Section 401.

20. These factors seem implicit in the concept of abuse, although they do not appear to have been carefully developed previously. Relatively similar dimensions have been utilized to measure seriousness of alcohol use: Don Cahalan, Ira H. Cisin, and Helen M. Crossley, *American Drinking Practices,* New Brunswick, N.J.: Rutgers Center of Alcohol Studies, 1969, pp. 10-17.

21. Alfred Lindesmith, *The Addict and the Law,* New York: Random House, Vintage Books, 1967, pp. 3-34, 222-242, and Howard S. Becker, *Outsiders,* New York: Free Press, 1963, pp. 129-163, suggest that our drug laws are due to the "moral enterprise" of the Bureau of Narcotics and its forerunner, the Treasury Department. However, David F. Musto, "The Marihuana Tax Act of 1937," *Archives of General Psychiatry,* 26 (Feb. 1972), 101-108, suggests the Bureau of Narcotics resisted making marihuana illegal, but grassroots support from local police and political pressure forced the regulation of marihuana. Also see, David Musto, *Narcotics and America: A Social History,* New Haven, Conn.: Yale University Press (in press).

22. Eddy et al., Ref. 7, pp. 721-733.

23. Harry J. Anslinger and William F. Tompkins, *The Traffic in Narcotics,* New York: Funk and Wagnalls, 1953, p. 22. Edward Bloomquist, "Marijuana: Social Benefit or Social Detriment," *California Medicine,* 106 (May, 1967), 352. Henry L. Giordano, "Marihuana—A Calling Card to Narcotics Addiction," *FBI Law Enforcement Bulletin,* 37 (Nov. 1968), 2-4. A recent and fair attempt to summarize findings and present basic ideas: Leo E. Hollister, "Marihuana in Man: Three Years Later," *Science,* 172 (April 2, 1971), 21-24.

24. Erich Goode, *The Marijuana Smokers,* New York: Basic Books, 1970. John Kaplan, *Marijuana: The New Prohibition,* Cleveland: World Publishing, 1970. Lester Grinspoon, *Marihuana Reconsidered,* Cambridge, Mass.: Harvard University Press, 1971. Joel Fort, *The Pleasure Seekers,* Indianapolis, Ind.: Bobbs-Merrill, 1969.

25. "Operation Impossible," *Time,* Oct. 17, 1969, p. 47, indicates that Operation Intercept was designed to force the Mexican government to start a program to control smuggling of marihuana. Also see *Life,* "Marijuana: The Law vs. 12 Million People," Oct. 31, 1969, pp. 27-31. The use of marihuana use continued upward, even in 1969; see *U.S. News and World Report,* "Latest Findings on Marijuana," Ref. 1, p. 27.

26. Eddy et al., Ref. 7, p. 729. Anslinger and Tompkins, Ref. 23. Giordano, Ref. 23.

27. Albert K. Cohen, *Delinquent Boys,* Glencoe, Ill.: Free Press, 1955, pp. 80-135, refers to middle-class values as roughly equivalent to the parent culture concept used here.

28. Milton Yinger, "Contraculture and Subculture," *American Sociological Review,* 25 (Oct. 1960), 625-635, mentions several different adult subcultures in America. Herbert J. Gans, *Levittowners,* New York: Random House, 1967, pp. 24-31, mentions three class-related subcultures to be found in a new suburb.

29. Ibid. For information about adult opposition to premarital sex, see Ira Reiss, *Social Context of Premarital Sexual Permissiveness,* New York: Holt, Rinehart, & Winston, 1967, p. 27.

30. Robert K. Merton and Robert A. Nisbet, *Contemporary Social Problems,* 2nd ed., New York: Harcourt, Brace and World, 1966, p. 805.

31. The peer culture concept used here is different from the use of the same term by Arthur L. Stinchcombe, *Rebellion in High School,* Chicago: Quadrangle Books, 1964, pp. 163-168. Our understanding of peer culture is similar to his concept of adult-orientation: p. 110. Our basic understanding of the peer culture concept is parallel to the notion of youth culture developed in two essays by Edmund W. Vaz, *Middle-Class Juvenile Delinquency,* New York: Harper and Row, 1967, pp. 131-147, 207-222.

32. Ibid., p. 211-214.

33. Stinchcombe, Ref. 31, pp. 121-122 shows that those who reject the importance of early marriage, smoking, and cars are most likely to participate in school clubs, and rank parents above friends. Vaz, Ref. 31, implies that participation in school clubs and activities increases the probability of delinquent activities but does not demonstrate so empirically.

34. Ibid., p. 214.

35. Ibid., p. 134.

36. Ibid., p. 214. Vaz borrows this concept from Robert Dublin, "Deviant Behaviour and Social Structure," *American Sociological Review,* 24 (Apr. 1959), 152.

37. Vaz, Ref. 31, p. 214.

38. Edwin Sutherland and Donald R. Cressey, *Principals of Criminology,* 8th ed.,

Philadelphia: J. B. Lippincott, 1970, pp. 75-77. This theory of differential association assumes the importance of contact with criminal role models, as does Clifford R. Shaw and Henry D. McKay, *Juvenile Delinquency and Urban Areas*, Chicago: University of Chicago Press, 1942, p. 165. The importance of mass media role models for middle-class youth, especially through rock music and political protest songs, has been discussed by Ralph J. Gleason, "Like a Rolling Stone," *American Scholar*, Fall 1967, reprinted in Glen Gaviglio and David Raye, *Society As It Is*, New York: Macmillan, 1971, pp. 115-126. See also Marvin F. Wolfgang, "The Culture of Youth," in President's Commission on Law Enforcement, *Task Force Report: Juvenile Delinquency and Youth Crime*, Washington, D.C.: Government Printing Office, 1967, p. 147.

39. Cohen, Ref. 27, pp. 24-32, discusses the delinquent subculture. Richard A. Cloward and Lloyd E. Ohlin, "Subcultural Differentiation," *Delinquency and Opportunity*, New York: Free Press, 1960, pp. 161-186, discuss three different kinds of subcultures that are likely to emerge in different urban neighborhoods. However, empirical research has been unable to locate clear examples of these three subcultures: James F. Short, Jr. and Fred L. Strodbeck, *Group Process and Gang Delinquency*, Chicago: University of Chicago Press, 1965, pp. 10-15. For an understanding of Violence, see Marvin E. Wolfgang and Franco Ferracuti, *The Subculture of Violence*, London: Travistock, 1967, pp. 95-163.

40. Cohen, Ref. 27, pp. 24-32. Cloward and Ohlin, Ref. 39, pp. 1-10. Wolfgang and Ferracuti, Ref. 39, pp. 95-163.

41. Howard S. Becker, Ref. 21; "Becoming a Marihuana User," *American Journal of Sociology*, 59 (Nov. 1953), 235-242; "Marihuana Use and Social Control," *Social Problems*, 3 (July 1955), 35-44; and "History, Culture and Subjective Experience: An Exploration of the Social Bases of Drug-Induced Experiences," *Journal of Health and Social Behavior*, 8 (Sept. 1967), 163-176. James T. Carey, *The College Drug Scene*, Englewood Cliffs, N.J.: Prentice-Hall, 1968. Harold Finestone, "Cats, Kicks and Color," in Becker, ed., *The Other Side*, New York: Free Press, 1964, pp. 281-297. Goode, Ref. 24, pp. 21-25, 183-202.

42. Wolfgang, "The Culture of Youth," Ref. 38, p. 146; see his broader discussion of a subculture in the *Subculture of Violence*, Ref. 39, pp. 99-113.

43. Ibid., p. 113.

44. Ibid., p. 101. This definition of conduct norms is more precise than the original definition by Thorsten Sellin, *Culture, Conflict and Crime*, New York: Social Science Research Council, 1938, pp. 22-32. Cloward and Ohlin, Ref. 39, p. 7, note that a group must be organized around a central activity to qualify as a delinquent subculture. We suggest that the group exerts a great deal of pressure on its members to participate in such an activity. More than anything else, the participants in the drug subculture are expected to use marihuana.

45. Wolfgang and Ferracuti, Ref. 39, p. 102.

46. Ibid., p. 100.

47. Lennard et al., Ref. 7, pp. 10-15.

48. Wolfgang and Ferracuti, Ref. 39, p. 103.

49. Travis Hirschi, *Causes of Delinquency*, Berkeley and Los Angeles: University of California Press, 1969, p. 226.

50. Richard Blum, *The Dream Sellers*, San Francisco: Jossey-Bass, 1972, p. 19.

51. Martin Gold, "Undetected Delinquent Behavior," *Journal of Research in Crime and Delinquency*, 13 (Jan. 1966), 31-34.

CHAPTER 2
Study Design and
Sample Selection

To make inferences about social relationships among people, many sociological studies utilize data obtained from a few randomly selected persons. It is also possible, however, to discern and understand social relationships by carefully selecting and analyzing data from a nonrandom sample. Lazarsfeld and Berelson imply that many conclusions obtained from limited studies of voting patterns in Sandusky, Ohio, and Elmira, New York, are true to national voting patterns.[1] They feel that inferences about voting patterns in the national population are not misleading, because relationships between dependent and independent variables (vote and class or religion) occur all over the United States. Their finding in Sandusky that Catholics are more likely to vote for Democrats and Protestants for Republicans has held up when tested by others using random samples of the U.S. population.[2] However, since the proportion voting Democratic in Sandusky and Elmira is not valid for the national population, they cannot predict who will win. The strength of their analysis rests upon the assumption that social factors associated with voting choice (or drug use, in this study) are very similar in widely different parts of the nation. If widely divergent findings emerge in two different studies, they must be empirically demonstrated and explained.

In a manner parallel to Lazarsfeld and Berelson, inferences can be made about social factors associated with college student drug use. The focus will be on the relationship between one or more independent variables and drug use. Other comparable studies will be shown to report similar relationships between variables. However, the incidence of drug use reported in this study is higher than that in the national college population. Nevertheless, the differences are not great. This study focuses upon why college students use drugs and what the consequences of use are, not on how many college students use drugs.

A. STUDY DESIGN

This book reports on the use of various drugs by students at twenty-one different colleges and universities. Most of the colleges and universities are located in the New York metropolitan area, but a few are located outside it. This highly urbanized area has a long history of drug use, although not among its college population. Since World War II, the illicit use of drugs has mainly been confined to heroin use among black and Puerto Rican populations and to some marihuana use among musicians and bohemians in the Greenwich Village area.

New York colleges were among the first affected by trends toward drug use. Samuel Pearlman noted in spring 1965 that 6% of Brooklyn College seniors had tried some drugs illicitly.[3] The drug use of these seniors was about two years ahead of that in the first national study of college students; in spring 1967, Gallup reported that 5% of the nation's college students had tried marihuana. Thus, New York students probably reflect emerging trends in drug use among college students that are likely to be followed by the rest of the country. Hence, the New York metropolitan area is an important location for a study of drug use among urbanized college students.

The institutions participating in this study will not be directly identified. In order to obtain the cooperation of an institution, the researcher promised officials at each college that their school would not be identified. In addition, assurances of anonymity were clearly stated on the cover letter attached to all questionnaires: "In the final report, there will be no identification of the classes, individual teachers, administrations, or the institutions (colleges, organizations, etc.) which take part in this study." Thus, all colleges and universities, and *even the department* from which the students were sampled, have been given pseudonyms.

The sampling design was influenced by three main considerations: (1) A need to obtain a large sample of persons exhibiting heavy drug use, a relatively rare form of behavior, to permit the empirical testing of various hypotheses that attempt to explain drug use. It was desirable to sample college classes where a high proportion of heavy drug users was apt to be found. (2) A need to protect the anonymity of the respondents. It was felt that only assurances of complete anonymity would enable heavy drug users to honestly report their heavy use. Complete anonymity would also make it impossible for police or college officials to trace respondents. (3) A need to reduce expenditures of time and money.

With meager resources a large sample of respondents had to be obtained, the data had to be coded, and then it had to be punched on cards. This restriction dictated the use of a precoded questionnaire to obtain the data and the use of mechanized card punching directly from mark-sense answer sheets. Despite restricted resources, 3500 usable questionnaires were obtained between February 4 and May 6, 1970. The data from these precoded questionnaires, recorded by the respondent on special mark-sense answer sheets, was then converted to punched cards with the aid of an Optical Scanning machine.

Pre-Judgment of sample

Since regular drug use is a reasonably rare phenonema and an increased proportion of such users in the sample was needed, the sample was taken from social contexts in which a higher than average proportion of drug users was known to exist. This was done by sampling from a department in each college that, on the basis of other studies of college drug use, was likely to have a higher than average proportion of drug users and by requesting students who had completed the questionnaire in class to ask heavy drug-using friends to complete the questionnaire and return it to the researcher. Although this sampling design should result in the overrepresentation of regular drug users, many students in a typical classroom will not be drug users. Thus, our sample was designed to increase the proportion of drug users so that important comparisons between regular and less-regular users or nonusers could be made. A random sample of college students in the New York metropolitan area should show a higher proportion of those who did not use drugs and a lower proportion of regular drug users than was the case in the present sample.

The basic instrument for measuring the use of drugs was a precoded questionnaire in which the respondent had to choose from the alternatives given. The questionnaire was similar to the Scholastic Aptitude Test (SAT), which most of the students had taken for admission to college. Each question had ten or less possible answers. The students selected the best answer(s) to the question and marked their response on a special answer sheet. (The Questionnaire and a typical completed answer sheet are provided in Appendix C.)

A precoded questionnaire has several advantages: (1) It protects the respondent's anonymity since all answer sheets look alike. (2) The questionnaire can be used several times, reducing expenses of duplication. (3) Very little recoding of vague answers is needed. (4) The expensive and time consuming task of coding and keypunching is reduced to a minimum. (5) The optical scanning device is extremely accurate (99.5%) in converting the student's answers into punched data; the random errors that ordinarily occur in the coding and keypunching process are drastically reduced.

There are also disadvantages to a precoded questionnaire: (1) Respondents have a severely limited choice of answers; the qualitative richness of open-ended questions is drastically reduced. (2) Students who do not read quickly or who have difficulty with written instructions will have difficulty reading the questionnaire and marking the appropriate response on a separate sheet. (3) Students may easily mark the wrong response or mark the wrong question. The advantages of this technique, however, are probably greater than the short-comings. The precoded questionnaire is most efficient when used to collect a large amount of comparable data in a short period of time. The researcher may proceed with data analysis more rapidly.

B. SELECTION OF THE SAMPLE

Colleges in America vary greatly in student-body composition. Different schools attract different kinds of students and, hence, have widely different rates of drug use.[4] It was therefore thought that the colleges selected should represent the range of variation that exists in institutional types. Two characteristics were used in selecting the colleges for the sample, the quality of students attending the college and the type of institutional control, private, religious, or public.

Obtaining an objective measure of the academic caliber of students in different colleges seems fairly difficult. However, most colleges in the New York area require and compile SAT scores for incoming freshmen. The average SAT scores for each college are presented in Singletary.[5] These scores permit the classification of colleges according to the quality of their incoming freshmen. This is probably a fairly reliable measure of the quality of the college as well.[6]

Singletary reports both the average verbal and average mathematical SAT scores. Although his statistics are for the freshman class of 1967, there has probably been little change in the relative positions of the colleges on mean SAT scores for incoming freshmen. The verbal SAT scores were selected as the best indicator of quality, mainly because the mathematical SAT scores are strongly affected by the sex ratio of the college. The cutting points were arbitrarily chosen, but they probably reflect differences in quality among the colleges in the sample:

Quality of College	Average Verbal SAT Score
Elite	over 630
High	585-630
Medium	531-584
Low	500-530
Lowest	below 500

The second major way in which colleges were classified was according to the type of institutional control. It is assumed that the agencies controlling colleges strongly affect the individual and social selection processes that bring students to a particular college. There are important Socio-Economic Status (SES) differences between students attending private and public secular colleges. Students at religious colleges are recruited disproportionately from their own religious denominations, and they are probably the most devout of those in that religion. Further, pretesting of the questionnaire indicated some important differences in drug use between religious groups.

Table 1 contains a list of colleges, none of which were in the sample, by quality and type of control so that the reader can obtain some idea of the kinds

Table 1. Colleges of the same quality and type of institutional control as those sampled in the present study

Quality of School; Average Verbal SAT Score	Private Nonsectarian	Public	Religious Schools (or religiously affiliated ten years ago)
Elite SAT = over 630	Amherst Harvard Sarah Lawrence Smith Yale		Brandeis
High SAT = 585-630	Boston U. Bard Tufts	SUNY-Albany Berkeley	College of New Rochelle (RC) Manhattanville (RC) Notre Dame (RC)
Medium SAT = 531-584	Briarcliff Hofstra Ithaca College	CUNY Rutgers U. Conn. SUNY-Cortland	Manhattan (RC) St. Peter's (RC) Yeshiva (Jewish) Keuka (Prot.)
Low SAT = 500-530	Conn. College C. W. Post Finch Fairleigh Dickinson	Glassboro State Newark State Southern Conn. State	Iona (RC) Houghton (Prot.) St. Joseph's (RC)
Lowest SAT = under 500	Pace Quinnipiac	N.Y.C. Comm. College: Bronx N.Y.C. Patterson State Eastern Conn. State	Bloomfield (Prot.) Nyack Missionary College (Prot.) St. Francis College (RC)

Table 2.   Pseudonym of colleges in sample, sample size, quality, control, institutional control, and % ever using cannabis

Pseudonym of College	Sample Size	% of Coll. Sampled[a]	Quality[b]	Instit. Control[c]	% Using Cannabis
Old University	60	2.2	1	PrM	83
Ivy University	252	7.7	1	PrM	61
Betty College	112	7.5	1	PrF	67
Terry College	81	4.3	1	PrF	68
Metro University	111	1.6	2	Pr	64
Urban University	274	5.5	2	Pr	58
Suburb University	139	4.3	4	Pr	37
James University	166	2.2	5	Pr	63
St. Paul University	122	2.3	2	R.C.	49
St. Luke's University	124	1.7	4	R.C.	31
Calvin University	221	18.5	2	Prot.	55
Christ College	132	5.8	4	Prot.	56
State University	37	.7	2	Pub.	68
State College	77	2.3	3	Pub.	57
High College	247	2.0	3	Pub.	44
Boro College	314	3.2	3	Pub.	45
Public College	240	2.2	3	Pub.	62
Park College	194	3.5	4	Pub.	41
Young College	92	9.2	4	Pub.	55
City Junior College	186	3.2	5	Pub.	50
Suburb Junior College	128	3.4	5	Pub.	55

[a]Approximate percent of total daytime undergraduate student population sampled.
[b]Quality of college: 1. Elite; 2. High; 3. Medium; 4. Low; 5. Lowest.
[c]Type of institutional control: PrM—Private, Male; PrF—Private, Female; Pr—Private; R.C.—Roman Catholic; Prot.—Protestant; Pub.—Public.

of colleges sampled in this study. Table 2 contains the list of colleges actually sampled, but only a pseudonym for the college is supplied. It also contains information about the quality, type of control, sample size, approximate proportion of the total daytime student population sampled, and the percentage who have ever used marihuana or hashish. It was possible to obtain between 2% and 8% of the total student population at each school, which constituted a fairly adequate sample of all schools but two (discussed in Appendix B). It is interesting to note that the colleges having the highest (Old) and lowest (St. Luke's) levels of cannabis use are both in New York City.

With the very limited resources available for the study, the decision was made to limit the sample to one major department in which many drug users might be found. The literature in the field of drug use indicates that persons majoring in the social sciences and humanities (or liberal arts) have higher rates of drug use

Pre Judge mental.

than those majoring in other fields,[7] although the evidence is not overwhelming. It was decided to randomly sample students enrolled in courses offered by one major social science department, henceforth referred to by its *pseudonym*, the *Ethics Department.* It was expected that gaining access to classes in other departments would be more difficult because they would be less willing to devote instructional time to a drug survey; this proved to be the case. Furthermore, the Ethics Department was very cooperative, the refusal rate of instructors was very low, and 75% of all Ethics instructors contacted agreed to let their class complete the questionnaire during a regular class period suggested by the researcher.

The Ethics Department provided a fairly broad spectrum of students. The introductory course in Ethics is taken by many who do not plan to major in Ethics; however, many major in other social sciences or the humanities. Since most colleges require a minimum number of social science credits for graduation, there were some students from every major. The Ethics majors did prove to have a high rate of illicit drug use, somewhat higher than majors from other social science departments and considerably higher than science, business, and education majors. Thus, the initial assumption of a high rate of drug use in the Ethics department proved to be correct. Random selection of Ethics Department classes should provide about the same kind of students in the twenty-one different colleges. It is assumed that students attending classes in the Ethics Department at college A are more like the student body of college A than they are like students in the Ethics classes of college B, where college A and B are very dissimilar.

The most efficient way to collect a large number of cases is to give the questionnaire during a regular class hour. Classroom administration has the advantage that most students present will complete the questionnaire. Only a few students (about 2%) will walk out or refuse to participate in the study. The major disadvantage is that many students (10-15%) will be absent on a particular day, with absenteeism being especially high toward the end of the semester.

After a college had been selected, the schedule of classes and room assignments for spring 1970 were obtained from the college registrar or Ethics Department secretary. All classes (and sections) listed by the Ethics Department were considered part of the sampling frame. These classes were divided into two strata: introductory classes, which can be taken without any prerequisites in the Ethics Department, and advanced classes, which usually require the student to have taken a previous course in the Ethics Department. This division was considered important because introductory classes have large numbers of students from other majors. They are therefore more representative of the student body as a whole than are advanced Ethics classes. However, a large sample of Ethics majors was desirable; pretest evidence suggested that a higher proportion of heavy drug users would be found in the advanced classes. Hence,

Testing a pre-text theory

about an equal number of introductory sections and advanced classes were sampled at each college, but more introductory students were actually obtained than advanced students (there were about three introductory students for every two advanced students sampled) because of differences in class size.

All introductory Ethics sections were numbered from 1 to N in the order that they were listed in the catalogue, where N is the number of introductory sections in the Ethics Department. Then, using a table of random numbers,[8] the first random digit equal to or less than N was the first section selected as part of the sample. Then, the next random number less than or equal to N was the next section chosen, and so on, until enough classes were sampled to provide 75-125 students attending introductory classes at the college. The same procedure was followed to select the advanced Ethics classes; 3-6 classes were usually sampled.

At the same time that the sample was being selected, the researcher made contact with the chairmen of the Ethics Department in order to obtain permission to contact instructors. Frequently the necessary permission to contact instructors was gained by a telephone call or a short personal visit to the department chairman in which the purpose and extent of the study was explained. At 50% of the colleges this contact was sufficient to gain the cooperation of the whole department. Other chairmen requested a copy of the questionnaire and/or a letter from the researcher's Ph.D. adviser before making a decision. A week or two later the chairman would either give permission to contact instructors or refer the researcher to the dean of students for his consent.

Once the consent of the chairman or dean was obtained, a form letter was sent to the instructor of each class in the sample. In this letter the researcher indicated the class he desired to sample and suggested a convenient date and time to give the questionnaire. An attached postcard allowed the instructor to indicate whether his class would cooperate or not. This was a most effective way of gaining cooperation, and little difficulty was encountered in gaining the consent of the teachers until midterm-exam time.

Once the cooperation of the department chairman and instructor had been obtained, a date and time convenient for both researcher and instructor (usually the time indicated in the letter sent to the instructor) was agreed upon. The researcher encouraged the teacher to inform the class about the study and let the students vote on whether or not they wished to participate. The instructor was requested not to inform the class of the exact date that the questionnaire was to be administered. This way the students would not feel that something had been forced on them by the instructor, since by voting they had chosen to participate in the study voluntarily.

On the date agreed upon, the researcher or an assistant attended the class, briefly explained the purpose of the study, handed out the questionnaires, answer sheets, and pencils, and told the students to begin. The students followed the written directions on the questionnaire. Since the questionnaire was complicated in some parts and very long (taking most students 40-60 minutes to complete), the researcher's presence was generally necessary to answer questions and to urge slow students to skip certain questions and complete other questions if they were obviously not going to finish in the class hour.

Two additional, nonrandom groups were included in the sampling design. First, the researcher tried to obtain the cooperation of some instructors and classes outside of the Ethics Department. It was hoped that this would give some indication of how biased the sample from the Ethics Department was. Unfortunately, considerable effort provided little cooperation from non-Ethics instructors. Second, in an attempt to obtain an even greater number of regular drug-using respondents, all students in class were requested at the end of the hour to give a copy of the questionnaire, an answer sheet, and a stamped self-addressed return-envelope to a friend who had used more than six times any of the following drugs: hallucinogens, methedrine, cocaine, or heroin. About 10% of the students in most classes took questionnaires home to friends. From such friends 165 usable questionnaires were returned to the researcher.

C. VARIATIONS IN DRUG USE BY MAJOR SAMPLING FACTORS

Graph 2.1 shows the proportion of students ever using marihuana by the major variables on which the sample was stratified. One finds that cannabis use increases with the quality of the college. But schools of the lowest quality have a fairly high rate of cannabis use. Likewise, the type of institutional control influences cannabis use, but differences are slight. Catholic colleges have a significantly lower incidence of cannabis use. The expectation that drug use among students in Ethics classes is greater than among students in non-Ethics classes and that students in advanced Ethics classes have higher levels of cannabis use than those in introductory classes is verified. But cannabis use is highest among the friends who mailed in the questionnaires. This group included a few who did not use drugs, despite directions to give the questionnaire only to regular drug-using friends. Thus, our expectations as to variation in drug use among subgroups specifically selected to be part of the sample are verified.

The sample actually obtained departs in some ways from the original sampling design but probably not enough to substantially alter any of the fundamental relationships between various independent variables and drug use. For example, 70% of all colleges that were ever part of the sampling frame participated in the study; 77% of the randomly selected Ethics classes and 97% of the students attending class on the day that the questionnaire was administered cooperated in this study. Thus, all indicators of participation in this study show that a relatively adequate sample was obtained.

Proportion Ever Using Cannabis

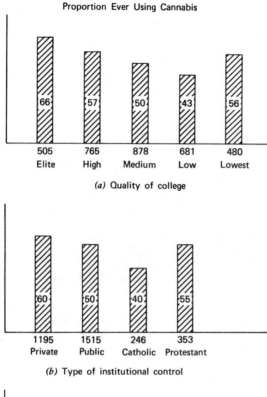

66	57	50	43	56
505	765	878	681	480
Elite	High	Medium	Low	Lowest

(a) Quality of college

60	50	40	55
1195	1515	246	353
Private	Public	Catholic	Protestant

(b) Type of institutional control

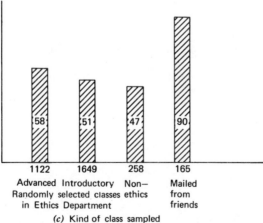

58	51	47	90
1122	1649	258	165
Advanced Randomly selected in Ethics Department	Introductory classes	Non— selected ethics	Mailed from friends

(c) Kind of class sampled

Graph 2.1. Cannabis use is associated with major sample selection variables. In (a) and (b), 165 friends of students and 23 students attending a church group are excluded. In (c), 23 cases in church group, plus 210 students attending nonrandomly selected Ethics classes are excluded.

Rather than present the technical problems of obtaining the sample in the main body of the book, the interested reader is referred to Appendix B, in which several data-collection problems, such as obtaining cooperation from colleges, classroom instructors, and students, are discussed. Difficulties that arose in obtaining cooperation from non-Ethics departments and from heavy drug-using friends are dealt with, as well as problems with mark-sense machines.

REFERENCES

1. Paul Lazarsfeld, Bernard Berelson, and Hazal Gaudet, *The People's Choice*, 3rd ed., New York: Columbia University Press, 1968. Berelson, Lazarsfeld, and William McPhee, *Voting*, Chicago: University of Chicago Press, 1954, p. 297.
2. Ibid., pp. 331-347. Angus Cambell et al., *Elections and the Political Order*, New York: John Wiley and Sons, 1966, esp. chap. 6 by Philip E. Converse, "Religion and Politics: The 1960 Election," pp. 96-124. Similar religious differences emerge in other Anglo-American countries: Robert R. Alford, *Party and Society*, Chicago: Rand-McNally, 1963.
3. Samuel Pearlman, "Drug Use and Experience in an Urban College Population," *American Journal of Orthopsychiatry*, 38 (April 1968), 503-514.
4. Richard Blum et al., *Students and Drugs*, San Francisco: Jossey-Bass, 1969, p. 41. Edwin S. Robbins et al., "College Student Drug Use," *American Journal of Psychiatry*, 126 no. 12 (1970), 1747.
5. Otis Singletary, *American Universities and Colleges*, 10th ed., Washington, D.C.: American Council on Education, 1969.
6. Paul F. Lazarsfeld and W. Thielens, Jr., *The Academic Mind*, New York: Free Press, 1958, indicate that several different measures of college quality are relatively interchangeable.
7. Blum, Ref. 4, p. 65.
8. Samuel B. Richmond, *Statistical Analysis*, 2nd ed., New York: Ronald Press, 1964, pp. 595-596.

CHAPTER 3

Marihuana Enters the Peer Culture

This chapter will do six things. First, it will present operational definitions of the concept illicit drug use, discussed in the first chapter. Second, it will describe two important measures of illicit drug use, the Frequency of Cannabis Use Index and the Multiple Drug Use Index. Third, it will examine the relationship between drug use and various standard demographic indices, such as father's income, race, sex, and church attendance. Fourth, it will show that patterns of drug use in subgroups of our student population are similar to patterns of use discovered by other drug researchers, suggesting that our findings may be generalized to the entire U.S. college population. Fifth, it will establish that there has been a major increase in the illicit use of drugs. Finally, it will be shown that this increase has been most striking among those highly involved in the peer culture.

A. OPERATIONAL DEFINITIONS OF ILLICIT DRUG USE

A respondent is considered to have used drugs illicitly if he used a substance defined by law as illegal for any citizen to possess in the United States. Drugs such as marihuana, hashish, hallucinogens, cocaine, and heroin are specifically illegal according to federal law.[1] To measure this illicit use, respondents were asked to "indicate the greatest frequency [at any time] with which you have used each of the following substances: marihuana, hashish, LSD, other hallucinogens, cocaine, and heroin." People who indicated that they had ever used one of these drugs were classified as having illicitly used that drug.

29

The problem of defining illicit drug use is more difficult, however, when considering the use of drugs that, as of 1971, are widely prescribed by doctors and pharmacists. Amphetamines, barbiturates, tranquilizers, legal opiates, and combinations of these drugs can be legally prescribed to patients for a wide variety of medical reasons.

Chapter 1 discussed four points that may help to distinguish between the medical and nonmedical use of prescription drugs: (1) using drugs for euphoric purposes, (2) using drugs in larger doses or more frequently than prescribed by the doctor, (3) buying drugs from illicit (nonmedical or nonpharmaceutical) sources, and (4) selling the drug. However, the illicit purchase or sale is not here included in the definition of the illicit use of prescription drugs.

To measure the first two dimensions of illicit prescription drug use, respondents were asked, "Which of these substances have you used with the specific intention of getting high: methedrine, other amphetamines, barbiturates, and tranquilizers?" Second, to determine whether students had obtained prescriptions for medical reasons but used them in a nonmedical manner, they were asked, "Which of these substances have you had prescribed for you by a physician or received during medical treatments?" They responded to a list of drugs that physicians may prescribe: methedrine, amphetamines, barbiturates, tranquilizers, cough medicines with codeine, darvon, morphine, opium, and paregoric. They were then asked, "Which of these substances have you had prescribed for you by a physician, but you used in larger doses or more frequently than directed?" Students who choose any substance in answering the last question were classified as having illicitly used that prescription drug. Thus, these two questions allow us to distinguish between those who have used drugs only as directed medically and those who have intentionally used these same drugs in an illicit manner.

However, it is not enough to know that a person has illicitly used drugs during his life. A person who has used every single drug only once is probably not a serious drug user but a heavy experimenter. One must also know something about the frequency of use of each drug, the recency of use, and the kind of drug used.

Measures of the frequency of use of various drugs appeared at two points in the questionnaire. People were asked to indicate the greatest frequency with which they had ever used each drug, but were told "do not include the use of medically prescribed drugs." The respondents could choose among ten possible frequencies, from never using the substance to using it more than once per day. As a further check on the frequency of use and to measure the recency dimension, students were asked, "How recently and how often did you usually use each of the following substances?" The response categories were divided into two time periods. The respondent was to indicate whether he had used a drug before June 30, 1969 and the frequency with which he had used the drug prior to that date. If he had used a drug at any time between July 1, 1969 and taking the questionnaire, he was to indicate how frequently he was currently using it. These two questions permitted a double check on the frequency of use of important drugs and also provided a measure of whether respondents had reduced their frequency of use or stopped using a drug in the seven to ten months prior to the administration of the questionnaire.

By relating the frequency and recency of use to the medical or illicit (nonmedical) use of the drug, one can classify the respondents into four different patterns for each prescription drug: (1) "never" used the drug; (2) "medical," used a legally prescribed drug only as directed by the doctor; (3) "illicit," used the drug to get high or in larger doses or more frequently than prescribed; (4) "marginal," responded positively to the questions dealing with the frequency of use, but failed to indicate medical use or illicit use of prescription drugs. This marginal use of drugs may include persons who have obtained pills from friends or parents to aid in studying for exams, in weight reduction, or in sleeping.

Table 3 presents the various patterns of drug use for major drugs in the study. Among prescription drugs, the legal opiates are the most likely to be used according to medical direction, while methedrine is almost never used for strictly medical purposes. On the other hand, of those who have ever tried sedatives or amphetamines less than 40% have confined themselves to strictly medical usage. Furthermore, about 15% of the sample has intentionally used these substances for nonmedical reasons. About an equally large proportion of the population has been marginally involved with these drugs.

Table 3. Patterns of drug use for various drugs

Drugs	Patterns of Drug Use				Total (N = 3498)
	Never Used	Medical	Marginal Use	Illicit Use	
Prescription drugs					
Legal opiates	37.0	49.0	4.0	10.0	100.0
Sedatives (barbiturates, tranquilizers)	57.0	17.1	12.4	13.6	100.1
Amphetamines	63.7	5.2	16.1	15.0	100.0
Methedrine	86.0	0.7	4.9	8.6	100.2
Illegal drugs					
Cannabis (marihuana, hashish)	44.8			55.2	100.0
Hallucinogens	80.6			19.4	100.0
Cocaine	92.6			7.4	100.0
Heroin	95.8			4.2	100.0

Since Chapters 6 and 7 will analyze why students illicitly use prescription drugs, the criteria to be used in defining the "illicit" use of these drugs must be determined. When examining the use of methedrine, amphetamines, and sedatives, one could reasonably use two different criteria to classify persons as illicitly using these drugs. The "soft" criterion would combine marginal users with those who intentionally use the drug for euphoric reasons. The "hard" criterion would exclude marginal users and include only those who use the drug for euphoric purposes. This study will employ the hard criterion. Although the data are not presented, it can be shown that persons who intentionally use these drugs for euphoric reasons are much more likely to use them on a regular (monthly or more) basis than persons using them medically. Marginal users are even less likely to be regular users of these drugs than those using them for medical reasons only.[2] Thus, to include marginal users would weaken the definition.

For similar reasons, the use of other prescription drugs will generally be ignored. The only way of determining the respondent's illicit use of cough medicine, Darvon, morphine, and Demerol is his admission of using them in larger doses or more frequently than prescribed.[3] Respondents were not asked about the use of these drugs to get high or about involvement in the illicit buying or selling of these drugs. In addition, data not presented indicate that persons who use these drugs in larger doses or more frequently than prescribed are very unlikely to become regular (monthly or more) users of these drugs, when compared to those using them as directed by a medical doctor.

In the rest of this book, then, the "illicit" use of drugs will refer to either the use of illegal drugs (marihuana, hallucinogens, cocaine, and heroin) or the intentional use of methedrine, amphetamines, and sedatives to get high or use in larger doses or more frequently than prescribed by a doctor. Frequently the term "illicit" will be dropped and "drug use" employed to mean "illicit drug use" as defined here.

B. FREQUENCY OF CANNABIS USE INDEX AND THE MULTIPLE DRUG USE INDEX

In this section two important indices will be developed. Both attempt to operationalize the central idea, promoted by the official position, that the use of marihuana or hard drugs is an important factor in explaining certain outcomes (use of other dangerous drugs, crime, political militancy, poor grades, etc.) not completely explained by social or psychological factors.[4]

The Frequency of Cannabis Use Index attempts to measure what the official position means by marihuana use. In the early part of the questionnaire, respondents were asked to indicate "the greatest *frequency* with which you have ever used: (a) marihuana and (b) hashish." In the latter part of the questionnaire, students were asked, "How *recently* and how often do (did) you usually use marihuana or hashish?" Answers to both questions permitted a double check on the respondent's truthfulness. In comparing the question about the greatest frequency of use with the question about the recency of cannabis use, the data demonstrate that about 1.5% of the total sample were "highly inconsistent."

A person was highly inconsistent if he indicated that he had used cannabis in one question but not in the other or if he indicated a much greater use in the recency question than in the frequency question. It is probable that some of the 1.5% simply marked the wrong answer in one question or the other. Indeed, an inconsistency level of 1.5% could almost happen by random marking. This is especially true when the complex nature of the response categories on the question about the recency of cannabis is considered. Hence, overt lying on the questionnaire was probably rare.

Respondents were classified on the Frequency of Cannabis Use Index as (a) "nonusers" if they marked the "never" response in all three questions; (b) "experimental users" if they indicated in all three questions that they had used marihuana or hashish less frequently than once per month; (c) "moderate users" if they were not at the time using marihuana as often as once per week but had used cannabis at some time in their life with the frequency of once a month or greater or if they had regularly (weekly) used cannabis at one point in time but had stopped or reduced their use of cannabis; and (d) "regular users" if they were then using marihuana or hashish at least once a week. Because the definitions of experimental, moderate, and regular users are easily forgotten, other terms will be used interchangeably: "less-than-monthly users" for "experimental users"; "less-than-weekly users" for "moderate users"; and "weekly-or-more users" for "regular users."

"Cannabis use" and "marihuana use" will also be interchangeable in the following pages but will refer to the Frequency of Cannabis Use Index. In the total sample, 45% of the respondents were nonusers of cannabis; 21% less than monthly users; 16%, less than weekly cannabis users; and 18%, weekly cannabis users. Only one respondent out of 3498 could not be classified, because he had failed to answer the three questions on marihuana or hashish use.

Thus, 55% of the sample had ever used cannabis, but the sample was intentionally designed to overestimate the amount of cannabis use on college campuses in the New York metropolitan area.[5] Even so, the proportion of students who reported ever using cannabis is not too different from findings reported elsewhere. Goode and McGlothlin present similar levels of cannabis use in samples of social science classes.[6] In the spring of 1968 at a California college Blum determined that 57% had used marihuana or hashish at some point in their lives, while 16% indicated regular or considerable use.[7] It must be noted that the levels of cannabis use in California and New York are probably higher than they are in the rest of the country.[8] Gallup reports that in December 1970, 44% had used marihuana and 17% were using it once per week.[9] Groves and Rossi's national college student sample conducted in the same semester as the present study (spring 1970) found that 31% had tried marihuana, while 14% used it every week or two.[10]

Despite the biased nature of the sample obtained in the present survey, the level of marihuana use compares very well with one of the best and most widely quoted surveys of drug use ever conducted. In August 1970 (four to six months after the present data were collected), the New York State Narcotics Addiction Control Commission (NACC) conducted intensive interviews with a random sample of 7500 New York State households with persons ages fourteen and older. The results of this statewide survey were reported by Carl Chambers.[11] With the permission of NACC, the present author was permitted to examine some of the tables upon which the Chambers report was based. Fortunately, unpublished tables present data about the drug use among college students in New York City, a population that is roughly similar to the present sample. The statewide study found that 50% of the New York City college students had tried cannabis and that 19.5% had used cannabis six or more times in the past thirty days. Thus, the incidence of cannabis use in New York City was only about 5% lower than the present sample. Although the definitions of "regular" use are somewhat different, it appears that both studies report comparable levels of regular cannabis use.

Even more impressively, both studies find similar sex differences in cannabis use. The NACC survey found that 57% of the males versus 36% of the females in city colleges had tried cannabis; similar figures for the present study reported in Graph 3.1 show that 63% of the males versus 48% of the females had tried cannabis. In addition, the NACC study finds that males are 12% more likely than females (24% versus 12%) to be regular users; this is almost precisely the same difference in regular use found in the present study (25% males versus 13% females). Further, roughly similar incidences of hard-drug use were obtained. The NACC survey found the following percentages of city students using hard drugs: LSD, 16%; methedrine, 11%; cocaine, 8%; and heroin, 1.2%. The present study yields hallucinogens, 19%; methedrine, 14%; cocaine, 8%; and heroin, 4%. Comparison of amphetamine and sedative use is not possible, since the NACC survey separates the use of drugs that have been combined in the present study.

The basic conclusion emerging from the comparison of the NACC survey with the present survey is that despite all the biases built into the study design, the present sample closely reflects the incidence of drug use among the college population in New York City. The author is at somewhat of a loss to explain such convergence when he expected a greater difference. Perhaps the actual incidence of cannabis use among city college students in spring 1970 (when the present data were collected) was 4-5% lower than in August 1970. (See the discussion of national college student drug use trends below, section D.) But it is more likely that college students attending classes in almost any department are relatively heterogeneous in terms of social background, life style, and drug use. But particular colleges attract certain kinds of students. If a researcher samples from a wide variety of institutional types, he will obtain a fairly good cross section of the entire student population in a given geographical area. Thus, the small differences in drug-use rates between the present survey and the NACC survey suggest that the relationships between variables and results reported in succeeding chapters are probably a good approximation of the actual behavior of New York City college students.

The other major variable, the Multiple Drug Use Index, is an attempt to measure what public officials mean by "drug use." This index is a combination of the Frequency of Cannabis Use Index and the illicit use of hard drugs (hallucinogens, methedrine, amphetamines, sedatives, cocaine, and heroin). The number of hard drugs that respondents had used illicitly was computed and related to the frequency of cannabis use.

Table 4. Number of hard drugs used by frequency of cannabis use

Frequency of Cannabis Use	Number of Hard Drugs Used							Total %	No. of Cases
	0	1	2	3	4	5	6		
None	95	4	1	.1	0	0	0	100	1567
Experimental	80	15	3	2	.1	.1	0	100	725
Moderate	50	23	12	7	3	3	2	100	559
Regular	21	21	16	14	11	10	7	100	646
Total	71	12	6	4	3	2	2	100	3497

Table 4 shows that cannabis use is strongly related to the illicit use of hard drugs (this finding is discussed at length in Chapters 6 and 7). The present chapter will use Table 4 to construct the Multiple Drug Use Index. Categories based on respondents' varying degrees of involvement with drugs were set up: (1) "nonuser" if they had not used cannabis or any hard drugs; (2) "cannabis only" if they had used marihuana or hashish but not hard drugs; (3) "hard drugs/1-2" if they had illicitly used one or two of the six hard drugs (about 90% of this category had also used cannabis); and (4) "hard drugs/3+" if they had illicitly used three or more hard drugs (all but one of the respondents in this category had used cannabis). The proportion of the total sample in each category of the Multiple Drug Use Index is as follows:

```
Nonuser . . . . . . . . . . . . . . . . . . . . . . .  43%
Cannabis only . . . . . . . . . . . . . . . . . .  28%
Hard drugs/1-2 . . . . . . . . . . . . . . . .  18%
Hard drugs/3+ . . . . . . . . . . . . . . . .  11%
        Total . . . . . . . . . . . . . . . . . . . . .100%  (N = 3497)
```

This index was originally conceptualized as a typology that would isolate "pot heads," "acid heads," and "narcotic users." However, such distinct types did not emerge. Those who were the heaviest cannabis users were most likely to use all hard drugs.

C. FACTORS RELATED TO THE FREQUENCY OF CANNABIS USE INDEX AND MULTIPLE DRUG USE INDEX

This study is most interested, of course, in why persons use drugs. Most researchers approach this question by relating (sociologists use the term "crosstabulating") many independent variables to one or two measures of drug use. Generally the independent variables are background characteristics such as sex, race, socioeconomic status, age, and religious preference. Chapter 4 will attempt to analyze further why such factors are related to drug use, by holding constant certain factors that increase our understanding of the social processes at work. The present section will restrict itself to demonstrating that (1) various background variables are related in almost the same way to the Frequency of Cannabis Use Index as they are to the Multiple Drug Use Index; and (2) that other competent random studies of drug use obtain relationships between background variables and drug use that are highly comparable to those reported here.

The graphs that follow present the relationship between each independent variable and these two indices of drug use. The number of cases may not add to the total (N = 3498) because some respondents refused or failed to indicate their sex, race, or family income and have been excluded from analysis.

Data in Graph 3.1 demonstrate that there is virtually no racial difference in the use of cannabis. Blacks are as likely as whites to try cannabis. Whites are slightly (11% versus 7%) more likely to try three or more hard drugs. To the best of our knowledge, there is no other study of a college population that has reported the relationship between race and drug use. Langrod shows that there is virtually no racial or ethnic difference in the use of marihuana among institutionalized narcotics addicts.[12] Nor do racial differences appear among high school students or the New York State population.[13]

Males are more likely than females to use marihuana and to be multiple drug users. Further, 25% of the males in our sample are weekly marihuana smokers, while only 13% of the females are. Males are also almost twice as likely as females to be multiple drug users. Similar findings are reported by Blum, Gallup,

Chambers, Goode, and Kaplan.[14] However, the national surveys of high school drug use find no significant sex differences.[15]

The data here demonstrate a positive relationship between family income and drug use. Students from the high-income families were 24% more likely to try cannabis than students from low-income families. Class-related differences are not too strongly related to the use of three or more dangerous drugs. The same conclusion obtains when father's occupation or education are related to drug use. The relationship between socioeconomic status (SES) and drug use is paralleled by results from other studies. Gallup, Blum, Goode, Chambers, and Josephson show similar increases in the use of cannabis according to the SES of the parents, although the differences are not as strong as in the present study.[16]

In Graph 3.2 is found an even more striking relationship between drug use and the frequency of religious observance.[17] Those who attend church weekly or more are much less likely to use drugs than are people who never attend church. Weekly churchgoers are 50% (77% vesus 26%) more likely to abstain from marihuana than people who never attend religous services. Further, only 4% of present weekly churchgoers, but 31% of nonattenders, are weekly cannabis users. Those who never attend church are also more likely to use multiple drugs. Only Boggs does not support this finding.[18]

There seems to be no relationship between age and drug use. Blum and Gallup indicate that freshmen may be somewhat less likely than juniors and seniors to try marihuana but do not indicate statistical significance.[19] However, there are important age differences outside of the college population. Gallup found that 12% of young adults (ages 21-29) versus 1% of those over 50 had ever used marihuana.[20] Manheimer found that 49% of the males aged 18-24 and 1% of males 55 and older had used marihuana; the corresponding levels of use for females were 32% and 0% in his San Francisco area sample.[21] In high school populations, the proportion of students ever using cannabis increases with age.[22]

It is demonstrated elsewhere that many other factors such as living arrangements, college major, and high school background are significantly related to the use of cannabis and other drugs.[23] The relationships between independent variables and drug use here are generally consistent with other surveys. For some variables, such as year in college, sex, and church attendance, one finds a strong relationship where another researcher finds a nonexistent or weak relationship. But such disagreements between drug researchers are rare.

Even though the studies to which the present one has been compared are based on different samples of college students, high school students, or adults, there is a remarkable similarity between such studies and the present study in the proportion of marihuana triers and weekly users as well as the strength of the relationships between certain standard variables and drug use. The conclusions to be drawn from this study, although not based on random-sample

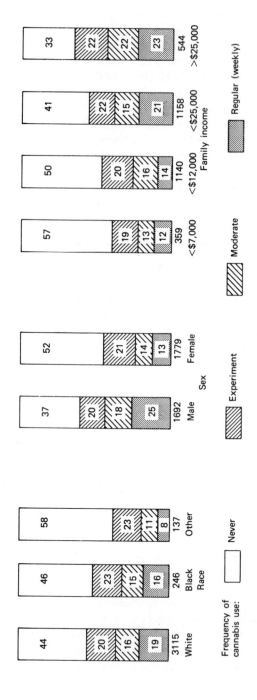

Frequency of cannabis use: ☐ Never ▨ Experiment ▨ Moderate ▨ Regular (weekly)

Race: White 44 / 20 / 16 / 19 — 3115; Black 46 / 23 / 15 / 16 — 246; Other 58 / 23 / 11 / 8 — 137

Sex: Male 37 / 20 / 18 / 25 — 1692; Female 52 / 21 / 14 / 13 — 1779

Family income: <$7,000 57 / 19 / 13 / 12 — 359; <$12,000 50 / 20 / 16 / 14 — 1140; <$25,000 41 / 22 / 15 / 21 — 1158; >$25,000 33 / 22 / 22 / 23 — 544

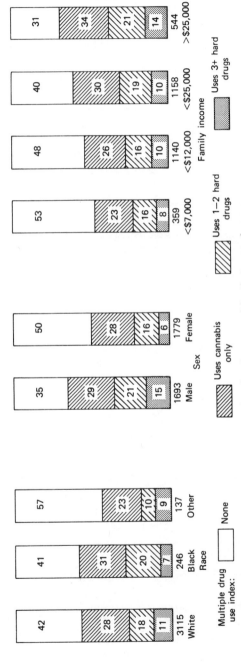

Graph 3.1. Both measures of drug use are positively related to sex and family income but not to race.

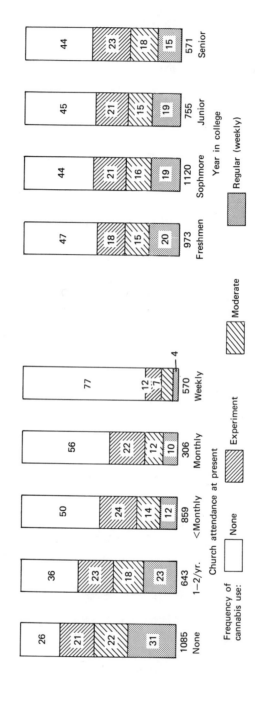

Church attendance at present

Year in college

Frequency of cannabis use:

None

Experiment

Moderate

Regular (weekly)

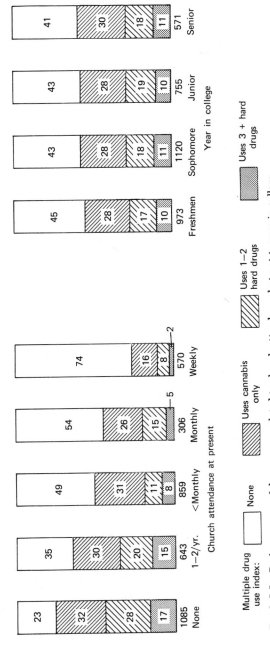

Graph 3.2. Both measures of drug use are related to church attendance but not to year in college.

data, are certainly based on data comparable to that in other well-known studies
of drug usage among college students.

D. INCREASING USE OF DRUGS AMONG HIGH SCHOOL
     AND COLLEGE STUDENTS

Drug use has increased greatly in the past five years among middle-class college
students. Blum notes about a threefold increase in the use of marihuana and
LSD during a period of less than three years.[24] Goode presents evidence
showing that since 1967, there appears to be "*a monthly increase* in the
percentage of college students who have tried marihuana of *just under one
percent.*"[25]

If there has been an increase in drug use, the data here should reflect this
increase. Although this study did not have samples at two or more different
points in time from the same population, it did record the year in college of each
student. One can, then, approximate a trend study by comparing students who
are presently at different phases in their education. This approach assumes, of
course, that about the same kinds of students are recruited each year and that
comparing class in college is like comparing similar samples.[26]

Data on the year in college and the use of cannabis are presented in the last
part of Graph 3.2. There is no significant difference in the use of marihuana or
other drugs when the four classes of students are compared. This finding was
surprising to many students, especially upperclassmen, to whom the finding was
presented. One dismayed senior remarked, "How can that be? When I started
college, no one had heard of the drugs that freshmen today use regularly."
Nevertheless, our data show no differences between freshmen, sophomores,
juniors, and seniors in cannabis use and multiple drug use. This evidence would
tend to indicate that there has been no change in drug use in the last few years.

Nothing could be further from the truth, however. There has been a great
increase in the illicit use of all forms of drugs; but to discover this change, one
must examine, not the present use of drugs, but rather levels of use at some
constant point in the past. The increase in drug use is occurring before students
get to college; to measure such a change we asked our respondents to indicate
which drugs they had used before graduation from high school.

Graph 3.3 shows a striking trend in the use of drugs. Take marihuana, for
example. Of those who were seniors in the sample (most were in the high school
class of 1966), 9% had tried cannabis, while 34% of the freshmen (high school
class of 1969) had tried cannabis before graduation from high school. For
comparison purposes, 53% of those who were college freshmen when they took
the questionnaire, about nine months after graduation from high school, had
ever tried cannabis. Thus, about 20% of the freshmen had "turned on" between

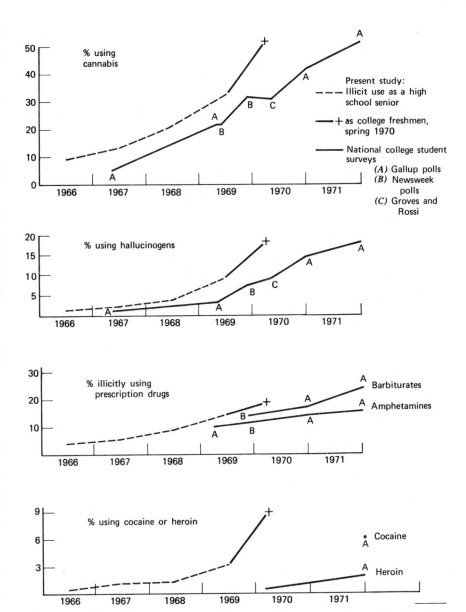

Graph 3.3. Illicit drug-use trends in the present study are similar to trends in drug use among the national college population. (These graphs are based upon data presented in Table 17, Appendix A.)

high school graduation in June 1969 and taking the questionnaire in the spring of 1970. However, if the trend in high school cannabis use is projected to 1970, about 40% of the high school class of 1970 should have tried cannabis by the spring of 1970. Thus, it appears that the college freshmen sample may have a cannabis-use level that is 10-15% greater than the high school seniors behind them at the same point in time; this differential may be due to the effect of attending college or the biased nature of the Ethics Department sample.

However, the most striking feature about Graph 3.3 is the great similarity between the trends obtained from students' reports of drug use in high school and the trends obtained from national surveys of marihuana use in the U.S. college population.[27] It appears that the students in this sample were, as high school seniors, about one year ahead of the national college population; but the rate of increase in marihuana use is just about the same in the two groups.

This is the strongest possible evidence supporting the contention that the present sample is adequate and compares favorably with data based upon national surveys. Although the actual level of drug use is higher in the sample than in the nation, this is what was expected. But the patterns of drug use and rates of change are just about identical.

These trends also hold for the use of other drugs. When the present freshmen were high school seniors (June 1969), 9% reported trying hallucinogens, exactly the same rate reported by Groves and Rossi in the spring of 1970.[28] It is more difficult to make comparisons for prescription drugs. Groves and Rossi asked their students to include the medical as well as nonmedical use of "pills." Gallup presents the evidence separately for barbiturates and amphetamines. Gallup has not asked questions about cocaine and heroin use, while Groves and Rossi only report information for heroin.[29] It is probable that college students in the New York area are somewhat ahead of the national college population in using various hard drugs.

One can conclude that since 1966 there has been a massive increase in the use of marihuana and, recently, of hard drugs. Evidence not presented here shows that this increase in drug use is not due to drug users being more likely to drop out of college.[30] The trends in drug use among the national college population are similar to trends in the sample.

E. THE PEER CULTURE AND MARIHUANA USE

The question arises, how did marihuana use become prevalent in the high school population? An attempted answer to this question must turn to one of the main theoretical ideas suggested in the first chapter: the peer culture. The basic hypothesis holds that those who spend a great deal of time with peers in settings in which adult controls are weak are more likely to engage in a wide variety of unconventional activities than those who do not spend so much time with peers. In addition, it holds that those who are highly involved in the peer culture are the most likely to accept the operating innovation of cannabis use.[31] Thus, a large proportion of those who are highly involved in the peer culture should use cannabis at an earlier time than persons who are less involved in the peer culture.

In order to test this theory, an indicator of peer culture participation at an earlier point in life is needed. The study has tried to operationalize this concept by concentrating upon indicators of commitment to a peer group while respondents were in high school and earlier. The students were asked, "While you were in high school, did you ever?" and "Which did you do *five* or more times?" Two of the possible responses were "Drive around with friends" and "Spend time around a local 'hangout' " (a store, drive-in, or the street). At another point in the questionnaire, they were asked, "Did you ever date at an early age (14 or younger)?" Respondents were classified on the "Peer Culture Index": (1) "none" if they never "drove around," "hung out," or dated at an early age; (2) "some" if they had done only one or more of these things, but were not high; (3) "high" if they had done two or more of the following three things: (a) dated at an early age, (b) "drove around" five or more times, and (c) "hung out" five or more times while in high school. The basic intention of this index is to classify a person according to the degree of involvement with peers *prior* to attending college.

This index has certain weaknesses. More than half of the sample grew up in New York City, where the legal driving age is eighteen; many teenagers thus have little opportunity to drive around. Even as college students, a third of the sample did not have a driver's license. But the lack of a driver's license probably does not affect many highly peer-oriented persons. If the peer group theory is correct, one member of the peer group would probably have been eighteen and had access to a car before graduation from high school. But even if the legal driving age kept many from being classified as high on the Peer Culture Index, they would fall into the "some" category. Thus, the category "high" may be short some cases. Nevertheless, a sizable proportion (about 25%) of the sample are high on the Peer Culture Index. At the other extreme, persons who are somewhat peer-oriented may be misclassified under "none," since driving around and hanging out are predominately male activities. The "date at an early age" item is included to increase female involvement in the peer culture.

Despite the weaknesses of the Peer Culture Index, it will serve to demonstrate that cannabis has entered the peer culture. Graph 3.4 presents information about cannabis use in high school among those who are highly involved and not involved in the peer culture. Data about those who are somewhat involved are presented in Appendix A, Table 18, and fall between the two extreme categories. Also, race is held constant and among whites, sex. The sample of white males and females is probably adequate.

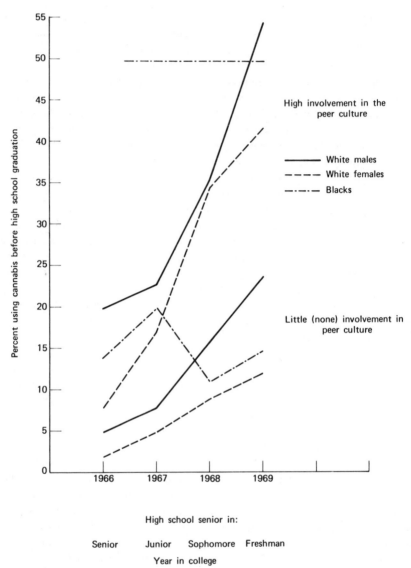

Graph 3.4. Students who are highly peer-oriented began using cannabis earlier and more rapidly than those who are less peer-oriented. (This graph is based upon data presented in Table 18, Appendix A.)

However, blacks in the sample are by no means representative of the black population. The blacks are female disproportionately and less involved in the Peer Culture Index than white females. Perhaps the sample is somewhat valid for middle-class blacks. Despite the small sample, it will be demonstrated that the blacks show a different trend in marihuana use than the more representative sample of white college students.

Graph 3.4 provides a striking demonstration of the early and rapidly increasing cannabis use among those highly involved in the peer culture. For example, among white males in the high school class of 1966 who were high on the Peer Culture Index, about 20% had used cannabis before high school graduation. But cannabis use was much higher among their successors in the class of 1969;[32] about 55% had tried cannabis in high school. A similar trend is noted among white females who were highly involved in the peer culture: less than 10% in the class of 1966 versus more than 40% in the class of 1969 had tried cannabis in high school. Thus, there has been an increase of about 30% in the use of cannabis among high school students who were highly involved in the peer culture between 1966 and 1969.

Among those who were not involved in peer-culture activities in high school, the level of cannabis use is much lower: 5% of white males of the class of 1966 had tried cannabis, while about a fourth in the class of 1969 had tried cannabis in high school. Similar findings hold for white females; few (about 10%) of the non-peer-culture-oriented white females in the class of 1969 had tried cannabis in high school. Thus, those highly involved in the peer culture began at an earlier age and have "turned on" more rapidly than their peers who are not involved in the peer culture.

But it remains to be demonstrated that cannabis has entered the peer culture rather than that cannabis use created new kinds of social groups. Despite a small number of cases, the evidence demonstrates that the black students in our sample have not been a part of this trend towards the increasing utilization of cannabis. Among the blacks who were highly involved in the peer culture, about half of those in the high school classes of 1966 and 1967 ($N = 12$) have used cannabis; the same proportion of their successors in the class of 1968 and 1969 had tried cannabis in high school. In a similar fashion, there is no sizable increase among the black students who were not involved in the peer culture; about 15% of all four classes had tried cannabis in high school. The explanation for this finding is that cannabis use has long been a feature of the black peer culture. Indeed, our data, despite their limitations, on black college students compare reasonably well with the one major study of a normal black population. Robins and Murphy found that 30% of a sample of St. Louis black males had tried cannabis before reaching the age of 20 (in 1950-1954),[33] while 23% of the college blacks (predominately female) had tried cannabis before high school graduation. Thus, the little evidence there is tends to demonstrate that the use of marihuana may have remained relatively stable in black populations over long periods of time in urban areas as diverse as New York and St. Louis.

But there is another reason why cannabis has entered the peer culture. Although not presented here, evidence suggests that freshmen were as likely as seniors in college to have been involved in skipping school, buying or selling liquor or cigarettes, defying parents, and committing minor theft before graduation from high school. While those highly involved in the peer culture were more likely to participate in these activities than those less involved, the null relationship between year of high school graduation and involvement in such activities was not affected when the Peer Culture Index, race, and sex were held constant.[34] The basic idea is that involvement in behaviors such as skipping school, minor theft, and defying parents have long been institutionalized as legitimate activities of those who are involved in the peer culture. Each year, about the same proportion of high school graduates at each level of peer-culture participation has been involved in these activities.

The only activity that shows a striking change between the high school classes of 1966-1969 is the use of cannabis. The increasing utilization of marihuana has been most striking among whites who are highly involved in the peer culture. Cannabis use has been incorporated into the white high school peer culture as a legitimate activity. However, our evidence demonstrate that cannabis use among blacks has not significantly changed in the same time period, probably because cannabis use has long been institutionalized as a black peer cultural activity.

It is important to note that this new operating invention[35] of cannabis use has probably entered peer groups that were relatively cohesive prior to the use of cannabis and has not occurred because of a general change in adolescent behavior. This conclusion is warranted because whites who were high on the Peer Culture Index had a stable, but high, incidence of involvement in minor theft and school truancy; seniors were as likely as freshmen to be involved in minor theft and truancy in high school. Furthermore, information that can be recomputed from Appendix A shows that about the same proportion of college students in the sample (27% of freshmen, 26% of sophomores, 31% of juniors, and 26% of seniors) were high on the Peer Culture Index before leaving high school. Thus, over these four years, peer-culture participation in high school has remained relatively constant, as have truancy and theft among those highly involved in the peer culture. From this, one may conclude that there has been little shift in adolescent behavior in the high school population as a whole. The peer culture has remained relatively cohesive and stable during these four years. The only behavior that has changed is the use of cannabis; the greatest use has occurred among those who are highly peer-oriented. From this, peer groups have added cannabis to their repertory of unconventional behaviors. Cannabis has entered the peer culture and is becoming institutionalized as a legitimate behavior to those who are highly involved in the peer culture and, to a lesser extent, to those who are less involved in the peer culture.

As shown in Graph 3.3 the use of drugs other than cannabis is also growing.[36] But the increasing use of hard drugs has emerged from the development of the drug subculture. Evidence about this concept will be found in the following chapters.

REFERENCES

1. Comprehensive Drug Abuse Prevention and Control Act of 1970, 84 Stat. 1236-1296 (1970).
2. Bruce D. Johnson, *Social Determinants of the Use of "Dangerous Drugs" by College Students*, Ph.D. thesis, Columbia University, privately published by author, June 1971, p. 68.
3. Ibid.
4. Gene R. Haislip, "Current Issues in the Prevention and Control of Marihuana Abuse," Paper presented to the First National Conference on Student Drug Involvement, U.S. National Student Association, Aug. 16, 1967, p. 4.
5. See Chap. 2.
6. Erich Goode, *The Marijuana Smokers*, New York: Basic Books, 1970, p. 204. Recomputation of data provided by a psychology class at U.C.L.A. shows that 59% have ever tried marihuana: W. McGlothlin, K. Jamison, and S. Rosenblatt, "Marijuana and the Use of Other Drugs," *Nature*, 228 (Dec. 19, 1970), 1228.
7. Richard Blum, *Students and Drugs*, San Francisco: Jossey Bass, 1969, p. 189. Blum does not indicate what he means by "regular or considerable use."
8. John Kaplan, *Marijuana—The New Prohibition*, Cleveland: World Publishing Company, 1970, pp. 23-28.
9. For a convenient summary of Gallup data on college student drug use, see "Latest Findings on Marijuana," *U.S. News and World Report*, Feb. 1, 1971, p. 27.
10. W. E. Groves, P. H. Rossi, and D. Grafstein, "Study of Life Styles and Campus Communities," Johns Hopkins University, Baltimore, Dec. 1970, p. 4.
11. C. D. Chambers, *An Assessment of Drug Use in the General Population*, New York State Narcotic Addiction Control Commission, May 1971. We thank Dr. Douglas Lipton, director of research, NACC, for permission to publish information on drug use among New York City college students.
12. John Langrod, "Secondary Drug Use among Heroin Users," *International Journal of Addictions*, 5(4) (Dec. 1970), 626.
13. Merit Publishing Co., *Merit Publishing Company's National Survey of High School High Achievers*, Northfield, Ill.: Merit Publishing Co., 1970. Chambers, Ref. 11, p. 100.
14. Blum, Ref. 7, p. 64. Gallup International, "Special Report on the Attitudes of College Students," Gallup Opinion Index, Report No. 48, Princeton, N.J., June 1969, p. 30. Goode, Ref. 6, pp. 33-34. Kaplan, Ref. 8, pp. 23-25. Chambers, Ref. 11, reports that men are more likely to use nonprescription drugs, but women are more likely to use prescription drugs.

15. E. Josephson et al., "Adolescent Marijuana Use: Report on a National Survey," Paper presented at the First International Conference on Student Drug Surveys, Newark, N.J., Sept. 14, 1971, p. 7. National Commission on Marihuana and Drug Abuse, *Marihuana: A Signal of Misunderstanding, Appendix II,* Washington, D.C.: U.S. Government Printing Office, 1972, p. 947 (henceforth, Schafer Report).

16. Gallup, Ref. 14, p. 30. Blum, Ref. 7, p. 66. Goode, Ref. 6, p. 37. Chambers, Ref. 11, p. 100. Josephson, Ref. 15, p. 6.

17. Goode, Ref. 6, p. 42.

18. R. A. Boggs et al., "Drug Dependence in Michigan, Part III: A Study of Attitudes and Actions of the Young People of Michigan," Lansing, Michigan House of Representatives, Special House Committee on Narcotics, Dec. 1968, Table IV.

19. Blum, Ref. 7, p. 64. Gallup, Ref. 14, p. 30.

20. Gallup Poll, "One Young Adult in Eight Has Tried 'Pot' " (American Institute of Public Opinion), Princeton, N.J., Oct. 25, 1969.

21. D. I. Manheimer, G. D. Mellinger, and M. Balter, "Marijuana Use Among Urban Adults," *Science,* 166 (Dec. 19, 1969), 1544.

22. R. G. Smart, "Illicit Drug Use in Canada," *International Journal of Addictions,* 6(3) (Sept. 1971), 394.

23. Johnson, Ref. 2, Appendix B.

24. Blum, Ref. 7, p. 189.

25. Erich Goode, "Drug Escalation: Marijuana Use as Related to the Use of Dangerous Drugs," Paper prepared for the National Commission on Marihuana and Drug Abuse, Oct. 31, 1971, p. 80.

26. This kind of analysis by year in college is utilized by H. C. Selvin, and W. O. Hagstrom, "Determinants of Support for Civil Liberties," *British Journal of Sociology,* 11 (1960), repr. in S. M. Lipset and S. S. Wolin, *Berkeley Student Revolt,* Garden City, N.Y.: Doubleday, 1965, p. 502.

27. Gallup, Ref. 9, p. 27. Groves, Rossi, and Grafstein, Ref. 10, p. 4. "The Marijuana Problem," *Newsweek,* July 24, 1967, pp. 46-52; and "The New Mood on Campus," ibid., Dec. 29, 1969, p. 44; Linda Charlton, *New York Times,* Feb. 10, 1972, p. 16.

28. Groves, Rossi, and Grafstein, Ref. 10, p. 4.

29. Ibid. Gallup, Ref. 9, p. 27.

30. Johnson, Ref. 2, pp. 85-88.

31. E. W. Vaz and J. Scott, "A Perspective on Middle Class Delinquency," in Edmund W. Vaz, *Middle Class Juvenile Delinquency,* New York: Harper and Row, 1967, p. 214.

32. When we refer to the high school class of (year) we are really referring to students who are freshmen, sophomores, juniors, and seniors in the present sample.

33. Recomputed from Lee N. Robins and G. E. Murphy, "Drug Use in a Normal Population of Young Negro Men," *American Journal of Public Health,* 57 (Sept. 1967), 1589.

34. We hope to document this point in a later paper.

35. Vaz and Scott, Ref. 31, p. 214.

36. The evidence for this conclusion is meager. See Erich Goode, "Trends in College Drug Use: Report from One Campus," Paper delivered at the First International Conference on Student Drug Surveys, Newark, N.J., Sept. 14, 1971. See a summary of trends: Bruce D. Johnson, "Student Drug Use: Implications of Drug Surveys for a Dangerous Drug Policy," Paper presented to the 30th International Congress on Alcoholism and Drug Dependence, Amsterdam, Netherlands, Sept. 7, 1972.

CHAPTER 4

The "Primary" Factor in Marihuana Use

Why do students use marihuana? This question is really two different questions: Why do students begin to use marihuana and why do students become regular marihuana users? Two different answers are encountered; one psychological and the other sociological.

In 1958 David Ausubel, an authority in the field of drug use could state that a habitual marihuana user comes "from a poverty-stricken broken home or a home marked by domestic strife. Frequent nightmares, enuresis, and other symptoms of emotional tension and disturbed interpersonal relationships are typical of his early childhood history."[1] More recently a government booklet entitled *Answers to the Most Frequently Asked Questions About Drug Abuse* asked why people continue to use marihuana and concluded, "the consistent user, the 'pothead,' is likely to be emotionally disturbed, according to many studies of this group. He is using the drug to treat his personality problems."[2]

This emphasis on the psychological aspects of drug use appears to be fundamental to the official position. Almost all statements from the medical associations, law enforcement officials, and drug "information" literature emphasize psychological factors.[3] In spite of the official importance attached to psychological explanations, definitive empirical proof is lacking. A psychiatrist, Lester Grinspoon, examined many studies attempting to link personality factors with marihuana use. He found that most clinical studies in the United States or other countries are badly misleading or methodologically insufficient. He concludes that "there can be no doubt that certain personality types are more

51

attached to the use of marihuana."[4] But he does not specify what these personality types may be. Increasingly, surveys of college and high school students are beginning to demonstrate that various neurotic indices are associated with drug use.[5] Grinspoon points out that this kind of data must be interpreted with care. Many drug users are quick to admit confusion and anger in an attempt to be "open" to their shortcomings. They respond positively to items indicating psychopathology to which equally disturbed, but less open, students respond negatively.[6] Another difficult problem is that many psychological scales are based upon conventional social values that drug users reject. Such personality measures are mainly a reflection of the dominant group ideology and yet are arbitrarily defined as indicators of mental health or pathology. Since many drug users disagree with the value assumptions expressed in questionnaire items, they provide answers that are interpreted by authorities as indicative of psychopathology.[7] Given the problems with psychological scales, it is not surprising that marihuana use is associated with indicators of psychological difficulties. However, personality variables are probably not as strongly related to marihuana use as the social variables discussed below.

In contrast to the limited evidence supporting personality explanations of marihuana use, there are many large-scale methodologically sound surveys of drug use in nonclinical populations. Although such researchers seldom investigate personality factors, they manage to demonstrate that many social factors are strongly related to the use of marihuana and other drugs. Using survey research, Blum, Goldstein, and Smart present 25-100 different variables significantly related to marihuana use. Some of the variables these sources and others[8] have found to be related to marihuana are sex, socioeconomic status, religiosity, authoritarianism, alienation, peer and parental drug use, self-social identification, cigarette and alcohol use, familial instability, political activism, and premarital sexual involvement. To the layman and professional researcher, the implication of these statistical associations is that drug use is "a complex behavior with multiple causes."[9]

This "multiple cause theory" implies an additive model of drug use. If several of the variables correlated with cannabis use could be added together, one could predict with a high degree of probability whether a person will use marihuana or not. Cisin and Manheimer found that combining sex, marital status, cigarette use, religious preference, and the nonmedical use of prescription drugs allows one to predict marihuana use quite successfully. Among San Francisco area adults, 91% of those without children, with no religious preference, and having obtained a prescription drug from nonmedical sources had tried marihuana. At the other extreme, only 2% of the married females with children and having a regular doctor have tried marihuana.[10] These findings are parallel to the findings reported below.

This study suggests that it really does not matter what background factors are used as the independent variables. Since the multiple cause theory holds that there are many other variables, as noted above, selecting and combining a few such factors increases the accuracy of predicting whether certain extreme social groups will or will not use cannabis. For this study, the four background factors that are most (not true for sex) highly correlated with marihuana use were selected. When these factors were applied simultaneously, almost 100% of those subject to all factors were shown to use cannabis. These variables are the respondent's religiosity, subjective political orientation, cigarette use, and sex.[11] A brief discussion of three of these variables is necessary.

Our measure of religiosity is not intended to indicate differences in personal beliefs or theology. It measures the degree of affiliation with conventional religious institutions. Persons have been classified on the religiosity variable as follows. (1) "Not religious" if they are nonaffiliates or never had a religious preference. Most of these persons indicate that while they were raised as a Jew, a Catholic, or a Protestant, they presently have no Judeo-Christian preference. They have given up organized religion. (2) "Some religiosity" if the respondent maintains the religious preference in which he was raised but has greatly decreased his attendance at religious services since being a high school senior. Also included here are a few persons who have changed from one major faith to another. (3) "Very religious" if the respondent maintains the religious preference in which he was raised and attends religious services about as frequently as he did while a high school senior.

The variable "cigarette use" (which does not include smoking pipes or cigars) classifies respondents using cigarettes: (1) "daily"; (2) "less than daily" if the respondent had used cigarettes at least once after July 1, 1969, or smoked cigarettes more than monthly before July 1, 1969, but has not used them since that time; and (3) "never" if the person claims never to have used cigarettes or had used them less than monthly prior to July 1, 1969.

Respondents were classified on "political orientation" according to their own evaluation of where they stood on a continuum from "radical" to "very conservative." Persons were classified as follows: (1) "left" if they said they were "radical" or "very liberal"; (2) "liberal" if they said "moderately liberal," "indifferent," or "don't know" or if they refused to answer or left the question blank;[12] and (3) "moderate" if they considered themselves "moderate," "moderately conservative," or "very conservative."

The dependent variable is the Frequency of Cannabis Use Index, described in Chapter 3. For the most part, experimental (less than monthly) and moderate (less than weekly) users are not considered because the concern here is to analyze why students ever try and become regular (weekly) users of cannabis.

The relationship between these four background variables and the use and regular use of cannabis is found in Graph 4.1. At the top of each section the strength of the relationship is noted. Hence, the percent difference in the

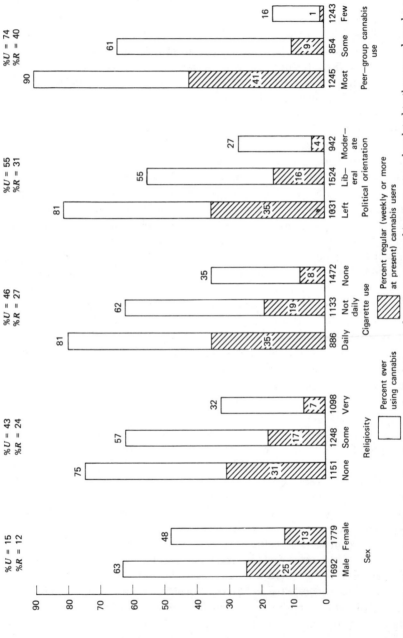

Graph 4.1. Sex, religiosity, cigarette use, political orientation, and peer-group cannabis use are strongly related to the use and regular use of cannabis.

use of cannabis (symbolized by %U) between males and females is 15% (63%-48%). In addition, the sex difference in regular cannabis use (%R) is 12% (25%-13%). Other factors are even more strongly related to cannabis use than sex. Nonreligious persons are 43% (%U = 75%-32%) more likely to ever use cannabis and 24% (%R = 31%-7%) more likely to be regular cannabis users than very religious persons. The 46% difference between daily smokers versus noncigarette smokers in marihuana use is virtually identical to the 47% (50%-3%) difference, reported by Josephson, in the national high school population.[13] The 55% difference between those who consider themselves left, versus moderate, is somewhat stronger than the 40% difference reported by Gallup in a national college population.[14] But the direction of the relationship is the same in this survey as in other major surveys. The most important factor, discussed in much greater detail below, is peer-group cannabis use. Respondents who claim that most of their friends use cannabis are 74% (90%-16%) more likely to use marihuana themselves than persons who claim to have few cannabis-using friends.

The basic intention here is to demonstrate the validity of the multiple cause theory by showing that four background variables (sex, religiosity, cigarette use, and political orientation) predict with great precision whether students will use marihuana or not. An attempt will be made to show that each background variable is additively and independently related to the use of cannabis. In Graph 4.2, these variables are held constant; different combinations of religiosity, smoking, and political orientation for men (p. 56) and women (p. 57) are presented.

For those students in the extreme groups one can predict with virtual certainty the use or nonuse of cannabis, because of the independent and additive effect of these four background variables. Among the 119 nonreligious, politically left, daily cigarette-smoking males (upper left), 97% have tried cannabis and 62% are weekly cannabis users. At the extreme lower right, only 4% of the 180 very religious, politically moderate, noncigarette-smoking females have ever tried cannabis and none are weekly cannabis users. These findings are not the result of statistical accidents; the numbers of cases (119 and 180) are sufficient to provide stable percentages. This finding is parallel to the Cisin and Manheimer data cited previously.

In addition, these data appear to be the result of social forces at work. Each of the four factors contributes independently and in relatively predictable ways to the use and weekly use of cannabis. Although there are a few exceptions, the level of marihuana use and the regular use of cannabis declines steadily as one goes from the upper left corner to the lower right corner of Graph 4.2.

As expected from the multiple cause theory, by combining only four background factors one can predict with great precision whether a person will or will not use cannabis. The important thing about these four variables is that they are essentially social variables. One need not consider personality or psycho-

Sex: males

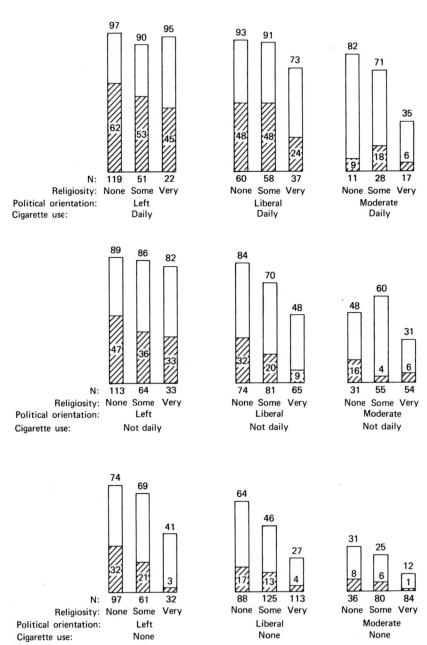

Graph 4.2. Combining the four background factors of sex, religiosity, cigarette use, and

Sex: females

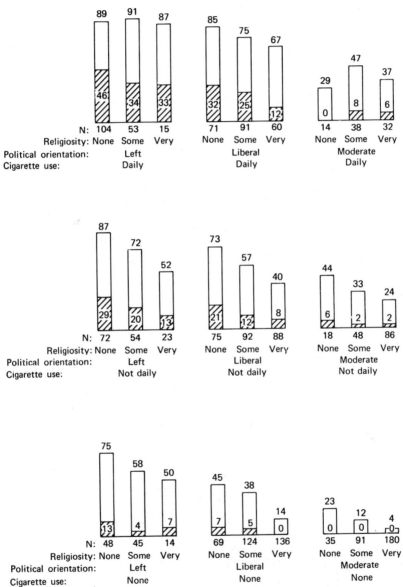

political orientation increases the predictability of the use and regular use of cannabis.

logical factors to be extremely accurate in predicting marihuana use. There is no need to hypothesize a drug-prone personality or psychological disturbance. This does not mean that personality factors may not be important, but they are not necessary to understand marihuana use.

Nevertheless, the above multiple cause theory is greatly misleading. Howard Becker, as long ago as 1953, recognized the fallacy of this theory. What we call the multiple cause theory, Becker called predispositional theory. He felt that a theory built upon such background variables was basically inadequate because such "predispositional theories cannot account for that group of users (whose existence is admitted) who do not exhibit the trait or traits considered to cause the behavior and such theories cannot account for the great variability over time of a given individual's behavior with reference to the drug."[15]

Instead, Becker's early writings suggest that involvement in marihuana-using circles was essential. Becker indicates that a marihuana-naive person must learn from someone, usually a friend, how to smoke the marihuana cigarette and how to recognize and enjoy the effects of the drug. In order for the person to become a regular marihuana user, the person must insulate himself against pressures not to use marihuana, which come from the definitions of morality of nonusing friends, family, and public. Insulation is usually facilitated by disaffiliation with family and friends who frown upon use and reaffiliation with persons who use and rationalize the consumption of cannabis and other drugs. [16]

Although the concept of insulation is used or suggested by Becker and others,[17] no writer carefully defines what is meant. This study will define "insulation" as occuring when almost all of one's friends engage in a particular activity—in this chapter, when almost all friends use marihuana. Evidence indicates that a person is not insulated if even 25% of his friends are nonusers. Having a few nonusing friends is probably the most important factor limiting the regular use of cannabis, although some marihuana use may occur.

In order to test Becker's ideas, respondents were asked, "Among your present friends, about how many have tried marihuana?" Respondents were classified as having: (1) "few" if less than a quarter of their friends used marihuana; (2) "some" if a quarter but less than three-fourths of their friends used it; and (3) "most" if almost all or all of their friends used cannabis. This variable, peer-group cannabis use, appears to be a good indicator of insulation from nonusing friends and involvement in marihuana-using circles.

This variable is really a measure of perception by the respondent of his friends' use of marihuana. It is not a measure of whether his friends actually use marihuana or not. However, with a highly visible activity such as marihuana use, there is likely to be a high correlation between the respondent's perception of, and his friends' actual use of, cannabis. Hence, peer-group cannabis use variable appears to be a good indicator of involvement in cannabis-using groups. Graph 4.1 demonstrated that those with most of their friends using cannabis were 74%

more likely to try cannabis than those with few cannabis-using friends. In addition, weekly cannabis use is common (41%) among those with most of their friends using marihuana. Respondents with some cannabis-using friends (9%) are much less likely, as are those with few friends (1%), to become regular cannabis users. The data seem to demonstrate, therefore, that having some cannabis-using friends is conducive to trying cannabis but not to regular use. For weekly cannabis use to occur, the user must insulate himself in a group where most friends use cannabis. Exposure to even a few (about 25%) friends who do not use cannabis appears to inhibit strongly regular cannabis use.

Having briefly described the variable peer-group cannabis use, the study will now attempt to demonstrate the weakness of the multiple cause theory. Although not presented, data show that each of the four background variables is significantly and strongly related to peer group cannabis use when used as a dependent variable. For example, 55% of the nonreligious versus 17% of the very religious respondents have friends most of whom use cannabis. Similar findings hold for political orientation: 61% of left versus 14% of moderates have most friends using cannabis. Hence, these four background factors greatly increase the probability that a student will have cannabis-using friends. If Becker's logic is generally correct, the relationship between each of the background factors and marihuana use should be reduced when peer-group cannabis use is held constant. This is precisely what happens. For example, Graph 4.3* shows that the

*This highly complex graph demonstrates the kind of analysis that will be used throughout the rest of the book. Readers are urged to study carefully this footnote to understand how the relationship between an independent variable and a dependent variable is altered by holding constant a test factor. One must first consider the strength of the relationship between the independent and dependent variables (sociologists refer to this as the original, or two-way, relationship). A simple and effective way to measure the strength of a two-way relationship is to calculate the percent difference. The percent sign [%U] before a letter symbolizes the percent difference between extreme catagories of the independent variable; the capitalized letter symbolizes the dependent variable (e.g., U = cannabis use) and the two-way relationship between an independent variable and this dependent variable. Thus, the %R is the *percent difference* in regular cannabis use due to the independent variable. For example, using religiosity as the independent variable, Graph 4.1 shows that nonreligious persons are 43% (%U = 75%-32%) more likely than very religious persons to have ever used cannabis and 27% (%R = 31%-7%) more likely to be regular cannabis users.

Why the nonreligious are more likely than the religious to use and to use regularly cannabis can be shown by holding constant the test variable peer-group cannabis use. This variable is held constant by splitting the sample into three subgroups, those with few, some, and most cannabis-using friends. Within each subgroup of the variable, the strength of the relationship between religiosity and drug use is examined. Lower-case letters (%u and %r) stand for the strength of the relationship between independent and dependent variables within a subgroup. Thus, among those most of whose friends use cannabis, the nonreligious are slightly (%u = 94%-80% = 14%) more likely than the very religious to try cannabis. Religiosity has some effect upon cannabis use among those with some cannabis-using friends

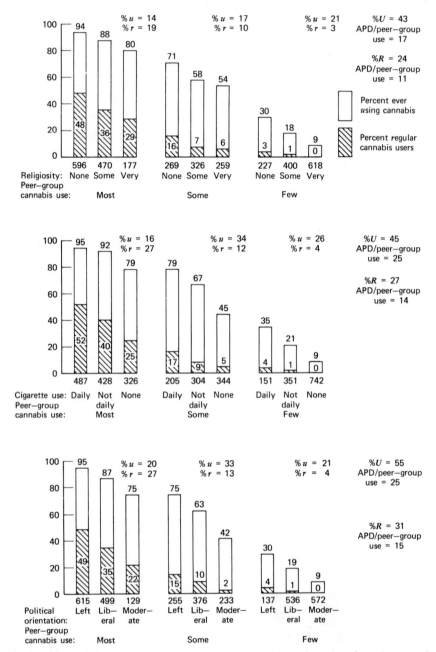

Graph 4.3 Cannabis use by friends is the primary factor in the use and regular use of cannabis; religion, cigarette use, and political orientation are considerably less important.

religiosity difference ($\%U$ = 43%) in cannabis use is reduced to an average percent difference (APD) of 17% when peer-group cannabis use is held constant. This tends to indicate that the strong relationship between religiosity and cannabis use exists mainly because less-religious persons become involved in peer groups where cannabis is used and hence use the drug themselves. The direct effect of religiosity on cannabis use is much less important. Similar findings hold for the other factors. Thus, the 46% difference in cannabis use due to cigarette use is reduced to 25% and the 55% difference due to political orientation is reduced to 25% when peer-group cannabis use is held constant. Only the sex differences are not greatly reduced. Thus, the 15% difference in cannabis use between males and females is reduced to 7% and 3%, respectively, among those with friends few and most of whom use cannabis. However, among those with some cannabis-using friends males are 16% more likely to use cannabis than females. This may indicate that when persons are pressured by some friends who want them to use cannabis and by other friends who would prefer that they avoid it, males will try cannabis and females will avoid it.

Graph 4.3 also allows a better understanding of regular cannabis use. For example, the 27% difference in regular cannabis use due to daily versus noncigarette use appears to be reduced by half (APD = 14%) when peer-group cannabis use is held constant. However, this is misleading. Among those with most of their friends using cannabis, daily cigarette users are 27% ($\%r$ = 52%-25%) more likely to be regular cannabis users than noncigarette users. This tends to demonstrate that in cannabis-using groups, being a noncigarette user is

($\%u$ = 71%-54% = 17%) and with few friends ($\%u$ = 30%-9% = 21%). One can average these religious differences in cannabis use by adding the differences ($\%u$'s) in each subgroup and dividing by the number of subgroups; this is called the average percent difference (APD). The APD due to religiosity while *holding constant* (symbolized by /) peer-group cannabis use is

$$\text{APD} / \text{ peer-group use} = \frac{14\% + 17\% + 21\%}{3} = 17\%$$

This 17% has a specific meaning, which is easily related to the original relationship. The strong [$\%U$ = 43%] relationship between religiosity and cannabis use is reduced to 17% when peer-group cannabis use is held constant. Another way of understanding the meaning of the APD is that religiosity has an independent effect of 17% upon cannabis use when peer-group cannabis use is held constant. For all practical purposes, religiosity has an independent effect which is about a third (17%/43%) of its original strength. What this means is that having cannabis-using friends, and not religiosity, is the important factor in determining cannabis use. Generally a reduction of two-thirds to 50% from the original relationship is sufficient to arrive at this conclusion.

In the following chapters and graphs the percent differences among subgroups [$\%u$'s and $\%r$'s] will be eliminated because they make the graphs confusing and are not central to the argument. For the most part, the original relationship ($\%U$) will be presented and compared to the APD holding constant some theoretically important independent variable.

associated with inhibiting the regular consumption of cannabis. Similar findings emerge from the analysis of other background variables. Background characteristics that mitigate against cannabis use (female, political moderation, and very religious) tend to inhibit the weekly use of cannabis, especially among those who have most of their friends using cannabis. Among those with few or some cannabis-using friends, the background characteristics seem to have much less influence in curbing or increasing the probability of regular use.

The basic weakness of the multiple cause theory can now be dealt with. The four background variables are accurate in predicting cannabis use, because they are closely associated with having cannabis-using friends. Graph 4.2 showed that there were 119 persons who were nonreligious, daily cigarette-using, politically left males. Two of these persons did not indicate their friendships with cannabis users. Of the remaining 117, 76% claimed that most of their friends use cannabis; 18%, some friends; and 6%, few friends. At the other extreme, one respondent did not indicate how many friends used cannabis. Of the remaining 179 very religious, noncigarette-using, politically moderate females, 86% have few, 12% have some, and only 2% have most friends using cannabis. Hence, these background variables are important in determining whether persons will have cannabis-using friends or not.

Once something is known about the cannabis use of a person's friends, knowing a great deal about the background variables does not greatly increase the ability to predict cannabis use. Thus, the primary factor in understanding why a college student used marihuana is the proportion of his friends who use it. The important sociological question becomes, Why do students have marihuana-using friends? An adequate answer to this question is beyond the scope of this book. However, the multiple cause theory suggests that background variables, especially when several are combined, increases greatly the probability of having many cannabis-using friends.

Nevertheless, the background variables have a slight effect on cannabis use that is not explained by friend's cannabis use. Graph 4.4 presents information about those 117 persons who are most likely and the 179 persons who are least likely to use cannabis while holding constant peer-group cannabis use. The most impressive feature of the graph is the amazing accuracy with which cannabis use is determined by the five independent variables. Thus, 100% of the 89 nonreligious, daily smoking, politically left males with most friends using cannabis have themselves tried cannabis and 74% are regular cannabis users. At the other extreme, only 2% of the 154 very religious, nonsmoking, politically moderate females have tried cannabis and none are regular cannabis users. A difference of this magnitude, 100% versus 2%, is seldom seen in the social science literature. Nor, to the author's knowledge, has other research been able to predict as accurately why people are regularly involved in a particular behavior or not (74% versus 0%). In short, cannabis use and regular use is a

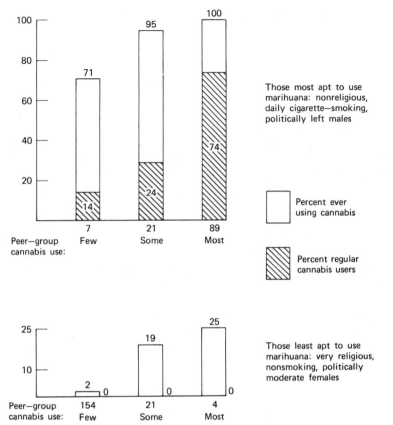

Graph 4.4. Background variables affect the level of cannabis among those least and most likely to use cannabis even when the peer-group cannabis use is held constant.

highly predictable phenomenon. Given information on just five predominatly sociological variables, one can predict with a high degree of accuracy whether a person will or will not use cannabis.

Graph 4.4 also shows that the background factors have some effect independent of friends. Although there are not enough cases for stable percentages, the results are suggestive. Among students who are likely to try cannabis (nonreligious, daily smoking, left males) but who have few or some cannabis-using friends, most have tried cannabis (71% and 95%, respectively) but are unlikely to be regular cannabis users (14% and 23%). Perhaps such persons participated in cannabis-using circles at an earlier time but they were not involved in such groups when completing the questionnaire. If this is the case, there is a need to analyze such change over time.

At the other extreme, those least likely to use cannabis (religious, nonsmoking, moderate females) are unlikely (19% and 25%) to use cannabis even though some or most friends use cannabis; however, the numbers of cases (21 and 4) are too small for generalization. Having a very conventional life style appears to inhibit the use of cannabis, even among those who have several cannabis-using friends.

For the most part, the discussion has been confined to extreme groups and has ignored the 90% or more of the population that is not so highly predictable. There is an important reason why cannabis use is not so easily determined for a majority of the students. While many persons are exposed to social pressures that should lead to drug use, they are exposed at the same time to pressures to avoid drug use. For example, evidence not presented here shows that daily cigarette smoking, politically liberal, very religious females have intermediate rates of cannabis use (66%) and mixed friendships (35% have few, 28% have most friends using cannabis). Thus, many persons are exposed to conflicting pressures that hold down the level of marihuana use. But, as noted in Graph 4.2, the general trend is clear: when various combinations of background factors are known, both the level of marihuana use and friendships with cannabis users are generally predictable within certain limits.

The data indicate that background factors are linked to cannabis use by the cannabis use of one's friends, but it has not been established which factor, peer-group cannabis use or the respondent's use of cannabis, is predominantly causal. According to Becker, a person is generally introduced to cannabis by a friend. However, in order for marihuana use to become regular, the prospective user must increasingly insulate himself from those who would disapprove. This insulation, if it occurs, is necessary before heavy marihuana use is possible. Furthermore, increasingly regular cannabis use is facilitated the more one becomes friends with cannabis users.[18]

Fortunately, there is a technique available by which one can determine the time order of cannabis use and having friends who use marihuana. The basic methodological technique is the sixteenfold table.[19] In the questionnaire respondents were asked to report their marihuana use and friends' use during their senior year in high school. There is also data, of course, on the use of cannabis and friends' use at the time of questioning. Four variables were developed and dichotomized in the following manner: (1) marihuana use in high school, yes or no; (2) present use of cannabis, yes, if the students had used it after July 1, 1969, and no, if only before July 1, 1969, but not since or never; (3) peer-group cannabis use in high school, "few" if less than a quarter of friends used it and "many" if more than a quarter of friends used marihuana; and (4) peer-group cannabis use at present, the same code as for high school use.

The basic logic of a sixteenfold table is that it allows the researcher to examine the relationship between the same two variables at two different points in time. By doing this the researcher can determine which of the two factors is most important in determining the other factor. Table 5 permits a test of whether friendships with marihuana users are shifted to accord with the respondent's use or whether his marihuana use changes because of peer-group pressures. In this kind of analysis raw numbers are used rather than percentages.

In Table 5, one cannot determine which variable is the cause of the other by examining the cells on either diagonal, since the upper left to lower right diagonal (1117, 18, 150, 393) is composed of persons who have not changed, while the lower left to upper right diagonal (2, 2, 34, 706) is composed of those who have changed on both variables between high school and college. It should be noted that the direction of changes is to gain friends and begin cannabis use (706 and 34); very few (2 and 2) give up friends or cannabis. By examining the other eight cells in the table, one can determine which of the variables have the greater "generating" and "preserving" effects.

Let us first examine the generating effect. This effect occurs when persons who are inconsistent on the two variables at time 1 (in high school) become consistent at time 2 (the present). For example, persons who are in the middle two rows of Table 5 are inconsistent in their friendships or cannabis use in high school. Those who became consistent at time 2 are found in the first and fourth columns.

If one assumes that pressure from friends determines the respondent's use, then high school cannabis users with few marihuana-using friends should give up their cannabis use; there are 17 such persons. Furthermore, nonusers in high school with many marihuana-using friends should take up marihuana later; there are 119 such persons. Thus, 136 (17 + 119) persons have adjusted their

Table 5. *Change over time in friends' cannabis use and respondents' cannabis use (retrospective data)*

			At Present Time (Time 2)			
Peer-Group Cannabis Use			Few	Few	Many	Many
		Own Can-nabis Use	No	Yes	No	Yes
	Few	No	1117	85^b	537^b	706
In High School	Few	Yes	17^a	18	34	197^a
(Time 1)	Many	No	33^a	2	150	119^a
	Many	Yes	2	8^b	78^b	393

[a]Cells for determining the generating effect.
[b]Cells for determining the preserving effect.

marihuana use to their friends' cannabis use. For these persons, pressure from friends "caused" the respondent's nonuse or use of marihuana.

Now assume that the respondent's marihuana use determines his friendships with cannabis users. If this is the case, nonusers in high school with many marihuana-using friends should give up such friends; there are 33 such persons. Further, high school marihuana users having few cannabis-using friends should acquire many cannabis-using friends in college; there are 197 such persons. Thus, for 230 (33 + 197) persons, their own marihuana use has "caused" them to drop or gain cannabis-using friends. Hence, the predominate direction of causality (230 versus 136) is the latter outcome. Persons change their friendships to accord with their own drug use rather than alter their use of drugs because of pressure from friends. The preserving effect holds that persons who are consistent at time 1 will tend to give up the least powerful factor by time 2, thus "preserving" the strongest factor. Essentially, Table 5 shows that more persons gain or give up their friendships to accord with their own marihuana use (8 + 537) than shift their marihuana use to accord with their friendships (85 + 78). Thus, for both the generating and preserving effects the respondent's own use of cannabis is a more important determinant of having cannabis-using friends than vice versa. Although the predominant tendency is for friendships to be adjusted to the respondent's own use, one must not forget that in many cases the opposite occurs. This tends to support Goode's assertation that

> a dynamic and dialectical relationship obtains between friendships and the amount one smokes. One does not generally acquire a great many marijuana-smoking friends until one already smokes. Yet the fact that one has friends who smoke further increases the likelihood that one will smoke more. . . . Rather than one or another being causal here, the two mutually influence and feed into each other. [20]

The evidence presented in this chapter indicates that cannabis use is a highly predictable phenomenon when four background variables (sex, religiosity, political orientation, and cigarette use) and peer-group cannabis use are combined (five independent variables); extreme groups are almost perfectly predicted. Thus, of the 89 (2.5% of the total sample) nonreligious, left, daily smoking males with most of their friends using cannabis, 100% have ever used marihuana and 74% are weekly cannabis users. At the other extreme, of the 154 (4.5% of the sample) very religious, moderate, nonsmoking females with few cannabis-using friends, only 2% have ever used marihuana and none are weekly cannabis users.

In addition the data help integrate the multiple cause theory with Becker's theory of social interaction in explaining cannabis use. Background factors strongly influence the probability of participating in peer groups where cannabis is utilized. However, membership in a peer group where marihuana is used, no matter what the background factor, greatly increases the chances that the individual will begin to use marihuana.

Once students begin using marihuana, two major factors affect the frequency of use. First, the proportion of the peer group using marihuana will greatly affect the frequency of use. If even 25% of one's friends do not use marihuana, the respondent's use of cannabis will tend to be irregular. However, if almost all or all friends use it, the respondent's use will become increasingly regular. Furthermore, there appears to be a tendency for novice marihuana users to seek new friends and social circles where almost everyone uses marihuana.

Second, the background factors also affect the regular use of cannabis. Each background factor increases the likelihood of gaining cannabis-using friends and hence progression to regular cannabis use. If the background variables indicate that persons should not use marihuana, respondents will be unlikely to have cannabis-using friends and hence unlikely to become a regular user. In addition, students having most friends using cannabis are unlikely to become regular marihuana users if one or more of the background variables indicate that students should not use cannabis.

These findings have important implications for drug subculture theory. First, the data demonstrates the enormous importance of social factors in determining marihuana use. This study has not resorted to psychological explanation to understand cannabis use. While the importance of personality factors has not been disproven, their importance is challenged. The present logic suggests that persons who are emotionally disturbed (however this is defined) are unlikely to try marihuana if few of their friends use it, while psychiatrically normal persons with cannabis-using friends are likely to try it.

Second, the basic conclusion of this chapter is that the most important factor in explaining the respondent's marihuana use is the use of cannabis among his friends. Among those with most friends using cannabis, 90% have used it; the 10% who have not tried marihuana are restrained by other social factors, such as noncigarette use or a moderate or liberal political orientation. Hence, the peer-group cannabis use variable is an important measure of what is meant by participation in the drug subculture. This variable measures the effects of social interaction centered around the consumption of cannabis. The greater the involvement of students in cannabis-using circles, the more students are subject to the conduct norm, "Thou shalt use marihuana." Very few students can resist this insistent, but supportive, pressure from friends to use marihuana unless they are exposed to other pressures against marihuana use from their background and general environment; even so, friends usually win.

Third, if one views the four background variables as indicators of commitment to the parent culture, one can understand how this culture is connected to marihuana use and, by inference, to initial and increasingly regular participation in the drug subculture. The parent culture structures and defines appropriate behavior for those occupying various statuses in society. Such statuses, or background factors, become important selector criteria for membership in cannabis-using peer groups and the drug subculture. In a similar fashion, background factors or statuses, such as the parental socioeconomic status, alcohol use, Peer Culture Index, familial instability, alienation, and parental drug use, which have not been dealt with here, are connected to the drug subculture.

If cannabis use and initial drug-subculture participation is the result of social interaction that is structured by the behaviors and ordinary social statuses of college students, it is difficult to imagine how laws and governmental action may greatly alter such patterns of use. Few government or college officials in the United States would try, for example, to get students to go to church. Nor could laws greatly affect political liberality. Indeed, many colleges in this study are proud of their role in instilling liberal values in their students. While many persons would like to end cigarette smoking, the policy on campus and elsewhere is to tolerate smoking; laws against smoking by minors are almost completely unenforced. And finally, laws can do little to alter the patterns of friendship formation, especially in the direction of nondrug use.

Although drug laws are intended to prevent cannabis use, the evidence here indicates that the opposite effect is more probable. Present drug laws, by defining drug use as a criminal act and promoting the idea that cannabis use is immoral, may drive marihuana use underground, so that users give up nonusing friends and insulate themselves in circles of cannabis-using friends. In addition, such laws may regularize cannabis use by insulating cannabis users from nonusers who might reduce the respondent's use of cannabis.

While it is hard to demonstrate convincingly and empirically that the drug laws are important in determining the use and regular use of cannabis, it is far easier to demonstrate that the illegality of cannabis plays a crucial role in the illegal sale of marihuana and hard drugs, the topic of the next chapter.

REFERENCES

1. David P. Ausubel, *Drug Addiction,* New York: Random House, 1958, p. 99.
2. *Answers to the Most Frequently Asked Questions About Drug Abuse* (pamphlet), Washington, D.C.: Government Printing Office, 1970.
3. Nathan B. Eddy et al., "Drug Dependence: It's Significance and Characteristics," *Bulletin of the World Health Organization,* 32 (1965), 721-733. American Medical Association, "Dependence on Cannabis," *Journal of the American Medical Association,* 201 (Aug. 7, 1967), 368-371; "Marihuana and Society," *JAMA,* 204 (June 24, 1968), 91-92. Jerome LaBarre, "Harms Resulting from the Use of Marihuana," *The Prosecuter,* 6 (Mar.-Apr. 1970), 91.
4. Lester Grinspoon, *Marihuana Reconsidered,* Cambridge, Mass.: Harvard University Press, 1971, pp. 253-290.
5. Ronald A. Steffenhagen and Patrick J. Leahy, "A Study of Drug Use Patterns of High School Students in the State of Vermont," unpublished, University of Vermont, 1968.

C. P. McAree et al., "Personality Factors in College Drug Use," *International Journal of Social Psychiatry*, 15(2) (1969), 92-106. Joel Goldstein et al., *The Social Psychology and Epidemiology of Student Drug Usage: Report on Phase One*, Department of Psychology, Carnegie-Mellon University, June 1970, pp. 67-71. Ulla Ahrens, Magnus Kihlbom, and Nils Nas, "Students and Narcotics: An Investigation of Students at the University of Stockholm in Spring, 1968" (translated title), in Statens offentliga utredningar, Socialdepartementet, *Narkotikaproblemet* ("The Drug Problem, Part IV, Sociomedical and Clinical Investigations"), Stockholm, Sweden, 1969, pp. 173-178. Richard Blum, *Students and Drugs*, San Francisco: Jossey-Bass, 1969, pp. 233-241. Robert Hogan et al., "Personality Correlates of Undergraduate Marijuana Users," *Journal of Counseling and Clinical Psychology*, 32(1) (Aug. 1970), 58-63.

6. Grinspoon, Ref. 4, p. 286.

7. Erich Goode, *Drug Escalation: Marijuana Use as Related to the Use of Dangerous Drugs*, Paper prepared for the National Commission on Marihuana and Drug Abuse, Oct. 30, 1971, p. 50.

8. Blum, Ref. 5, pp. 63-167. Goldstein et al., Ref. 5, pp. 18-48; Reginald Smart et al., "Preliminary Report on the Attitudes and Behavior of Toronto Students in Relation to Drugs," Toronto, Canada: Addiction Research Foundation, Jan. 1969. Bruce Johnson, *Social Determinants of the Use of "Dangerous Drugs" by College Students*, Ph.D. thesis, Columbia University, privately published by author, June 1971, Appendix B. Ahrens, Kihlbom, and Nas, Ref. 5, pp. 109-192. Gallup International, "Special Report on the Attitudes of College Students," *Gallup Opinion Index*, Report No. 48, Princeton, N.J., 1969. Leonard Goldberg, "Drug Abuse in Sweden," *Bulletin on Narcotics*, 20 (1968), 1-31. Kenneth Eells, "Marijuana and LSD: A Survey of One Campus," *Journal of Counseling Psychology*, 15(5) (1968), 459-467. Lillian Imperi et al., "The Use of Hallucinogenic Drugs on Campus," *Journal of the American Medical Association*, 204 (June 17, 1968), 1021-1024. Paul M. Kohn and G. W. Mercer, "Drug Use, Drug Use Attitudes, and the Authoritarianism-Rebellion Dimension," *Journal of Health and Social Behavior*, 12 (June 1971), 125-131. Lillian Robbins et al., "College Students Perception of Their Parents; Attitudes and Practices Toward Drug Use" (unpublished), New York, 1970. Edward Suchman, "The Hang-Loose Ethic and the Spirit of Drug Use," *Journal of Health and Social Behavior*, 9 (June 1968), 146-155. Lawrence S. Linn, "Social Identification and the Use of Marijuana," *International Journal of Addictions*, 6 (Mar. 1971), 79-107.

9. Joel Goldstein, "Motivations for Psychoactive Drug Use Among Students," Paper presented to Eastern Psychological Association, New York, N.Y., April 15, 1971.

10. Ira H. Cisin and Dean I. Manheimer, "Marijuana Use Among Adults in a Large City and Suburb," Paper presented at the New York Academy of Sciences, May 21, 1971. An earlier report of the San Francisco sample indicates a fairly high (.62) multiple correlation coefficient and that religious affiliation is one of the single most important variables: Dean I. Manheimer et al., "Marijuana Use Among Urban Adults," *Science*, 166 (Dec. 19, 1969), 1554-1555.

11. In personal conversations with the author, Eleanor Carroll of NIMH expressed a desire to know more about the drug use patterns of females. Hence, we have included sex as an independent variable, although it is not as highly associated with marihuana use as the other three variables. On the basis of our evidence, we feel that females behave almost the same but have slightly lower levels of marihuana use than males.

12. The question on political orientation was at the end of the questionnaire; about 425

students left it blank, were indifferent, or could not classify themselves. Since we wish to compare extremes (left versus moderates) and include all cases for detailed analysis, these 425 cases have been included in the intermediate "liberal" category. It must be noted that our New York City sample is more "left" than the national college population. Comparison with Groves et al., "Study of Life Styles and Campus Communities: Preliminary Report," Johns Hopkins University, Dec. 1970, shows that 9% of our sample, but 5% of the national college population, consider themselves radical. About 27% of our sample, but 56% of the national college students, consider themselves moderate or conservative.

13. Eric Josephson et al., "Adolescent Marijuana Use: Report on a National Survey," Paper presented to the First International Conference on Student Drug Surveys, Newark, N.J., Sept. 14, 1971, p. 9.

14. Gallup, Ref. 8, p. 30.

15. Howard S. Becker, "Becoming a Marihuana Smoker," *American Journal of Sociology*, 59 (Nov. 1953), 236.

16. Ibid., pp. 235-242. Howard S. Becker, "Marihuana Use and Social Control," *Social Problems*, 3 (July 1955), 35-44.

17. Erich Goode, "Multiple Drug Use Among Marijuana Smokers," *Social Problems*, Vol. 17, Summer 1969, pp. 54-62. James Carey, *The College Drug Scene*, Englewood Cliffs, N.J.: Prentice-Hall, 1968. Alan G. Sutter, "Worlds of Drug Use on the Street Scene," in Donald Cressey and David A. Ward, eds., *Delinquency, Crime and Social Processes*, New York: Harper and Row, 1969, pp. 802-829.

18. Becker, Ref. 15, p. 237; and Ref. 16, p. 35. Goode, Ref. 17, p. 56.

19. Paul F. Lazarsfeld, "Mutual Effects of Statistical Variables" in Paul F. Lazarsfeld, Ann K. Pasanella, and Morris Rosenberg, *Continuities in the Language of Social Research*, New York: Free Press, 1972, pp. 388-398. This kind of analysis is based upon having data from the same respondents at two different points in time (panel data). The data we report here is pseudo panel data because we use retrospective data, asking the respondent to report his activity in the past. Thus, our findings may be misleading.

20. Goode, Ref. 17, p. 56.

CHAPTER 5
College Student Drug Sellers

The U.S. public is concerned about drug sellers. In recognition of this concern, the present drug laws making drug possession illegal are generally aimed at the drug peddler. The Bureau of Narcotics and Dangerous Drugs and other enforcement agencies insist that they are only after heavy drug sellers.

The official description of drug dealing assumes the existence of a highly profitable, well-organized, pyramid-structured criminal underworld controlling the distribution of drugs.[1] While this description may be true at the upper levels of cocaine and heroin selling, it is probably not true at the street level. Information on marihuana and hallucinogen dealing indicates the absence of a pyramidal structure. Even at the high levels of dealing, several marihuana dealers may import large quantities from Mexico. At the lower levels of selling, there are many sellers, but few profit significantly.[2] If anything, the average dealer of marihuana, hallucinogens, and pills probably earns a relatively low income compared to his earning potential in the "straight" world. Income from selling is further reduced by the sellers own use of drugs, gifts of drugs to friends, and informal constraints of the subculture such as demands in underground newspapers for dealers to "lower their prices and hand out more free drugs."[3]

The antimarihuana position and the vast majority of the public maintain and strongly believe that the crucial motivation for student drug selling is the desire for profit; marihuana sellers also sell hard drugs to enhance their wealth. Selling drugs is usually the means of making a living for long periods of time. Students who are marginal sellers are only a front for the real criminals controlling the drug market.[4] Also common to the public image of drug sellers is the assumption that a nonusing adult is doing the pushing. Advertisements sponsored by Blue Shield show a picture of a handsome white man standing in a suburban setting with his eyes blacked out. The caption reads, "If you don't talk to your kid about drugs, this man will. Better you than the pusher on the corner" and urges the parent to send for a pamphlet published by Blue Shield.[5] This conveys the impression that pushers are adults who spend all their time selling drugs to children who are essentially nonusers and uninformed about drugs (like the parents' child).

Close observers of drug dealing attempt to show the public's image of drug pushing does not accord with actual practice, especially among the student, hippie, and professional worlds. Although the profit motive is not denied, Carey and Goode note many other factors that affect patterns of selling. The most important variable, neglected by the official position, in the selling of marihuana is the frequency of use. Goode demonstrates a powerful linear relationship among 200 marihuana smokers: 11% of the less than monthly versus 92% of the daily marihuana users have ever sold marihuana.[6] He also indicates that having regular marihuana-using friends increases the probability of selling. Goode feels that selling marihuana is really a function of involvement in the drug subculture: "The fact that a given individual sells—whether it be done once, occasionally, or frequently, specifically for a profit—is determined mainly by his involvement in the drug, in its subculture, with others who smoke."[7] The same argument holds for other drugs. The more frequently a person uses the drug, the more likely he is to buy and to sell it.

Although the frequency of use is perhaps the most important variable, having contact with many regular users increases the likelihood of selling. Within drug-using circles, being a seller is associated with having knowledge about "what's happening" and occupying a prestigious position in the group. Selling also gives the person a chance to promote other drugs that he feels are beneficial and a chance to indoctrinate others to his point of view.[8]

The Blue Shield image of a drug pusher as a nonusing adult is also unacceptable, especially to Carey. The seller resembles his clientele and sells mainly to close friends who are very much like himself: "The anticipated customers are friends or friends of friends, so totally profit oriented motives are rare. Small users will decide to push anticipating profiting from small sales to their friends. Heads will figure to sell to fellow heads, Hell's Angels to Hell's Angels, professors to professors."[9] In short, the seller, at least at the lower levels of dealing, is not a distant adult that the user buys drugs from on a few occasions. The seller is someone of the same age and much like the user, if not a close friend.

If this similarity between users, buyers, and sellers really exists, what is the process through which users become sellers? The transition from user to buyer and then to seller is a function of normal socialization into the subculture. Although many marihuana users never progress beyond the point where they share a joint with a circle of friends, many persons increase their use of cannabis and feel an obligation to supply the group of friends with marihuana. If the user buys in small quantities of individual joints or a "nickel" ($5) bag (about 1/5 ounce, enough for eight to fifteen joints), he pays a high price per joint. But buying small quantities on a regular basis greatly increases the risk of arrest. Furthermore, a buyer is likely to be offered an ounce on a "take it or leave it" basis; this is a larger quantity than he actually needs. The chance of being arrested with an ounce is about the same as with a nickel bag, and the purchase of a larger quantity saves money on a per joint basis. However, an ounce will provide fifty to seventy joints, more than a weekly user and his friends would generally consume in three months. If caught possessing this amount of marihuana, the person is subject to relatively heavy penalities (intent to sell rather than possession).[10] Thus present drug laws encourage the sale of an ounce.

A more important reason for selling is that friends may want some marihuana and offer a reasonable price for part of the ounce; it is then extremely difficult not to sell. Indeed, Carey indicates that "hardly anyone thinks of himself as crossing a line that makes him a pusher," because he may be selling part of something he does not really want.[11] If he has marihuana-using friends, a buyer quickly learns that he can sell enough marihuana to cover his expenses and have enough left over for his own use; he can "smoke free."

Frequently, the person who sells at one point in time may later buy from the person he sold to previously. The person who sells is determined by who has the contact with a higher-level seller. The decision to move to a higher level of selling (pounds or kilograms or selling hard drugs) is a function of one's use, the size of one's circle of friends and friends of friends, the desire to be in the center of the drug scene, and the potential profit.

Carey and Goode suggest that a meaningful typology of drug sellers can be constructed. Although the data to develop a detailed typology are not available, dimensions that might differentiate different levels of drug selling will be discussed. The various types of sellers overlap to some extent, but each type indicates increasingly greater involvement in the selling of drugs.

The "trader" drug seller appears to be equivalent to Carey's "give-and-take barter system."[12] The trader sells to close friends mainly because he wishes to smoke free. The profit obtained is so minor that he gains no more than spending money; he probably cannot live on what he obtains from selling. Furthermore, the trader is very likely to buy from someone to whom he has sold previously; the person who sells is the one with a contact who can supply the drug desired. The trader usually sells marihuana, although he may sell other drugs if he has them when a friend requests them.

The "dealer" has a wider circle of buyers. He probably sells to close friends for little profit and to friends of friends and those who can establish that they are not police for profit at current market prices. Usually the dealer will sell LSD and pills as well as cannabis but probably will not sell methedrine, heroin, or cocaine.[13] The dealer usually makes enough profit from his sales to use drugs free and to have enough money left over to provide a living. He probably clears (after expenses and gifts to friends are deducted) not much more than $100 per week, less than many factory laborers earn.[14]

The "pusher" may be divided into two types. The "hustler" is probably equivalent to Carey's "street pusher" or Goode's "nickels and dimes" hustler. The hustler actively searches for buyers whether they are friends or not. He actively sells to anyone who will buy and faces the greatest probability of arrest. The hustler will probably sell any drug he can obtain to those who wish to buy it. Although selling at the highest possible price, the hustler seldom makes much money because of competition from dealers and traders.[15]

The most important pusher is the "big pusher," who almost always sells to other dealers or hustlers and generally in large quantities. He is the equivalent of the wholesale merchant and seldom sells less than a pound or a kilogram of marihuana in one sale. He may employ persons to sell drugs at a lower level to increase his profit. He probably sells to those who have a consistent record of selling fairly large quantities of marihuana or other drugs. The big pusher generally buys drugs in large quantities (frequently more than $1000 worth), imports marihuana from Mexico, or buys other drugs from underground chemists or "rip-off" men (burglars). However, the proportion of big pushers in a drug-using population is probably very small. For example, about 5% of Goode's marihuana sellers usually sold pounds of marihuana: in 1968, 8% of Blum's sellers claimed incomes of $1000 per month; in 1970-1971, 31% claimed such profits.[16]

Each type of seller is likely to buy from the level immediately above him. Thus, traders will probably buy from dealers, and dealers and hustlers from big pushers. The higher the level of selling, the greater the number of different drugs sold. Thus, most traders infrequently sell small quantities of cannabis; the sale of LSD or a few pills is rare. Most dealers probably have a basic supply of cannabis, can sell hallucinogens and pills, and may be able to obtain methedrine, cocaine, or heroin upon request of their buyers. Big pushers may have several kilograms of marihuana available and can quickly obtain large quantities of other drugs if they do not have their own stock.

Thus, according to Goode and Carey, the crucial factor in the selling of drugs is the illegality of cannabis. The increasingly regular user of marihuana needs a supply for his use. If he is using on a regular basis, he cannot obtain the drug legally, as he can cigarettes and alcohol; he must buy it illegally. But unless he has a very good friend who will sell him a few joints or nickel bag, he will have to buy large quantities. Goode indicates that in 1970 the most common retail quantity was the ounce, or "lid."[17] However, an ounce is more than a weekly user needs, so smaller quantities are sold to friends. Once a person has sold, he is likely to be approached again by friends and friends of friends. In short, the lack of legal cannabis and the structure of an economically feasible black market in cannabis lead the regular cannabis user into selling cannabis.

The data will show the following points that demonstrate the crucial nature of the illegality of cannabis: (1) Students sell cannabis as they become increasingly regular users of the drug; no other factors strongly affect the relationship between using and selling of cannabis. (2) The selling of cannabis is almost a prerequisite for the sale of hard drugs. (3) Among cannabis sellers, students sell other drugs (LSD, pills, etc.) because of their increasingly regular use of these substances. (4) Involvement in the illicit buying and especially the selling of drugs is a very good indicator of the concept of drug subculture participation.

In order to measure involvement in the illicit buying and selling of various drugs, the following questions were asked:

(Mark all that apply)

Which substances have you purchased from friends, acquaintances, or illegal drug sellers:

Which substances have you sold to other persons (or acted as an intermediary):

0. None of these
1. Methedrine, desoxyn
2. Other amphetamines
3. Barbiturates or tranquilizers
4. Marihuana or hashish
5. LSD
6. Mescaline or peyote
7. Psilocybin, DMT, DET, STP
8. Cocaine
9. Heroin

A much larger proportion of the total population indicated involvement in the buying or selling of cannabis (marihuana or hashish) than in the buying or selling of any hard drug. Cannabis sales will be examined first.

Persons were classified with respect to cannabis as follows: (1) "sellers" if they had ever sold cannabis, regardless of whether they had ever bought it (there were forty-six persons who had sold but not bought);[18] (2) "buyers" if they had bought but not sold the drug; and (3) "none" if they had never bought or sold the drug. The data indicate a very simple answer to why students buy or sell cannabis. The more frequently students use marihuana, the more likely they are to buy and to sell cannabis. In the present sample, of the 1567 noncannabis users, 99% had neither bought nor sold cannabis; 40%, 82%, and 95%, respectively, of experimental, moderate and regular users had ever bought or sold cannabis. In a similar fashion, 0.8% of the noncannabis users, 10% of the experimental, 41% of the moderate, and 72% of the regular users had ever sold cannabis; a very strong relationship is thus obtained between the use and sale of cannabis.

Hence, one must now investigate whether the relationship between the use and sale of cannabis is strongly affected by other factors also significantly related to the sale of cannabis. Three variables that either are theoretically interesting or have an important impact upon the use-sale relationship have been selected.

Graph 5.1 contains findings that tend to disprove some of the assumptions about drug selling made by supporters of present laws. The study did not, unfortunately, have a good question that might tap the desire for profits as an important motivation in cannabis selling. However, if there is an actual need for profit or money, marihuana selling should be most common among students from low-income backgrounds. Instead, Graph 5.1 shows that the students from high-income (more than $25,000) families are 14% (%S = 29%-15%) more likely than those from low-income (less than $7000) families to sell cannabis. But the truth of the matter is that the 14% difference due to family income is greatly reduced to an average percent difference of 3% when the use of cannabis is held constant. Among regular cannabis users, students from low-income families are as likely (71%) to sell as high-income students (73%). The importance of profit as an important factor in initiating cannabis selling is somewhat suspect, at least among the college students in the sample.

Another tactic used to prevent selling is to pass strong laws and to enforce them strongly. Such tough laws should deter cannabis users from selling. However, the data show that weekly cannabis users who fear arrest are almost as likely (69% versus 73%) as those who do not fear arrest to sell cannabis. Data presented in Appendix A show, furthermore, that very high selling rates (91%) occur among regular users who have been stopped or arrested for a drug violation. This high incidence of selling occurs because police accurately stop those who sell. This evidence demonstrates that the fear of drug-related arrest seldom deters a regular marihuana user from selling (also see Chapter 10).

Goode's emphasis upon the drug seller's involvement in the drug subculture is partially verified.[19] In the third part of Graph 5.1 it is shown that having cannabis-using friends increases the probability of marihuana selling even when cannabis use is held constant. Among regular cannabis users, those with few, versus most, cannabis-using friends are less likely (50% to 74%) to sell cannabis. As can be seen in Graph 5.1, the use of cannabis is more important in determining cannabis selling than having cannabis-using peers. Appendix A presents additional information on other measures of subculture participation showing that the independent effect of marihuana use upon cannabis selling is about three times more powerful than the independent effect of other measures

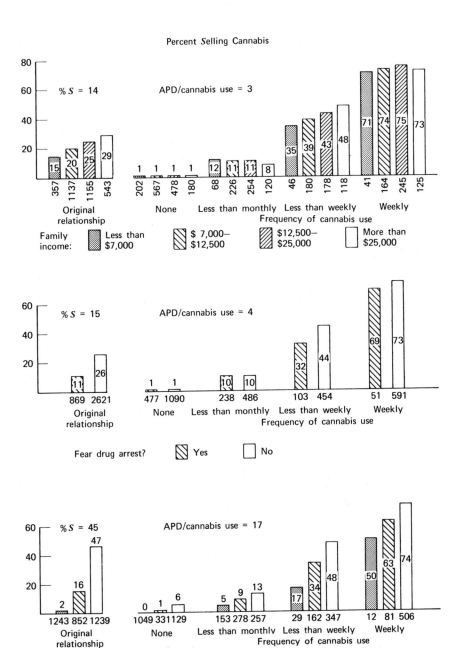

Graph 5.1. Student cannabis selling is primarily determined by the frequency of marihuana use, not by family income, lacking fear of arrest or cannabis use among friends.

of subculture participation, such as one's life style, exposure to hard-drug-using friends, and belief in the benefits of drug use.[20]

Hence, the data demonstrate that cannabis selling is a direct function of cannabis use. In an attempt to disprove this relationship, thirty or more other variables were held constant. Holding constant the sex, religiosity, peer-culture participation, cigarette and alcohol use, disobeying parents, bullying, theft, anomie, alienation, exposure to friends who use other drugs, the use of other drugs, political orientation, living arrangements, college major, and other factors does not strongly affect the positive linear relationship between the use and the sale of marihuana.

And here is a central conclusion of this book: the illegality of cannabis is a very important factor in understanding the sale of cannabis. The reasoning behind this conclusion is as follows: College students engage in cannabis selling for one main, very rational reason; they need to obtain a supply of the drug that they use regularly. In the process of gaining this supply, students must frequently buy a larger quantity of marihuana than they can reasonably use in four months and are likely to sell it to friends who want some. They quickly learn that they can smoke free by selling to a few friends. This cycle of use, purchase, and sale of cannabis could be successfully altered by a fundamental change in U.S. drug laws. If laws were changed so that cannabis users could legally obtain what they needed, few persons would have a concrete reason to illicitly buy cannabis, and since there would be few buyers, the illicit sale of cannabis would be substantially reduced.

There is a compelling historical precedent that indicates the central role that laws may have upon illicit drug selling: alcohol prohibition. During Prohibition there was probably a strong relationship between the frequency of alcohol use and illicit buying. It is not clear, however, whether heavy drinkers also became involved in illegal selling. What is clear is that after prohibition ended the illegal production and sale of alcohol reached negligable levels in a few years.[21] In a similar fashion, legal cannabis would probably reduce the illicit purchase or sale of cannabis to very low levels even among regular users; but this opinion, shared by Blum's drug sellers, cannot be proven at present.[22]

If the frequency of cannabis use is a major factor in the illicit purchase or sale of cannabis, may not a similar relationship exist between the frequency of use and the illicit purchase or sale of each hard drug? The study has classified students according to their use and nonmedical use of each drug and their source of each drug or involvement in illicit sale. Chapter 3 attempted to separate the nonmedical use of prescription drugs from medical usage. Respondents were asked to indicate whether they had ever used methedrine, amphetamines, or sedatives (barbiturates or tranquilizers) more frequently or in larger doses than directed by a doctor, or in an international attempt to get high. Persons who responded positively to either item were classified as illicitly using the drug.

Respondents were then classified on each prescription drug: (1) "nonusers" if they had never used the drug; (2) "marginal users" if they indicated ever using a drug but had not illicitly used it; (3) "illicit: less than monthly" if they had illicitly used the drug but had never used it as frequently as once per month; (4) "illicit: monthly or more" if they had ever illicitly used it once per month or more frequently. For drugs such as hallucinogens, cocaine, and heroin, the "marginal" category does not apply. There is no way to medically use these drugs; present laws define all use as illicit use.

In a similar manner, an attempt was made to classify the source from which each hard drug was obtained and/or whether a person had ever illegally sold it. Respondents were classified as follows: (1) "sellers" if they had ever sold the drug; (2) "buyers" if they had ever bought the drug from a friend or illicit drug seller but had never sold it; (3) "prescription source" if they had obtained the drug from a doctor or doctor's prescription but not illegally bought or sold it; and (4) "none" if they had not legally purchased or illegally bought or sold the drug. In many cases, persons who have illegally bought or sold the drug may have also legally obtained it. Indeed, data not presented here demonstrates that a quarter of those who illicitly use sedatives and about 10% of the illicit amphetamine users obtain these drugs only from legal prescriptions.

Nevertheless, the majority of illicit drug users obtain their supplies from the illicit market, and many become involved in selling drugs. The sale of hard drugs will prove central to the theory and main empirical findings of this book. The following chapter will demonstrate that it is involvement in selling drugs (especially hard drugs) and not marihuana use that explains how marihuana users become heroin users and perhaps users of other hard drugs.

One can analyze how students become hard-drug sellers in Graph 5.2. In the original relationship, there is, as for cannabis, a strong relationship for each hard drug between drug use and drug sale. For example, almost none (0.2%) of the nonamphetamine users, 6% of the marginal users, 25% of the irregular, and 51% of the monthly or more amphetamine users have sold amphetamines. Similar two-way relationships hold for all other hard drugs: the more regular the use of each drug, the greater the involvement in selling that drug.

However, unlike the cannabis use-sale relationship (which is not affected by other variables), there is one factor that strongly affects the use-sale relationship for each hard drug. Graph 5.2 demonstrates that involvement in selling cannabis, not hard-drug use, is the crucial factor in explaining hard-drug sales. The top section of Graph 5.2 shows that regular (monthly or more) amphetamine users who neither buy nor sell cannabis are unlikely (4%) to sell amphetamines. Likewise, among persons who only buy cannabis, the illicit users of amphetamines (5% and 14%) are relatively unlikely to sell amphetamines, especially when compared to the original relationship. It is only among cannabis sellers that regular amphetamine users are much more likely than less regular users to

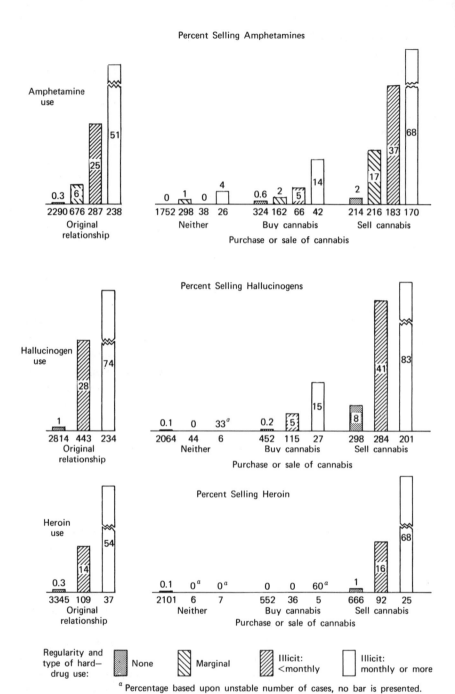

Graph 5.2. Students do not sell the hard drugs they use unless they are also involved in selling cannabis. (This graph is based upon data in Table 20, Appendix A.)

sell amphetamines. It should also be noted that cannabis sellers seldom become involved in selling drugs that they do not also use. Among cannabis sellers only 2% of the nonamphetamine users sell it; 8% of the non-LSD users sell hallucinogens; and 1% of the nonheroin users sell heroin. Similar findings hold true for sedatives, cocaine, and methedrine (see Appendix A, Table 20).

The bottom section of Graph 5.2 is particularly crucial to the theory in the following chapter. One finds no heroin selling among heroin users who only buy cannabis or who neither buy nor sell marihuana. But there are also very few heroin users (numbers at bottom of the bars) among those not buying or selling cannabis (6 + 7 = 13) or even among cannabis buyers (36 + 5 = 41). Thus, it appears that cannabis selling is strongly correlated with heroin use. It should also be noted that there are many cannabis sellers (666) who do not use heroin. The basic point is that the vast majority of college cannabis sellers are not supporting a heroin habit. A similar argument can be made for the methedrine and cocaine; however, similar conclusions for sedatives, amphetamines, and hallucinogens are less compelling.

Why is it that cannabis selling is such an important precondition for the sale of hard drugs? Although the following discussion is somewhat speculative, it is based upon what little evidence is presently available. In American society, there is considerable pressure, both legal and especially informal, against drug selling that affects all dealers.[23] In many respects, persons who become sellers must be emancipated, as Becker suggests, from societal controls that attempt to limit supply, to define selling as immoral, and to expose most drug sellers to nonusers who would negatively sanction selling activities.[24]

But the data show that large proportions of drug users become drug sellers. Thus, many persons manage to ignore or to become isolated from societal restraints against selling; the question becomes "How do students become increasingly involved in selling?" The data suggest that beginning involvement in the buying and selling of drugs is predominately a function of the use of cannabis. Blum finds that the first drug purchase and sale occurred with a neophyte dealer sharing or selling cannabis at cost to users or buyers at a social gathering; less than a quarter of first sales were to make a profit.[25] Thus, a budding drug seller generally makes his first sale in a setting that isolates him from pressures against selling and also provides social supports that he may find emotionally rewarding; he is supplying friends who want what he has to offer and who appreciate his services. The crucial point is that through the same supportive peer groups that induce the use of marihuana, increasingly regular users of cannabis are isolated from, and rewarded when they overcome, the social barriers that prevent drug sale. Without this peer-group support, most regular users would be unlikely to sell. So fundamental is cannabis use and sale to the drug subculture that it is mainly (or almost only) among such cannabis users and sellers that the users and sellers of hard drugs are recruited.

As a budding seller becomes known, he may be asked by others to supply cannabis or hard drugs. When approached by acquaintances (as opposed to friends), the person may consider the potentialities of making money and provide the drug on that basis.[26] Further selling activities may isolate him from nonusers and pressure against selling as well as provide him with a modest income (generally less than $100 per week) and free drugs.[27] In this sense, profit as a motivation for drug sales is about as important to the drug seller as to a small businessman; it is essentially a way to make a living and gain respect from important reference groups. There are, of course, some exceptions; big dealers, although few in number, may make exceptional profits from a few hours' work.[28]

Most importantly, cannabis is probably the bread-and-butter drug for sellers at all levels.[29] While providing a low profit per sale, the tremendous demand for cannabis generates a large number of sales, which makes cannabis economically feasible. Although there is no data presently available, student drug sellers would seem to depend heavily upon cannabis sales for a majority of their income. In addition, as the person becomes increasingly involved in selling cannabis, he is also likely to begin using hard drugs and perhaps to be asked to sell these drugs. If he sells hard drugs on a profit-making basis, he will probably depend upon contacts made from cannabis sales to meet customers willing to purchase hard drugs. However, as Graph 5.2 demonstrates, cannabis sellers are not indiscriminate hard-drug sellers; they sell only the hard drug that they use.

Nevertheless, economic motives play an important role in the illicit drug market. Student sellers, especially those selling upon a somewhat regular basis, seriously consider and attempt to maximize income. They do make money, although it is probable that the amounts are small for most sellers. Thus, despite the fact that few students amass great wealth from drug selling, there is definitely an economic motive in student drug selling. But it must be emphasized that this economic motive is secondary to the seller's own use of a given drug and, perhaps, to the rewards of prestige and respect conferred upon the seller by the subculture.[30] The individual seller's income is further reduced by the subculture's expectations that he will provide "free grass" (or drugs) at parties and to close friends, as well as dictating in what drugs he may deal (LSD and pills are acceptable; heroin is not). In addition, student sellers are constrained, like legitimate businessmen, by competition from other sellers, as well as by limited and irregular supplies.[31]

When all of these constraints upon sellers are taken into account, the progression from cannabis selling to hard-drug selling is frequently motivated by the desire for a higher income, since hard drugs have a higher profit per sale than cannabis.[32] However, among cannabis sellers, hard-drug sales are frequently motivated by the person's use of the hard drug; income is decreased because the seller uses drugs that would provide the profit margin. But it is doubtful that many college students give up selling cannabis when they begin selling hard drugs; cannabis sales probably continue to supply an important source of income and provide potential customers for the hard drugs.

Thus, most hard-drug sellers are probably recruited via cannabis use and cannabis sales. Further research into the motivations of drug selling is badly needed, however.

To further prove the centrality of cannabis sales to illicit purchase and sale of hard drugs and to develop the major indicator of drug-subculture participation, the number of hard drugs (methedrine, amphetamines, sedatives, hallucinogens, cocaine, and heroin) that respondents have purchased and sold were counted. Although not presented, data about the number of hard drugs purchased show a strong relationship between cannabis buying-selling and the purchase of hard drugs. Thus, among persons who have never bought or sold cannabis, 2% have illegally bought hard drugs, while 30% of the cannabis buyers and 67% of the cannabis sellers have purchased hard drugs.

Data in Table 6 demonstrate that 0.4% of the nonbuyers and nonsellers of cannabis, 6% of the cannabis buyers and 52% of the cannabis sellers have sold hard drugs. Looking at this result from the opposite direction, about 90% [(212 + 192)/(252 + 196) = 404/448] of those selling hard drugs have also sold cannabis. The main conclusion is that the purchase of cannabis precedes the purchase and sale of hard drugs and that the sale of cannabis is almost a prerequisite for the sale of hard drugs.

Table 6 has another very important function; from it will be derived a variable, the Illicit Marketing Index, with which one can prove the validity of subculture theory. This book asserts that the Illicit Marketing Index is a good measure of: 1) the different levels of participation in the illicit drug market, 2) the concept of drug subculture participation, both theoretically and empirically,

Table 6. Number of hard drugs sold by the purchase or sale of cannabis

Buy/Sell Cannabis	Number of Hard Drugs Sold							No. of Cases
	None		1-2		3 or More		Total	
	f	%	*f*	%	*f*	%	%	
None	2098	99.6	7	.3	2	.1	100	2107
Buy only	559	94	33	5.6	2	.3	100	594
Sell	379	48	212	27	192	25	100	783
Refuse	7							7
Blank	7							7
Total	3050	87	252	7	196	6	100	3498

and 3) the effects of present drug laws upon patterns of illicit drug use. Indeed, the rest of this book is an attempt to provide empirical proof of these three assertions.

While there are many ways in which this variable could be developed, the simplest is used here. The following pages will develop a measure of increasingly serious involvement in the activities of buying and selling drugs. In doing so, an attempt will be made to isolate groups that are crucial from both a policy viewpoint and a theoretical perspective and have sufficient cases for detailed analysis.

An examination of Table 6 reveals that 2098 respondents state that they have not bought cannabis or sold any drug.[33] To these nonbuyers, nonsellers are added the 7 respondents who left blank the questions on buying or selling of drugs; these respondents had never used cannabis or other drugs (data not presented). However, all of the respondents who refused to answer the buying or selling questions had used cannabis and some other drugs; the refusals have been excluded from the Illicit Marketing Index.

Some 559 respondents claimed to have purchased cannabis illicitly but not engaged in any selling activities. Persons who have bought drugs other than cannabis are intentionally excluded. The three reasons for not including these hard drug buyers along with cannabis only buyers are that there are fewer buyers of hard drugs only than *cannabis only buyers* (46 versus 559); that including them would not greatly alter the results; and most importantly, the data suggest that persons who only buy cannabis do not differ greatly from those who do not buy marihuana or sell drugs (nonbuyers, nonsellers). The drug scene's equivalent of the retail customer (cannabis buyer) is more like the nonbuyer than like those heavily engaged in illicit selling activities. If this conclusion emerges, then legalizing cannabis might not have a detrimental effect upon society. Thus, the study will here concentrate upon cannabis buyers.

In Table 6, there are 379 persons who have *sold cannabis only* and not hard drugs. Most (90%) of these persons have also bought cannabis. These students are interesting because they have confined their selling activities to cannabis and have not sold other drugs.

The last two categories isolate those *selling hard drugs*; those who sell three or more drugs are more involved than sellers of one or two drugs. The few persons who have sold hard drugs but not sold cannabis are included; their inclusion will have little effect upon the basic findings. About 85% of the sellers of one or two hard drugs have also sold cannabis, while 98% of the sellers of three or more hard drugs have sold cannabis. Some subsequent chapters will combine those who sell one or two hard drugs with those selling three or more into one category of "sell hard drugs," in order to have sufficient cases to prove a theoretical point when holding constant two or three other variables.

Our total sample is classified on the Illicit Marketing Index as follows:

	Number of Cases	Percent
None (nonbuyers, nonsellers)	2105	60
Buy cannabis only	559	16
Sell cannabis only	379	11
Sell 1 or 2 hard drugs	252	7
Sell 3 or more hard drugs	196	6
Total	3491	100

The categories of the Illicit Marketing Index are valid indicators of different levels of involvement in the college student drug market. Nonbuyers and nonsellers are essentially uninvolved in this market. Persons who only buy cannabis are marginally involved, while the last three categories indicate increasingly deep involvement in the illicit drug market. These three different levels of selling may correspond closely, although not perfectly, with the typology of sellers discussed earlier. The person who only sells cannabis may be the equivalent of the trader; he probably sells to close friends just enough to smoke free. He is losing nothing, but his monetary gain is very small. The person who sells cannabis and one or two hard drugs is probably intermediate between the dealer and trader. He probably sells to friends but also may have sold marihuana to friends of friends. He may occasionally sell hard drugs to friends at cost and hence be a trader. But a person who has sold one or two hard drugs to nonintimates or who is specializing in the sale of a particular drug, such as hallucinogens, while avoiding the sale of pills and narcotics, is more of a dealer. On the other hand, the person who sells three or more hard drugs (and cannabis) is probably fairly close to the concept of a dealer. Although it is possible for a person to "trade" that many drugs, most such persons probably sell on a regular basis and have contacts who can supply them with drugs they or their customers want. A small number of these dealers may even be pushers, supplying large quantities to other sellers. However, one can only speculate about the convergence between the number of drugs sold and the typology of drug sellers developed earlier; there is no data to prove how intimate a seller is with his buyers or the amount of drugs a person has sold.

The Illicit Marketing Index is theoretically independent of drug use, and yet both factors are strongly related because the present drug laws have made the nonmedical use of drugs illegal. Hence, involvement in selling is a good measure of the illegality of drugs. There is no natural law that requires students to use a drug before selling it. There is a concrete reason for the high correlation between use and sale; regular users of a drug have the greatest interest in obtaining the drug. Since they cannot legally obtain it, the task of illegally obtaining and distributing the drug becomes that of regular users by default. Thus, laws designed to discourage the use and the sale of cannabis and other drugs appear to have just the opposite effects: they induce a large number of persons to become sellers. If cannabis could be obtained legitimately, like alcohol, cigarettes, coffee, and tea, even very heavy users might be unlikely to sell it. Sedatives and amphetamines are legitimately dispensed by doctors, and as a result are somewhat less apt to be illicitly bought and sold than the drugs that can never be legally obtained (data not presented). Further, when a drug is very popular but illegal, such as cannabis and hallucinogens, almost three-fourths of the regular users are likely to become sellers.

The drug most crucial to the cycle of use, purchase, and sale is cannabis. It is by far the most popular drug, the most frequently used, bought, and sold. In the sample population, cannabis use appears to be a prerequisite for the use, purchase, and sale of hard drugs.[34] Thus, in many crucial ways, the illegality of cannabis becomes a central issue; the consequences of the illegality of cannabis will be explored in subsequent chapters.

The Illicit Marketing Index will be the central measure of the concept of drug-subculture participation. Heavy involvement in selling drugs is essentially an outgoing activity. The seller is likely to meet and befriend a wide variety of persons who use and sell a large number of drugs. Sellers are probably the first to learn about new drugs, new ideas, and new beliefs and in turn teach these new beliefs and behaviors to their customers. Because of the danger they face and the large market they supply, drug sellers are accorded considerable prestige in the drug community. Drug sellers are, in short, at the center of the drug subculture and of "what's happening" in the world of drugs.[35]

But most importantly, the Illicit Marketing Index is a better measure of drug-subculture participation than the other two measures of drug use. In the analysis to be reported in the following chapters, involvement in the purchase or sale of drugs, not the frequency of cannabis use, is the most important factor in understanding both exposure to hard-drug-using friends and involvement in delinquency, crime, sex, and plans to leave college. The following chapters will show that when the Illicit Marketing Index is held constant, there is a significant reduction in the relationship between the use of cannabis (as the independent variable) and hard-drug use, friendships with users of hard drugs, crime, premarital sex with four or more persons, and plans to leave college. Similar findings emerge from analysis of the relationship between the Multiple Drug Use Index and crime, delinquency, and sexual behavior.[36]

Several interesting questions arise, questions that the present study cannot answer. Rather, panel data about drug use and the purchase or sale of drugs at two different points in time for the same sample of persons is needed. However, the following questions are important and locate areas of concern for future research in this field: What is the relationship between the use of cannabis and the use of other dangerous drugs? Does a person need to sell cannabis before he begins to use other dangerous drugs? Or does his use of hard drugs lead a cannabis user to begin selling cannabis and then hard drugs? Does a regular user of a hard drug, such as heroin, methedrine, or hallucinogens, depend upon marihuana selling to support his heavy drug consumption? Answers to these questions are important but somewhat beyond the scope of the present book.

However, the data suggest some basic guidelines about certain patterns of events in this sequence of drug involvement: (1) The use of marihuana is almost essential for the nonmedical use of hard drugs (see following chapter) and involvement in the buying or selling of cannabis and other dangerous drugs. (2) The use of a hard drug is almost a prerequisite for the illicit purchase or sale of that drug. (3) Involvement in the buying or selling of cannabis is almost a prerequisite for the illicit purchase and especially the sale of other dangerous drugs. (4) The illicit buying of a drug probably preceeds the selling of that drug. (5) Only among cannabis sellers are increasingly regular users of a hard drug likely to sell that drug.

This chapter suggests that a possible and reasonable way to stop drug selling is to permit students to legally obtain cannabis. Before one can discuss the policy implications of these findings, one must investigate other controversies about drug use, the most important of which is whether marihuana use leads to hard-drug use.

REFERENCES

1. Robin Moore, *The French Connection*, Boston: Little, Brown, 1969 describes how the Mafia imported drugs into the United States in 1962. However, Charles Grutzner, "Mafia Is Giving Up Heroin Monopoly," *New York Times*, Sept. 2, 1968, claims that organized crime has gotten out of heroin. Rather than giving up, it appears that the Mafia has moved to South America: "Heroin: Now It's the Latin Connection," *Newsweek*, Jan. 24, 1972, pp. 24-26.

2. James I. Carey, *The College Drug Scene*, Englewood Cliffs, N.J.: Prentice-Hall, 1968, pp. 68-93. Erich Goode, *The Marijuana Smokers*, New York: Basic Books, 1970, pp. 243-263. Richard Blum, "Drug Pushers: A Collective Portrait," *Transaction*, July-August 1971, 18-21. Richard Blum et al., *The Dream Sellers*, San Francisco: Jossey-Bass, 1972, p. 39.

3. Goode, Ref. 2, p. 250.

4. Will Oursler, *Marijuana: The Facts, The Truth*, New York: Paul Erikson, 1968, pp. 113-120.

5. Blue Shield ad, Blue Shield, N.Y., N.Y.

6. Goode, Ref. 2, p. 252.

7. Ibid., p. 255.

8. Ibid., pp. 257-259. Blum, Ref. 2, pp. 49, 113, 140, 233.

9. Carey, Ref. 2, p. 73.

10. The legal distinction between simple possession and possession with intent to sell fluxuates considerably from state to state. A close reading of "The Criminal Penalities Under the Current Marijuana Laws," compiled by National Organization to Reform the

Marijuana Laws (NORML), Washington, D.C., July 1, 1971, shows that nine states (none with a population of three million) have made the possession of less than an ounce a minor offense or misdemeanor; many other states treat possession cases as felonies without regard to the amount of drug possessed.

11. Carey, Ref. 2, p. 70.

12. Ibid., p. 68.

13. Anonymous, "On Selling Marijuana," in Erich Goode, *Marijuana,* New York: Atherton Press, 1969, p. 94. This comes close to fitting the description of the dealer as we understand this concept. There are many such dealers working at legitimate jobs and selling marihuana to their coworkers: Nancy Mayer, "How the Middle Class Turn On," *New York Magazine,* Oct. 20, 1969, pp. 42-46.

14. Goode, Ref. 2, p. 260. Blum, Ref. 2, p. 140.

15. Carey, Ref. 2, p. 72. Goode, Ref. 2, p. 256.

16. Goode, ibid., p. 251. Blum, Ref. 2, p. 39.

17. Goode, Ref. 2, p. 248.

18. For forty-six respondents, it appears that a friend gave them marihuana, which was later sold to someone else.

19. Goode, Ref. 2, p. 255.

20. This finding is justified by the following facts, which can be verified in Table 19 presented in Appendix A: The average percent difference in cannabis selling due to cannabis use is reduced from 71% to about 60% (average percent difference) when measures of subculture participation are held constant. However, the 40%-50% differences in cannabis selling due to subcultural variables are reduced to less than 20% (average percent differences) when cannabis use is held constant. Thus, the independent effect of cannabis (60%) is three times as powerful as the independent effect of subculture variables (20%).

21. Robin Room, "The Effects of Drinking Laws on Drinking Behavior," Paper presented at the Society for the Study of Social Problems, Denver, Colorado, August 28, 1971, p. 5. Gerald Globetti, "Problem and Non-Problem Drinking Among High School Students in Abstinence Communities," Paper presented at the First International Conference on Student Drug Surveys, Newark, September 14, 1971, shows that problem drinkers were more likely (70% versus 30%) than nonproblem drinkers to obtain alcohol from "merchants and bootleggers" in Mississippi abstinence towns.

22. Blum et al., Ref. 2, p. 51.

23. Ibid., pp. 38, 142.

24. These ideas are borrowed from Becker's discussion of marihuana use but also apply to drug selling: Howard S. Becker, *Outsiders,* New York: Free Press, 1963, pp. 59-78.

25. Blum et al., Ref. 2, p. 33.

26. Ibid.

27. Ibid., p. 39. Goode, Ref. 2, pp. 249-251. Carey, Ref. 2, p. 90.

28. Blum et al., Ref. 2, pp. 39, 141. Carey, Ref. 2, pp. 99-117.

29. Carey, ibid., pp. 89-95.

30. Goode, Ref. 2, pp. 248-259.

31. Carey, Ref. 2, pp. 73-79.

32. Ibid., pp. 94-110.

33. Concealed among these 2098 cases are an unknown number of persons who failed to respond to the questions on buying and selling. In editing the answer sheets, the researcher marked such blank responses as "never" bought or sold. Hence, an unknown number of persons who may have actually bought or sold drugs are incorrectly classified as not involved. The ramifications of this editing mistake are discussed in the following chapter.

34. We will demonstrate in the following chapter that the use of cannabis appears to be a prerequisite for the use of hard drugs.

35. Goode, Ref. 2, pp. 257-259, and Carey, Ref. 2, p. 84, discuss the importance of the prestige motive among sellers. Jerry Mandel, "Myths and Realities of Marihuana Pushing," in J. L. Simmons, ed., *Marihuana: Myths and Realities,* North Hollywood, Calif.: Brandon House, 1967, pp. 58-110, feels that prestige is not an important motive.

36. See Chaps. 8-9.

CHAPTER 6

The Stepping-stone
Theory Stumbles

The use of drugs other than marihuana has become a source of considerable concern in American society in the 1970s. The use of illegal drugs (cocaine, heroin, and hallucinogens) and the illicit use of medically prescribed drugs (amphetamines, sedatives, and legal opiates) has probably increased two to five times since 1966 among U.S. college students.[1] Federal laws state that these drugs are "dangerous" because they "have a high potential for abuse." When abused, these drugs may cause physiological and psychological dependence, harm the physical health of the user, and perhaps cause persons to engage in behavior that is harmful to society.[2]

Regardless of the actual physiological harm caused by cannabis, the most important controversy involving cannabis is whether marihuana use "leads to" the use of other dangerous drugs. This chapter and the following one will interchangeably use the terms "other," "hard," or "dangerous" drugs to refer to the illicit use, as defined in Chapter 3, of amphetamines, sedatives (barbiturates or tranquilizers), methedrine, hallucinogens, cocaine, and heroin.

This stepping-stone theory derives from the now classic position of the Bureau of Narcotics, which connects marihuana to heroin use. The stepping-stone theory has an interesting history. In testimony before the House of

Representatives in 1937, the commissioner of the Federal Bureau of Narcotics, Harry Anslinger, was asked whether "the marihuana addict graduates into a heroin, an opium, or a cocaine user." Anslinger replied, "No sir; I have not heard of a case of that kind. I think it is an entirely different class. The marihuana addict does not go in that direction."[3] The Bureau of Narcotics position began to change in the late 1940s and early 1950s. The stepping-stone theory became, under a new director, Giordano, the main reason for maintaining the illegality of marihuana. In a pamphlet printed as late as 1965, the Bureau of Narcotics set forth the "simple" stepping-stone theory:

> It cannot be too strongly emphasized that the smoking of the marihuana cigarette is a dangerous first step on the road which *usually leads to* enslavement by heroin. . . . *Most* teenage addicts started by smoking marihuana cigarettes. *Never let anyone persuade you to smoke even one marihuana cigarette. It is pure poison.*[4]

This simple stepping-stone theory directly blames marihuana use for heroin use and ignores the social and psychological factors that may affect this progression. Former attorney general John Mitchell linked marihuana and heroin by a psychological concept: "A kid gets into steady use of marijuana. After a while he gets less charge from it, and this psychological dependency causes him to move on to the harder stuff."[5] The director of the Bureau of Narcotics and Dangerous Drugs (BNDD) in 1970 held that

> . . . the overwhelming majority of those who use heroin or LSD in the U.S. and England have had prior experience with either marijuana or hashish. Thus, . . . if many individuals did not get involved with marijuana, they would never get around to using the more potent and dangerous drugs.[6]

With one exception,[7] support for this simple progression theory comes from studies demonstrating that institutionalized heroin addicts used marihuana before using heroin. Ball, Glazer, and Weppner analyze the patterns of drug use among institutionalized heroin addicts and discover that more than a majority of heroin addicts have used marihuana prior to heroin use, although all studies find much variation by various demographic characteristics such as sex, urban-rural, North-South, race, and age.[8] One problem with such evidence is that the population selected for study is predominantly urban slum dwellers who have been contacted by the law for their drug habits. Very few middle-class drug users are included in such studies. A second problem is that the wrong comparison is being made. Instead of a sample of heroin users, a sample of marihuana users in a noninstitutionalized population is needed. Data that show how many marihuana users have tried heroin and how many have not tried heroin is needed to demonstrate the correct progression.

A further problem is that proponents of the stepping-stone theory tend to ignore evidence from societies where there is much cannabis use and little heroin (or hard-drug) use or where heroin (or other drug) use is common and marihuana use is unknown. For example, cannabis use is legal and sold by government monopolies in India and most predominantly Moslem countries. Important segments of such populations use cannabis but never touch opiates.[9] Even India, which supplied much of the opium for Chinese opium smokers between 1830 and 1900, has few opiate addicts when compared with the probable number of cannabis users. The Chopra brothers (who are frequently cited by U.S. public officials to support anticannabis laws) did not carefully consider the stepping-stone theory in a 1957 article on cannabis. In a study of habitual cannabis users in 1935 (and cited in their 1957 article), the Chopras found that the "habitual use of alcohol as well as opium along with cannabis drugs occurred in about 9% of the cases."[10] Hence, the use of other drugs appears uncommon among cannabis users in India.

On the other hand, in Hong Kong, where perhaps one out of every eight males is addicted to opium, cannabis use is virtually unknown.[11] Likewise, Vancouver, Canada, has had a high level of opiate use for many years; cannabis was virtually unknown until the late 1960s.[12] Ball and Chambers found that a large number of southern opiate addicts had not used marihuana or heroin.[13] In addition, it appears that Anslinger may have been correct in 1937; many heroin and opiate users had apparently not used marihuana prior to their heroin use.[14]

Although marihuana use is not always associated with the use of other drugs in the U.S. or foreign countries, it is very clear that marihuana is somehow related to the use of hard drugs in many Western countries, especially among youth populations. The American public appears to have accepted the stepping-stone theory. A Louis Harris poll in May 1969 found that 85% of the U.S. population agreed that "pot leads to habit forming drugs."[15] Gallup found that 12% of the adult population spontaneously mentioned that marihuana "leads to the use of stronger drugs," when asked what the effects of marihuana are by interviewers.[16]

This belief has considerable basis in fact.[17] Supporters of present laws against marihuana and proponents of marihuana legalization are likely to agree that marihuana smokers are significantly more likely to use heroin or other drugs than nonmarihuana users. However, diverse groups draw different conclusions from this correlation; BNDD officials support marihuana criminalization, while drug users feel that marihuana should be legalized. How is it that such diametrically opposed conclusions can be drawn from the same basic statistical relationship?

The answer to this dilemma lies in the different interpretations given to the concept "leads to" and other factors that are seen as affecting the marihuana-to-hard-drug progression. There are at least six distinct theories that attempt to explain how marihuana use leads to the use of dangerous drugs: the (1) pharmacological, (2) disturbed-personality, (3) euphoria, (4) increased benefits,

(5) sophisticated stepping-stone, and (6) subculture theories. The last two theories are much more important than the other four.

The pharmacological theory holds that the use of cannabis "invariably causes" the use of heroin or other drugs. According to this theory, the pharmacological effects of cannabis on the body are such that the user needs some other drug in order to remain stable or to keep from becoming sick. Opiate addiction is a good example of the basic principles of this pharmacological theory. After the daily use of sizable doses of heroin, the body becomes physically dependent upon that drug. If the drug is not used, the person will suffer serious withdrawal symptoms. Yet the heroin addict's misery can be easily alleviated by the administration of some other opiate such as morphine, Demerol, or methadone.[18] A similar dependency on cannabis may lead to hard drugs.

There are certain basic flaws in the pharmacological theory as it applies to marihuana. While there has been no scientific research that shows physiological dependence upon cannabis, a great deal of research demonstrates the lack of such physiological dependence upon marihuana.[19]

The theory can be disproved by showing that other factors affect the relationship between the frequency of marihuana use and heroin use. If, on the other hand, all social and psychological variables do not affect the marihuana-to-heroin relationship, this theory might be more plausible. It does not figure prominently in the scientific literature dealing with the marihuana controversy. No known reputable scientist holds to the theory; even the BNDD and other public officials no longer support the pharmacological theory.

The other five theories treat "leads to" as a statistical association to be explained. This statistical association holds that more cannabis users will use heroin or other drugs than nonmarihuana users. This statistical association happens to be true and has been uncovered in several studies of different populations. Among St. Louis black males, Robins and Murphy found that 26% of the marihuana users also used heroin, while none of the nonmarihuana users did so.[20] Several surveys of drug use in college populations find that the more frequently marihuana is used, the greater the likelihood of using a wide variety of other drugs.[21] Josephson, investigating a national high school population, found that less than 2% of the nonmarihuana users had tried (nonmedically) any of the psychoactive drugs. However, among the "occasional and frequent users" (ten or more times) of marihuana, 12% had tried heroin, 55% had tried LSD, and about 70% had tried barbiturates or amphetamines.[22] This information, in widely differing populations, demonstrates that the more frequently marihuana is used, the greater the probability of using dangerous drugs. All of the following theories assume the truth of this relationship, but they disagree about why this statistical association is true. Each theory proposes different variables that are hypothesized to intervene between the use of marihuana and the use of hard drugs.

The second major theory for explaining the association between marihuana use and the use of harder drugs, which the data will not be able to disprove directly with the data, is the disturbed-personality theory. Blaine, for example, sees psychological deficiencies as precipitating drug use:

> An individual who feels inadequate or perhaps perverted sees in drugs a way out of himself and into a totally new body and mind. . . . Often this search for a new self is what leads to escalation and a frantic search for new drugs which lead to addiction. [23]

According to this approach, the individual uses drugs in a "clumsy and misplaced effort to cope with many of one's most pressing and seemingly insoluble problems."[24] Kaplan, a lawyer, probably states most clearly how this personality theory may account for hard drug use:

> A person who has a predisposition to take drugs would probably use different drugs in succession until he found one that satisfied his particular predisposition. . . . Marijuana is used before the dangerous drugs, since it is the least dangerous and usually the most available of the illegal drugs. [25]

Although the present study cannot disprove this theory, it can show that psychological variables are not necessary to explain the progression from marihuana use to heroin use; social factors do the job quite adequately.

A third theory, promoted by the BNDD, holds that the link between marihuana and hard drugs revolves around the search for euphoria, hence the name euphoria theory. This theory was directly endorsed by an attorney of the BNDD in a speech still distributed by the BNDD to interested citizens:

> One particularly grave danger of habitual marihuana use is that there is often a clear pattern of graduation from marihuana to the stronger addictive opiates. Those who seek personal well-being and exhilaration through the stimuli of drugs ultimately discover that opiates have more to offer. [26]

The former director of the BNDD also directly endorses this theory: "The use of marijuana develops a taste for drug intoxication which, in turn, leads many people to the use of more potent drugs—even heroin."[27] It is possible to demonstrate empirically the validity of the euphoria theory by developing an indicator of the desire to get high. Examination of the relationship between the frequency of marihuana use and hard-drug use while holding constant the desire to get high or not will allow a test of this theory.

A fourth theory is exposed by pro-marihuana commentators. The increased benefits theory holds that marihuana users will experience certain beneficial effects, which are even more intense when other drugs are used. DeQuincey (opium), Gautier (hashish), Ginsberg (marihuana), and Leary (LSD)[28] have attributed to these drugs a large array of benefits. It is possible to find writers and users ascribing to the opiates, cannabis, hallucinogens, and amphetamines but not barbiturates and tranquilizers the power to expand consciousness, increase creativity and sensitivity to music and color, serve as a releaser of inhibitions and an aphrodesiac, enhance pleasure and sociability, turn hostility into friendship, and see past the artificiality of middle-class culture.[29] Specifically, nonusers and marihuana users are urged to turn on to drugs other than marihuana because of the increased potential benefit to the user. It is possible to test the increased benefits theory to a limited extent. If this theory is correct, those who report experiencing such benefits from marihuana should be more likely to graduate to other drugs, independent of their own marihuana use.

A fifth theory, increasingly promoted by officials from the BNDD and World Health Organization, is the sophisticated stepping-stone theory. The basic tenet of this theory is that the link between marihuana and hard-drug use cannot be fully explained by psychological and social factors.[30] Thus, this theory admits that nonpharmacological or nonbiological factors may influence the progression, but marihuana use still has some independent influence upon hard-drug use.

In addition, the sophisticated stepping-stone theory increasingly accepts the sociological idea of subcultures but blames marihuana for leading persons into drug subcultures:

> Abuse of cannabis facilitates the association with social groups and subcultures involved with more dangerous drugs, such as opiates or barbiturates. Transition to the use of such drugs would be a consequence of this association rather than an inherent effect of cannabis.[31]

A similar note is sounded by a BNDD pamphlet entitled *Fact Sheets,* under the section on marihuana:

> Researchers point out that a person predisposed to abuse of one drug may be likely to abuse other, stronger drugs. Also, users of one drug may be exposed to a variety of other drug users and sellers and through this association may be encouraged to experiment with more potent drugs.[32]

This theory implies that marihuana is undesirable because the person will gain friends who use other drugs. This is essentially a new version of the idea that marihuana use helps one gain "evil" associates. The important implication is that marihuana use, and not some other social factor, is the basic reason persons gain friends who use hard drugs. One may prove or disprove this theory by investigating the relationship between using marihuana and having friends who use other drugs, while holding constant other social factors.

The sixth theory, and most crucial for our purposes, is the subculture theory. This position sets itself in opposition to most of the above theories. The strongest statement of this basic position is found in the introduction to a paper prepared for the National Commission on Marihuana and Drug Abuse by sociologist Erich Goode. In this paper, Goode attempts to demonstrate the overwhelming importance of social and cultural forces operating in all drug use . . . it is the social settings themselves which determine the form that behavior will take, and not the drug itself. People do not "escalate" from the use of marijuana to more dangerous drugs because of any property resting within the chemistry of marijuana itself. If and when escalation does occur, it is totally a function of the kinds of people who use these drugs, their attitudes and values, their friendship networks, activities related to drug use, and so on. When the data on this topic are presented, it will be clear that all of the variation in rates of progression from group to group and from individual to individual can be accounted for by nonpharmacological factors. [33]

Above all else, the subculture theory stresses social factors in explaining the progression from marihuana to hard drugs, while disavowing the importance of the use of marihuana. This theory attempts to explain how persons become differentially involved in drug using groups. Briefly, the novice drug user is recruited to marihuana use by close friends who teach him how to smoke the drug, experience the effects, and define it as a pleasurable high. In order to become a regular marihuana user, the person must insulate himself from various social control mechanisms, such as the family and public definitions of morality, and he must obtain a regular supply of the drug. [34] As demonstrated in Chapter 4, regular use is frequent among those persons who have insulated themselves in a small group of friends who also use marihuana.

The most important addition to a sociological theory of dangerous drug use has been made by Goode. His article "Multiple Drug Use Among Marijuana Users" is instrumental in specifying dimensions of drug-subculture participation and in attempting to present empirical indicators of these dimensions. [35] If a subculture of drug use exists in America, the participants in this subculture constitute the main core of the drug problem in America. In the course of his discussion, Goode excludes from this subculture physician addicts, housewives, and truck drivers who use drugs in nongroup settings. Although the persons who participate in this drug subculture may come from different parts of the country and have never met each other, they use drugs in similar ways and espouse similar values.

There are different degrees of involvement in the drug subculture. Few persons devote a major portion of their time to this subculture. Further, people may be involved in different aspects of the subculture. Goode lists several different dimensions of participation in the drug subculture as it governs marihuana use, but they may be applied here to the use of hard drugs:

1. [Marijuana use] is characteristically participated in a group setting;
2. The others with whom one smokes marijuana are usually intimates. . . .
3. One generally has long-term continuing social relations with the others;
4. A certain degree of value consensus will obtain within the group;
5. Value-convergence will occur as a result of progressive group involvement;
6. The activity maintains the circle's cohesion and reaffirms its social bonds by acting them out;

7. Participants view the activity as a legitimate basis for identity—they define themselves, as well as others, partly on the basis of whether they have participated in the activity or not. [36]

A person's participation in each of these dimensions can vary from no involvement to much involvement, but heavy involvement in two or three of the dimensions usually implies some involvement in the other dimensions.

But Goode is not satisfied with simply listing dimensions of subcultural involvement. He attempts, in addition, to analyze the process by which individuals become progressively involved in the drug using subculture. He notes that almost all persons begin smoking marihuana with intimate friends and they they continue to use it, mainly with intimate friends. Involvement in this illegal activity then reaffirms subcultural values, intensifies emotional commitments to the group, and regularizes the individual's use of marihuana. In addition, the more an individual smokes, the greater his need for a regular supply of the drug. This may lead to involvement in buying and selling marihuana. [37]

Most important for this chapter is Goode's assertion that heavy marihuana use also "increases the likelihood of taking drugs in addition to marijuana *which the subculture approves of.* (Even daily use of marijuana will not involve the individual in heroin use if it is absent from the group in which he interacts and finds his significant others.)" [38] The use of hard drugs will be associated with heavy marihuana use due to favorable definitions within the group about drug experiences and increased opportunities of making friends with persons who use hard drugs. Then, in a direct attempt to refute the euphoria theory, Goode maintains,

> Often marijuana use "leads to" experimenting with narcotics in a working-class urban area not because of the search for an even-bigger and better "kick," but because the associations one makes as one's use level moves upward are increasingly also likely to experiment with narcotics.
>
> In contexts other than the slum, marijuana use does not imply experimentation with narcotics; on the college campus, for example, heroin use involves a very tiny segment of even the drug-using contingent, and its use is distinctly frowned upon. [39]

He states further, however, that "heavy marijuana use on the college campus almost *implies* at least one-time use of one of the heavier psychedelics" [40] because the middle-class college drug subculture tends to value the stimulation of the mind that hallucinogens reputedly have.

The subculture theory has another emphasis. In his lengthy and informative treatment of Haight-Ashbury, Carey seems to indicate that another important factor in understanding the drug scene or the drug subculture is involvement in the buying and especially in the selling of marihuana and other drugs. [41] Goode suggests a possible mechanism by which progression occurs:

> By buying marijuana, one often interacts with, forms friendships with, comes to respect the opinions of, the seller of the drug, who is generally older, more

> experienced and sophisticated, involved in a daring and dangerous life, and is
> respected and eagerly sought after by many members of one subcommunity. . . . the
> neophyte drug user gradually acquires the seller's favorable definition of, and accepts
> opportunities for, heroin use.[42]

Similar logic leads Kaplan, in arguing for the controlled legalization of
marihuana, to state that "the illegal selling of marijuana will continue to provide
an entry into the drug culture and thus a ready distribution network for other
more dangerous drugs."[43] Thus, the subculture position suggests that the
illegality of marihuana exposes neophyte marihuana users to drug sellers and
new friends who use hard drugs and hence to use the drugs themselves. If
marihuana were legally available, the progression from marihuana to hard drugs
would occur less frequently than it does at the present time, because marihuana
users would be unlikely to meet drug sellers and to gain friends who use hard
drugs.

Thus, the subculture theory maintains that if drug use among friends, class
background, drug buying and selling, and other indicators of drug-subculture
involvement are held constant, the positive linear relationship between marihuana use and the use of hard drugs should substantially decrease, if not vanish
altogether. This is a proposition that the present chapter will attempt to test.

Techniques of multivariate analysis may be used to "explain away" or
interpret the positive linear relationship between the frequency of cannabis use
and the use of hard drugs. If attempts to explain or interpret the marihuana-hard
drug relationship do not succeed, the conditions under which dangerous drugs
will or will not be used subsequent to marihuana use will be investigated.[44] In
addition, an attempt will be made to determine which of the six theories are
essentially incorrect and which theories provide the most complete understanding of hard-drug use.

This chapter will use two important measures of drug use. The Frequency of
Cannabis Index will be the major independent variable; the dependent variables
are measures of the illicit use of hard drugs as defined in Chapter 3. A
respondent was classified as illicitly using a prescription drug (amphetamines,
methedrine, and sedatives) when he admitted to having used it in an attempt to
get high or used it more frequently or in larger doses than prescribed by a
doctor. A respondent had illicitly used illegal drugs (hallucinogens, cocaine, and
heroin) if he admitted to ever using these drugs.

It is more difficult to develop good measures of the theories discussed above.
While there was no attempt to measure the disturbed-personality theory, there
was to measure the euphoria theory. The Euphoria Index was formed from the
question: "What are (or might be) the most important reasons for your using
marihuana?" The respondent could mark any or all of nine possible answers, one
of which was to "feel good, get high." The 57% who chose this item indicated a
desire for euphoria. In retrospect, this is a weak indicator of euphoria. The

question should have allowed students to select "getting high" as the most important reason for using drugs when contrasted to other possible reasons. However, such a question was not asked.

An indicator of the increased benefits theory was obtained by measuring the degree of orientation to values favorable to drug use with the following five "agree" or "disagree" items (the proportion of the total sample agreeing with each item is indicated in parentheses):

1. Most drug users in college are among the more independent, thoughtful, and creative students. (23%)
2. A person who uses illicit drugs should encourage nonusers to try these drugs. (1.4%)

Gave as a reason for using marihuana:

3. Aid in "socializing" or communication with others. (28%)
4. The "in thing" to do. (20%)
5. Improve my creativity or performance, to better understand other people or my inner self. (18%)

According to the response to these items, a respondent was classified on the Increased Benefits Index as follows: (1) "none" if he agreed with none of the items; (2) "some" if he agreed with one or two items; and (3) "much" if he agreed with three or more items.

Measures of drug-subculture participation will also serve as measures of the sophisticated stepping-stone theory. Three indicators of differential participation in the illicit drug subculture were developed: (1) Peer Group Cannabis Use Index, the proportion of friends who use marihuana; (2) Illicit Marketing Index; and (3) exposure to hard-drug-using friends. The first measure of differential involvement in the drug subculture, the Peer-Group Cannabis Use Index, was developed in Chapter 4. The second measure of subculture participation, the Illicit Marketing Index, was developed in Chapter 5.

As noted above, Goode discusses the importance of having "intimate friends" or "significant others" who use dangerous drugs in introducing the individual to these other drugs. Hence, on the third measure of involvement in the drug subculture, exposure to hard drug-using friends, respondents have been classified according to their intimacy with persons who use various hard drugs. Respondents were asked to indicate what drugs their friends, close friends, and siblings used; they were differentially exposed to each drug as follows: (1) "none" if none of these three reference groups used the drug; (2) "friends" if only a friend or an acquaintance used the drug (but not a close friend or sibling); and (3) "intimate friends" if a close friend or sibling used the drug. Thus, a person reporting that a brother or sister used hallucinogens is seen as very exposed to hallucinogens.

Having developed the major variables, one can now begin an analysis of the stepping-stone theory. First, it will be established that a statistical relationship between the use of marihuana and the use of each hard drug does exist. Graph 6.1 shows a strong positive, linear relationship between the frequency of cannabis use and the illicit use of each of the hard drugs. The more frequent the use of cannabis, the greater the illicit use of each dangerous drug. Thus, while less than 1% of the nonmarihuana users have tried hallucinogens, 68% of the weekly marihuana users have used hallucinogens, a difference of 67%.

The independent variable, frequency of cannabis use, appears at first glance

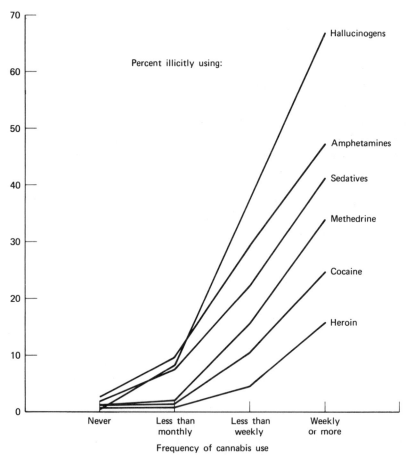

Graph 6.1. The more frequent the use of cannabis, the greater the use of each hard drug. (This graph is based upon data presented in the "total" rows of Table 22, Appendix A.)

to influence most strongly the use of hallucinogens and amphetamines, while having a lesser effect on the use of cocaine and heroin. However, when the proportion of the total sample using each drug is taken into account, the heavy use of cannabis is still an important factor in determining heroin use. Thus, 4% of the total sample but 0.3% of the noncannabis users and 17% of the regular cannabis users have tried heroin.

This positive linear relationship between marihuana use and dangerous-drug use has been found in all studies that have investigated the relationship. In addition, no matter what definition of "frequent" marihuana use is employed, the strength of the relationship is very similar. In a national study of high school students, Josephson found that 1% of the noncannabis users had tried LSD, heroin, and "downs" or "ups." But among those who had used marihuana ten or more times, 12% had tried heroin (similar to 17% of weekly marihuana users here), 55% had tried LSD, 71% had nonmedically used "downs," and 74% had tried "ups."[45] Josephson's patterns of drug utilization are virtually parallel to the levels of drug use in the sample in this study. One difference Josephson reports is that more persons have used the amphetamines and sedatives nonmedically. This difference may be due to the definition of "illicit" use adopted in Chapter 3, which Josephson does not use.

As mentioned earlier, there is agreement that such a statistical relationship exists; the BNDD and subculture theorists agree on this point. The disagreement deals with why this relationship is true. In order to decide which theory best explains the relationship, one must consider the effect of other factors.

Although the data will not be presented, each of the measures of various theoretical positions is positively and significantly related to the illicit use of each of the dangerous drugs. Thus, the greater the agreement with the Euphoria Index, the Increased Benefits Index, and each of the subcultural indices, the greater the probability of illicitly using hallucinogens, amphetamines, sedatives, methedrine, cocaine, heroin, and cannabis.[46]

Now the study must try to show whether any of the theories proposed above can explain or interpret the relationship between the frequency of marihuana use and the use of hard drugs. Since it wishes to investigate the relationship between marihuana and the use of six different drugs while holding constant five variables to test these theories, it needs to present thirty different graphs, many more than are needed to demonstrate the important findings. Thus, only graphs on heroin will be presented and occassionally, the data for hallucinogens. Similar findings, not presented, hold true for other drugs.

The selection of heroin for intensive analysis is made for four reasons. First, evidence presented in Graph 6.1 demonstrates clearly that, as Goode asserts, "on the college campus heroin use involves a very tiny segment of even the drug-using contingent."[47] Among weekly marihuana users, few (17%) have tried heroin. Second, in the college population there appears to be less support for heroin use than for the illicit use of other drugs. Students were asked whether they agreed that "a person should be allowed to use this substance if he wishes." About a third of the sample agreed with the statement for hallucinogens, amphetamines, and sedatives, while only 13% agreed for heroin or cocaine. In addition, 64% agreed that heroin and cocaine should be controlled by strong laws. Hence, college students are generally opposed to the use of narcotics. Third, Loiselle and Whitehead have utilized Guttman scaling in an attempt to determine sequential patterns of drug use. They found that they could form an adequate scale only when they confined their analysis to marihuana users (nonusers were excluded). Among marihuana users, the use of stimulants, sedatives, hallucinogens, and opiates could be predicted by Guttman scaling techniques. They conclude, "We are empirically correct in saying that those who have used heroin have progressed through the series of items in the scale as well as marijuana."[48] If the criteria of illicit drug use adopted in the present study were used, the hallucinogen use might occur prior to the illicit use of stimulants and sedatives. Thus, it would seem that students becoming progressively involved in drugs are likely to try hallucinogens, then the illicit use of stimulants and sedatives, with heroin being the last drug utilized. However, since the Guttman scale has not been used on the present patterns of drug use, one cannot tell whether the illicit use of these drugs is scalable. Fourth, the public concern about heroin use is great; empirical evidence is badly needed.

The top sections of Graph 6.2 show that the Euphoria Index has no effect upon the relationship of marihuana use to heroin. That is, at each level of cannabis use, people who chose "to get high, feel good" are not more likely to use heroin than persons who failed to choose this answer. The same findings hold true for other drugs. However, the indicator of euphoria is probably a weak one; hence one cannot completely discard the Euphoria Theory. But the data do cast doubt upon the importance of this theory.

The increased benefits theory does not survive much better. Graph 6.2 demonstrates that the powerful effect of marihuana use upon heroin use is not significantly altered when the Increased Benefits Index is held constant. Marihuana use, and not the potential benefits of drug use, appears to be more important in determining heroin use.

However, the subculture variables do significantly affect the cannabis-hard drug relationship. Of the three variables, the Peer-Group Cannabis Use Index appears to have the least effect. Weekly marihuana users with few or some cannabis-using friends are unlikely (8% and 5%, respectively) to try heroin, while 18% of those with most friends using cannabis have tried heroin. It appears that if persons are not insulated in marihuana-using circles, they are unlikely to use heroin.

Percent Using Heroin

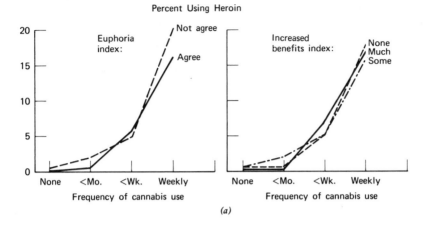

(a)

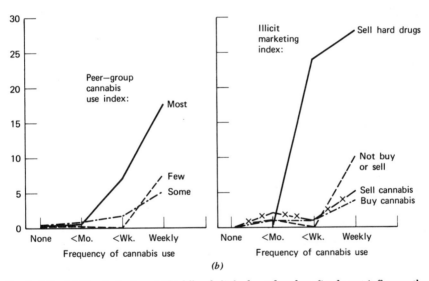

(b)

Graph 6.2. (a) The desire to get "high" or beliefs about drug benefits do not influence the marihuana-heroin use relationship. (b) Having cannabis-using friends and selling hard drugs strongly influence the marihuana-heroin use relationship. (These graphs are based upon data presented in Table 21, Appendix A.)

More importantly, when the Illicit Marketing Index is held constant, the relationship between marihuana use and heroin use is strongly affected. Those who neither buy nor sell, as well as those who only buy and/or sell cannabis, are most unlikely (10% or less) to use heroin, even among weekly marihuana users. On the other hand, those who have sold hard drugs are likely to have tried heroin (about 25%), even though moderate (less than weekly) cannabis users. There is one exception; of the twenty persons who are experimental (less than monthly) cannabis users but have sold hard drugs, 0.7% have tried heroin. However, a percentage based upon such a small number of cases is unstable.

By far the most crucial factor is having heroin-using friends. The upper left corner of Graph 6.3 (bottom line) shows that few (5%) of the weekly cannabis users have tried heroin if they have no heroin-using friends. In addition, persons with heroin-using friends (but not intimate friends) are not much more likely to use heroin (12%), regardless of their regular use of cannabis. However, those who have intimate heroin-using friends are likely to try heroin (45%) if they are weekly cannabis users. In short, marihuana use does not "usually lead to" heroin use. The marihuana-heroin relationship is contingent upon having heroin-using intimates; the probability that weekly cannabis users will try heroin is very low if they do not have such intimate friends.

The frequency of cannabis use is a less powerful factor than heroin-using friends in influencing the respondent's use of heroin. Data presented in Appendix A show that weekly marihuana users are 16% more likely to try heroin than noncannabis users. But 28% of those with intimate heroin-using friends versus 1% of those with no heroin-using friends have themselves tried heroin, a difference of 27%. Thus, friendships with heroin users is almost twice as powerful a factor as cannabis use in predicting heroin use (27% versus 16%).

The other charts in Graph 6.3 show similar findings for other hard drugs. In all graphs, noncannabis users are unlikely (less than 3%) to use hard drugs illicitly, even if they have intimates using that drug. There are two minor exceptions; if noncannabis users have intimates using sedatives and amphetamines, 8% and 6%, respectively, have tried these substances. On the other hand, having intimate friends using a particular hard drug greatly increases the probability that more frequent cannabis users will try that drug. Also, persons with friends, but not intimates, who use a particular hard drug are more similar to those without hard-drug-using friends in their use of hard drugs than those with intimate hard-drug-using friends. (For all drugs, the "friends" line is closer to the "none" line than to the "intimates" line.) This evidence tends to indicate that the college students' level of marihuana use or, as will be shown shortly, level of involvement in the subculture predisposes respondents to try hard drugs. Having intimate friends using a particular hard drug may be seen as the immediate cause, or precipitating factor, in the use of that drug. If students have no such intimate friends, even though weekly cannabis users, they are unlikely to use various drugs.

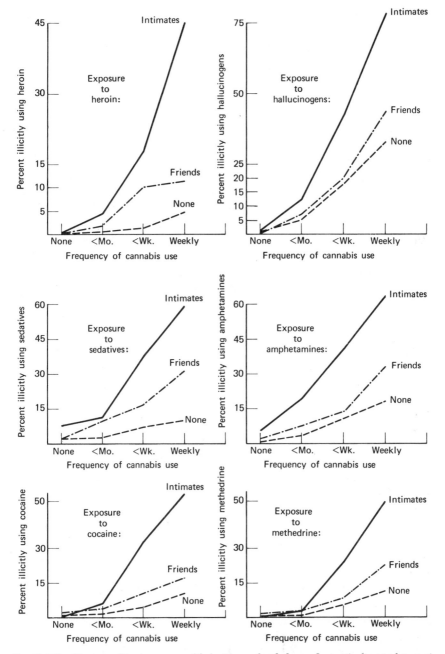

Graph 6.3. Noncannabis users are unlikely to use hard drugs. Increasingly regular marihuana users with intimate friends using a particular hard drug are likely to try that drug. Those without heroin-using friends are unlikely to try heroin, even if they are weekly cannabis users. (These graphs are based upon data presented in Table 22, Appendix A.)

There is one important difference between heroin use and hallucinogen use. For heroin, the "none" line demonstrates that having heroin-using friends is almost a sociologically "necessary" condition[49] for heroin use. However, among those without hallucinogen-using friends, the regularity of cannabis use has an important effect upon hallucinogen use; having hallucinogen-using friends is not so necessary a condition for hallucinogen use. Cannabis use has an effect independent of friendship. But hallucinogen use is the exception and not heroin use. Students without friends using sedatives, amphetamines, methedrine, and cocaine are unlikely (less than 20%) to use these drugs, even if regular cannabis users.

Thus, one major shortcoming of the simple stepping-stone theory is that it fails to consider the effect of friendships with users of each drug and involvement in drug buying and selling. The progression from marihuana use to the use of these drugs is very strongly affected by these social factors.

However, the data do demonstrate one aspect of the simple stepping-stone theory that is correct. A review of all of the graphs in this chapter and the tables in Appendix A reveals that noncannabis users almost never use other drugs, no matter what factors are held constant. For each drug, less than 8% of the noncannabis users have illicitly tried that drug no matter what variables are held constant. In order to investigate whether any other factor might increase the illicit use of drugs by nonmarihuana users, a wide variety of factors, such as sex, parental income, race, involvement in school truancy, unconventional behaviors (see Chapter 8), religiosity, and alienation were held constant. For all practical purposes, in a college student population, only those who use marihuana are likely to use hard drugs illicitly.

Hence the data tend to support the BNDD contention that "the smoking of the marihuana cigarette is a dangerous first step"[50] toward hard drugs. More recently, director of the BNDD, John Ingersoll, stated that: "if many individuals did not get involved with marihuana, they would never get around to using the more potent dangerous drugs."[51]

This statement is, of course, a reaffirmation of the stepping-stone theory and is a classic example of the logical fallacy of *post hoc, ergo propter hoc* ("after this, therefore because of it").[52] This kind of logic is analagous to the following statement, which might be used to explain prostitution. To paraphrase Ingersoll's basic reasoning: If many individuals did not get involved in premarital sexual intercourse, they would never get around to being prostitutes. Such logic is too simplistic to explain either hard-drug use or prostitution and unfairly condemns marihuana use or premarital sex.

There is a much better explanation for the lack of hard-drug use among nonmarihuana users. The use of marihuana is a *rite de passage* into drug using circles or into the drug subculture. The conduct norms of the subculture dictate, and the peer group in which a person participates expects, that a person will use marihuana first. Until the individual does so, there will be little pressure on him to use hard drugs. Once he uses marihuana, group pressures to use hard drugs depend greatly upon the social composition of his friendship group. If no one else uses hard drugs, the probability of trying such drugs will be low. If most friends use another drug, the person will probably graduate to that drug. Similar findings emerge from a study of Haight-Ashbury hippies. Davis and Munoz (1968) state that it was a matter of chance "whether a novice hippie turned to 'acid' or 'speed' or some other drug or a combination of several. Whose 'pad' he 'crashed' on arrival or who befriended him . . . could have as much to do with his subsequent pattern of drug use as anything else."[53]

Further examination of the data tends to indicate that a willingness to try marihuana is not the only important norm in the subculture. A person is expected to use marihuana on a reasonably regular basis (at least monthly) before being expected to use hard drugs. Very few experimental cannabis users, generally less than 15%, have tried other substances even though they have intimate friends using it or are themselves engaged in selling drugs. It is only among the moderate (less than weekly) and weekly cannabis users that the subculture expects and maintains high levels of hard drug use. But the probability of progression to hard drugs among weekly marihuana users is strongly affected by the drug-use patterns of close friends and involvement in selling drugs.

Thus, the simple stepping-stone theory is essentially incorrect because social factors strongly affect the progression from marihuana to heroin. Marihuana use does not usually lead to hard-drug use; one must know something about the respondent's friendship patterns and involvement in drug buying and selling.

In addition, Graph 6.2 shows that the euphoria theory and the increased benefits theory do not explain the marihuana-heroin relationship. Similarly, Graphs 6.2 and 6.3 demonstrate the fundamental inadequacy of the pharmacological theory and, to a lesser extent, the disturbed-personality theory. These graphs demonstrate the great impact that social factors have on the relationship between marihuana use and hard-drug use. The pharmacological theory is disproven because both friendships with hard-drug users and drug buying or selling greatly alter the relationship between marihuana and hard-drug use. In addition, information about a respondent's personality is not needed to understand hard-drug use. However, the study did not measure personality variables and, hence, cannot completely discard the disturbed-personality theory.

There remain two theories that are more probable. The sophisticated stepping-stone theory cannot be discarded; among those with intimate friends using heroin (or other hard drugs), there is still a strong positive relationship between marihuana use and heroin (hard-drug) use. In addition, as will soon be shown, the use of marihuana is associated with having friends who use various hard drugs.[54]

The subculture theory, of course, receives impressive support from the above data. Factors identified by Goode and Carey do impressively affect the marihuana-hard drug relationship. The problem with the subculture theory at this point is that it seems identical to the sophisticated stepping-stone theory; each theory emphasizes a different aspect of the same data. For example, the sophisticated theory would emphasize that noncannabis users do not use hard drugs and that a strong relationship between marihuana use and heroin is obtained among those with intimate hard-drug-using friends. Subculture theorists would emphasize that there is almost no relationship between marihuana and heroin among those without heroin-using friends. In addition, Goode states that "intense and continuing involvement in marijuana use implies involvement in a drug using subculture."[55] Thus, it appears that what Goode means by "involvement" in the drug subculture and what the sophisticated position means by "marihuana use" are measured by precisely the same variable, the frequency of cannabis use. Since both theories can use the same set of data to support their position, is it possible to determine which theory is better?

It was noted earlier that these two theories seem to diverge with respect to how one becomes involved in subcultures or groups in which dangerous drugs are used. Eddy, as a representative of the sophisticated position, says that "abuse of cannabis facilitates the association with social groups and subcultures involved with more dangerous drugs such as opiates or barbiturates."[56] Thus, he implies that something about the use of cannabis causes persons to gain bad associates. The BNDD also notes that marihuana users "may be exposed to a variety of other drug users and *sellers*."[57]

Carey and Goode both agree that marihuana users are likely to gain hard-drug-using friends but indicate that this is because of the illegality of marihuana, not anything inherent in marihuana itself. Both authors point to the fact that persons get involved in selling because they use the drugs.[58] Because they buy drugs from sellers, they are likely to be turned on to hard drugs by such sellers. But something must be added to this model; a student who becomes involved in selling drugs is likely to gain friends who use dangerous drugs and hence to be turned on by such friends.

One can empirically measure the truth of these perspectives. The sophisticated stepping-stone theory would hold that the more frequently a person uses marihuana, the more likely he will be to have hard-drug-using friends. The subculture theory would postulate that some measure of subculture participation, independent of marihuana use, is the basic factor explaining hard-drug-using friends. One major measure of subculture participation, is the Illicit Marketing Index.

Graph 6.3 established that a very important factor in understanding heroin use (and other hard-drug use) is having heroin-using intimate friends. Thus, the study will use exposure to heroin or other drugs as the dependent variable and will attempt to show why students gain intimate friends who use heroin or other drugs.

Graph 6.4 shows that 2% of the noncannabis users have intimate friends using heroin. As suggested above, noncannabis users do not participate in the drug subculture. Likewise, only nineteen noncannabis have bought or sold illicit drugs; hence, they cannot be compared with those who use drugs and bought and/or sold drugs. The analysis will be confined to cannabis users.

In addition, the high level (27%) of exposure to heroin users among thirty weekly cannabis users who have not bought or sold drugs is misleading; data from all nonbuyers, nonsellers will be ignored in the analysis below for three reasons. First, there is no reason why these 30 cases should have a much higher level of exposure than regular cannabis users who only buy and/or sell cannabis. Second, respondents could easily lie by marking the "none" category on the drug buying or selling questions even though they had actually bought or sold. Third, the present author made a serious error in editing the questionnaire. When a student had left the questions on drug buying or selling blank, the author inserted the response "never." In reality, blank responses should be treated as refusals and excluded from consideration (as were seven persons who definitely stated a refusal; see Chapter 5). This error meant that persons who had actually bought or sold drugs but failed to report (left blank) their involvement in buying or selling are incorrectly classified in the category of not buying or selling. If only a few (five to ten) regular marihuana users who had actually bought or sold were incorrectly recoded, it would be sufficient to greatly inflate the level of exposure to heroin (and other drug) users among these 30 cases.

The "original relationship" in Graph 6.4 shows that weekly cannabis users are 18% ($\%I$ = 24%-6%) more likely than experimental users to have intimate heroin-using friends; this supports the sophisticated stepping-stone theory. Data presented in Appendix A, Table 23 shows that the Illicit Marketing Index is also related to having heroin-using intimates. Among cannabis users, 5% of those who do not buy or sell drugs and 7% of those who only buy cannabis have intimate heroin-using friends. But 34% of those selling hard drugs have intimate heroin-using friends. Thus, those selling hard drugs are 28% (34%-7%) more likely than those who only buy cannabis to have heroin-using intimates. This supports the subculture position and shows that drug dealing is about twice as powerful as cannabis use in determining friendships with heroin users.

However, the central finding of this chapter emerges from analysis of the relationship between cannabis use and exposure to heroin-using intimates when

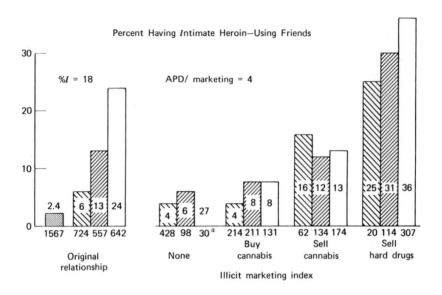

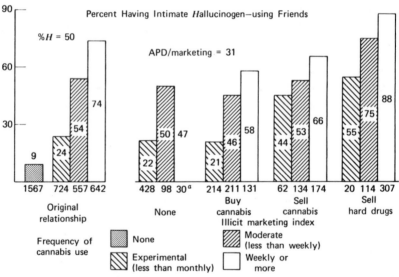

Graph 6.4. (a) Students gain heroin-using intimates by drug selling; marihuana use is unimportant. (b) Both drug dealing and cannabis use increase the probability of having intimate hallucinogen-using friends. (These graphs are based upon data presented in Table 23, Appendix A.)

the Illicit Marketing Index is held constant. Those who only buy cannabis are unlikely (4% to 8%) to have heroin-using intimates, regardless of their cannabis use. Nor does cannabis use appear to affect the friendship patterns of those who sell cannabis; experimental users are as likely to have heroin-using intimates as weekly users (16% versus 13%). In addition, among those who sell hard drugs, the weekly cannabis users are 11% (36%-25%) more likely than experimental users to have intimate heroin-using friends. Thus, holding constant the buying and selling of drugs, the 18% difference due to cannabis use is significantly reduced to 4% (APD). On the other hand, the 28% difference in exposure to heroin between buyers of cannabis and sellers of hard drugs is not affected (APD = 24%) when cannabis use is held constant. Thus, our evidence indicates that involvement in selling drugs is the crucial factor in understanding why students gain intimate heroin-using friends; the frequency of cannabis use is relatively unimportant.

The evidence tends to indicate that the sophisticated stepping-stone theory is basically incorrect because it ignores the important factor of illegal buying and selling of drugs and the role of friendships with heroin users. Far more impressive, and supported by empirical data, is the subculture theory. Essentially, this theory holds that heroin use occurs because persons gain heroin-using friends through increasingly heavy involvement in illicit buying and selling activities.

Given the above evidence, one may object that the selling of cannabis and hard drugs is a consequence of the heroin addict's need for money and that the present interpretation has the direction of causality completely wrong. This objection is particularly untenable because there are many more drug sellers than heroin users or addicts (bottom chart of Graph 5.2). In a sample of students attending college classes, there are few persons who could be classified as heroin addicts. Of our total sample, less than 1% has used heroin more than monthly, while 4% have ever tried it. A much larger proportion of the sample has sold cannabis, 22%, or hard drugs, 13%. The explanation presented in this chapter is both theoretically and empirically sounder than the addicts' desire for money to support his habit.

While it is clear that drug buying and selling is the important factor in understanding exposure to heroin-using friends, it is not as clear that drug selling determines exposure to hallucinogen-using intimates. Although the 50% (74% − 24%) difference due to marihuana is reduced in half (APD = 31%) when holding constant illicit marketing (bottom half of Graph 6.4), there is a steady increase due to cannabis use in exposure to hallucinogen users at each level of buying and selling drugs. Thus, among those who only buy cannabis, 21% of the experimental, 46% of the moderate, and 58% of the weekly cannabis users have intimate hallucinogen-using friends. A similar increase, but at higher levels, is found among cannabis sellers and sellers of hard drugs. Thus, it appears that cannabis use combines with illicit buying or selling in determining exposure to hallucinogen users. Despite this fact, it does not seem that any pharmacological factor in cannabis is responsible. Rather, the frequency of cannabis use is an indicator of early participation in the drug subculture; proof of this interpretation will be presented in the following chapter.

It must now be shown that drug dealing and heroin-using friends allow an adequate understanding of heroin use and that marihuana use is relatively unimportant. In addition, the data will test the one remaining assertion of the sophisticated stepping-stone theory: that social factors cannot fully explain the link between marihuana and heroin use.[59] If this is the case, then the relationship between marihuana and heroin use should be maintained when the Exposure to Heroin Users and the Illicit Marketing indices are simultaneously held constant. This is done in Graph 6.5. Because of an insufficient number of cases in extreme groups (such as experimental marihuana users who sell drugs), the categories of experimental and moderate cannabis use have been combined into an "irregular" category. Thus, "irregular" use combines all persons who were using cannabis less than weekly at the time they took the questionnaire. This will allow one to compare the heroin use of regular (weekly or more) and irregular cannabis users.

Graph 6.5 demonstrates that there is no marihuana-related differences in heroin use among persons who have no intimate friends using heroin. At each level of buying or selling, regular cannabis users are as unlikely to have tried heroin as irregular cannabis users. There does appear, however, to be a consistent finding that among students having intimate heroin-using friends, regular marihuana users are somewhat more likely than irregular users to use heroin. However, the number of cases is small (8, 11, 23) among regular cannabis users not selling hard drugs. But those who sell hard drugs and who have intimate heroin-using friends (two highest bars) are more likely to use heroin if they are regular, rather than irregular, cannabis users. Thus, it is only among those with intimate heroin-using friends that the marihuana-heroin relationship is not fully explained by social factors.

Such evidence can hardly be considered proof of the sophisticated stepping-stone theory. Since heroin use is strongly affected by subcultural factors (friendships and buying/selling), the regularity of marihuana use may also be an indicator of increased subculture participation. Or conversely, a person who has heroin-using intimates and engages in selling hard drugs but is an irregular cannabis user is, for some reason or other, not fully participating in the drug subculture.

Thus, the evidence demonstrates that the sophisticated stepping-stone theory, although not completely wrong, is badly misleading. It implicates marihuana use as the cause of heroin use and/or gaining heroin-using friends. The more important factor, a person's involvement in drug selling, is ignored. Thus, the

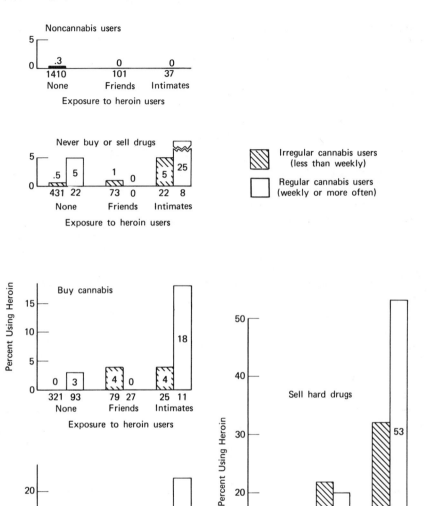

Graph 6.5. Marihuana-related differences in heroin use are found only among those with intimate heroin-using friends. Hard-drug sellers have high levels of heroin use. (This graph excludes 19 noncannabis users who have bought and/or sold drugs; none have used heroin.)

113

stepping-stone theory, both the simple and sophisticated versions, is essentially incorrect in explaining why college students use heroin.

The evidence in this chapter provides a great deal of support for the subculture theory. At every step in the analysis, factors identified by subculture theorists have been shown to be crucial to an understanding of heroin use. Particularly important factors in determining heroin use are exposure to heroin-using friends and involvement in selling hard drugs. The evidence further demonstrates the usefulness of the drug subculture concept. Progressive involvement toward the "core" of the subculture can be measured and traced in the data. Persons who do not use marihuana can be effectively considered nonparticipants in the subculture. Trying marihuana may be seen as a necessary *rite de passage* for subculture participation. The infrequent (less than monthly) use of cannabis indicates minimal participation in the subculture, as does the simple purchase of cannabis. Intermediate levels of participation in the subculture are indicated by cannabis selling and perhaps the weekly use of marihuana, which is not associated with the use or sale of hard drugs. Heavy participation begins when hard-drug-using intimates are gained and the individual begins to use hallucinogens and prescription drugs. One may be seen as a core participant when one becomes involved in selling hard drugs and gains intimates who use cocaine and heroin. However, this summary of drug-subculture participation is greatly simplified; the following chapter will demonstrate the complexity of progressive subculture involvement.

The present chapter also indicates how present drug laws are related to heroin use. Public officials fail to recognize how widespread drug selling is among those who use drugs as well as in the entire college population. Likewise, public officials fail to realize what the consequences of drug laws may be. Thus, our evidence indicts the present drug laws, and not marihuana use, as a major cause of heroin use.

This conclusion is arrived at by the following logic: marihuana is not legally available because of present drug laws. As a partial result of these laws, an underground drug market, centered around cannabis selling, has developed. Persons become involved in drug buying and selling for a rational reason: they wish to provide themselves with drugs which they use. Very high proportions of regular drug users become involved in selling cannabis. In particular, 72% of the regular cannabis users have sold cannabis and about half of the cannabis sellers have sold a hard drug (see Chapter 5 for details of this argument). If marihuana were legally available and weekly marihuana users could obtain what they need, they would have no rational reason to sell marihuana illegally. Persons who are presently drug sellers might be transformed into normal retail customers, as many bootleggers became alcohol buyers at the end of prohibition.

What might happen to persons who bought legal cannabis? It is probable that the illicit drug market's equivalent of the retail customer is the person who only buys cannabis. Cannabis buyers are unlikely (4% to 8%) to have heroin-using intimates and unlikely (7%) to use heroin themselves (Graphs 6.4 and 6.5). If marihuana were legally available, the majority of present drug sellers would probably soon give up drug dealing. They would have less reason to meet and befriend heroin users and, hence, to progress to heroin use. But the data demonstrate that under the present drug laws, just the opposite result occurs. Regular cannabis users are likely to become involved in selling marihuana and hard drugs, thus increasing the probability of meeting and befriending heroin users and being turned on to heroin. Legal cannabis might gravely undermine the illicit drug market and the cycle of events that recruits persons into the drug subculture. The present drug laws, more than marihuana use, are a major cause of heroin use among our college population. A similar conclusion cannot be so easily drawn for drugs other than heroin for reasons which will become apparent in the following chapter.

Before turning to the next chapter, one must note a serous difficulty in explaining hard-drug use. This difficulty has to do with the problem of time order. What factors come first, second, third, and last? Perhaps there is no clear cut sequence of events. Nevertheless, the data suggest that some such sequence exists, although it cannot be demonstrated with data obtained at one point in time. To solve the problem of time order and causality, information about the same students (panel data) at two or more different points in time is needed. Hence, the problem of time order cannot be resolved in the present book.

Despite the fact that it cannot unravel the time order of variables, this study makes assumptions about time order that must be made clear to the reader. It is hoped that future research can prove or disprove such assumptions. First, it assumes that marihuana use preceeds the use and sale of hard drugs. The present chapter has indicated that nonmarihuana users are unlikely to use any other drugs, no matter what other factors are held constant. In the previous chapter, noncannabis users were shown not to buy or sell any drugs, including cannabis. In addition, the more frequent the use of cannabis, the greater the likelihood of selling cannabis. Those who sell cannabis are likely to sell hard drugs. However, the time order between cannabis buying or selling and the use of hard drugs is not resolved. Persons who sell hard drugs appear to do so after having sold cannabis and after having used such drugs on a somewhat regular basis. Thus, one comes to a central, but unresolvable, dilemma. Do persons have to sell one hard drug in order to gain friends who use other hard drugs? But it has been shown that the sale of hard drugs may be a partial cause of exposure to hard-drug-using intimates and to the use of hard drugs. But selling hard drugs comes after the use of hard drugs (previous chapter). Thus, the whole chain of causality is open to question.

However, this study most closely analyzed heroin, and this is probably the last drug to which college students are exposed and use.[60] Thus, it is possible for students to sell drugs such as hallucinogens or pills prior to gaining heroin-using friends and to using heroin. What is more probable is that the use of different drugs may be the result of different causal chains. As indicated above, hallucinogen use may not be explained by the same processes that allow us to understand heroin use. The whole of the next chapter tries to unravel this problem.

The most critical assumption made in this chapter and the next, is that the influence of an intimate friend who uses a particular drug is frequently the precipitating (immediately causal) factor in the respondent's use of that drug. The contrary theory, that marihuana use leads to hard-drug use and then persons gain friends who use that drug, is rejected upon the basis of data presented in tables in Appendix A and Graph 6.5. If marihuana users first become heroin users and then gain heroin-using intimates, there should be more heroin users than persons with intimate heroin-using friends. Such is contrary to fact; there are 126 heroin users but 302 persons with intimate heroin-using friends. Of the 302 persons with heroin-using intimates, only 28% have used heroin. This evidence tends to indicate that having heroin-using intimates preceeds heroin use; similar findings emerge for other drugs. However, it is probable that once a person uses heroin or other hard drugs, he is likely to gain more friends who use that drug. Few (20%) of the 126 heroin users claim to have no heroin-using friends and two-thirds have intimate friends. But the most compelling evidence that hard-drug use by intimate friends precipitates hard-drug use is presented in Graph 6.3. At each level of cannabis use, hard-drug use is most common among those who have an intimate friend using that drug. Persons who have friends, but not intimate ones, are more like those with no friends in utilizing other dangerous drugs.

Finally, it is assumed that drug selling is an outgoing activity. Such selling, although frequently on a strictly commercial basis, is more frequently a social occurrence. The buyer and seller are likely to discuss topics of interest other than the particular drug sale.[61] This opens the way for the development of friendships. Since the seller is probably a somewhat more experienced drug user than his buyer (at each level of selling), the development of friendship will have important implications for the drug use of the buyer, especially among those at the lower levels of subculture participation. At higher levels of subculture participation, drug dealers are likely to meet and befriend each other on the basis of their common activity. In addition, those who specialize in selling certain drugs are likely to meet sellers specializing in other drugs, thus increasing the probability of each turning on the other. In many ways, then, the amount of involvement in drug buying or selling distinctly controls the kinds of friends that one is likely to make in the drug scene.

To summarize, the present chapter has discussed six possible theories that might explain the link between marihuana use and hard-drug use. By concentrating on heroin use, it has been able to disprove three theories, cast substantial doubt on two, and arrived at the conclusion that the subculture theory provides the most satisfactory explanation of the phenomena of hard-drug use.

The euphoria theory and the increased benefits theory were shown to have no, or minimal, effect upon the marihuana-hard drug relationship; at least, this was the case with the measures employed in the present survey. Perhaps superior measures would resurrect these theories, but it seems doubtful.

The simple stepping-stone theory, which is virtually identical to the pharmacological theory, is incorrect. If this theory were correct, then no other factors should affect the relationship between marihuana and hard-drug use. But it has been demonstrated that several social factors strongly affect this relationship.

The disturbed-personality theory maintains that something about the person's inadequate psyche leads him to progress from marihuana to hard drugs. This theory has not been disproven, mainly because there is no valid measure of what is meant by "disturbed personality." The evidence demonstrates that the marihuana-hard drug relationship can be well understood by social variables; personality factors may not be necessary. But, the disturbed-personality theory is either empirically untestable (and hence scientifically worthless), misleading, or wrong. Although the data is not presented, the author devised an alienation scale and adopted the Scrole Anomia Scale; neither of these social psychological scales had any important effect on the marihuana-hard-drug relationship. Future researchers are urged to develop valid measures of various personality deficiencies. It is doubtful that such measures will have much influence on the marihuana-hard drug relationship. Even if such factors do affect the relationship, it is probable that social factors are more important.

The sophisticated stepping-stone theory is the most difficult to disprove. But it suffers major damage from evidence presented. Although the relationship between the frequency of use and heroin use is not fully explained, it is shown that the relationship exists only among those with intimate heroin-using friends. In addition, the sophisticated stepping-stone theory does poorly in explaining how one gains heroin-using friends. It attributes to marihuana use the ability to influence friendship patterns. Instead, the data demonstrate that friendships with heroin users emerge from involvement in illicit drug selling. However, as demonstrated in Chapter 5, involvement in illicit selling is a function of the use of marihuana. Official explanations of the marihuana-hard drug relationship ignore a major, if not the crucial, factor: the illegality of cannabis. Thus, the stepping-stone theory stumbles badly on the question of the legality of cannabis.

Having shown the difficulty with five theories, one is left with the Subculture Theory. This theory does not win by default; it does a good job of identifying the important factors that help one to understand how some marihuana users progress to heroin use. This theory hypothesizes that the illegality of cannabis involves marihuana users in selling drugs; through drug selling, students gain friends who use hard drugs. Friends introduce students to hard drugs.

More than anything else, the subculture theory greatly aids one in understanding other factors such as sex and racial differences, which are related to hard-drug use. The next chapter will show the usefulness of the subculture theory in explaining findings not easily accounted for by other theories.

REFERENCES

1. See summaries of this data in Chaps. 1 and 3. Also see "Latest Findings on Marijuana," *U.S. News and World Report*, Feb. 1, 1971, p. 27; and "Gallup Finds a Continued Rise in the Use of Marijuana and LSD on Campus," *New York Times*, Feb. 10, 1972.
2. Comprehensive Drug Abuse Prevention and Control Acts of 1970, Public Law 91-513, Oct. 27, 1970; Section 201.
3. Anslinger's testimony is cited in Lester Grinspoon, *Marihuana Reconsidered*, Cambridge, Mass.: Harvard University Press, 1971, p. 236.
4. Federal Bureau of Narcotics, *Living Death: The Truth About Drug Addiction* (pamphlet), Washington, D.C.: U.S. Government Printing Office, 1965 (emphasis added).
5. "John Mitchell on Marijuana," *Newsweek*, Sept. 7, 1970, p. 22.
6. "Interview with John E. Ingersoll, Director, Federal Bureau of Narcotics: Dangers in Dope, Teen-Age Addicts: Drug Menace: How Serious?" *U.S. News and World Report*, May 25, 1970, p. 41.
7. Lee Robins and George E. Murphy, "Drug Use in a Normal Population of Young Negro Men," *American Journal of Public Health*, 57 (Sept. 1967), 1580-1596, show that none of the noncannabis users became addicted but that 20% of the marihuana users became heroin addicts.
8. John C. Ball; Carl D. Chambers; and Marion J. Ball, "The Association of Marihuana Smoking with Opiate Addiction in the U.S.," *Journal of Criminal Law, Criminology, and Police Science*, 59 (June 1968), 171-182. Daniel Glater, James A. Inciardi, and Dean V. Babst, "Later Heroin Use by Marijuana-Using, Heroin-Using and Non-Drug-Using Adolescent Offenders in New York City," *International Journal of the Addictions*, 4 (June 1969), 145-155. Robert S. Weppner and Michael H. Agar, "Immediate Precursors to Heroin Addiction," *Journal of Health and Social Behavior*, 12 (Mar. 1971), 10-17.
9. World Health Organization Scientific Group, *The Use of Cannabis*, World Health Organization Technical Report No. 478, Geneva, Switzerland, 1971, p. 10.
10. I. C. Chopra and R. N. Chopra, "The Use of Cannabis Drugs In India," *Bulletin on Narcotics*, 9 (Jan.-Mar. 1957), 18.
11. E. Leong Way, "Control and Treatment of Drug Addiction in Hong Kong," in Daniel M. Wilner and Gene G. Kassebaum, eds., *Narcotics*, New York: McGraw-Hill, 1965, pp. 275-278.
12. John Kaplan, *Marijuana—The New Prohibition*, Cleveland: World Publishing Company,

1970, p. 245. Ingeborg Paulus, "Psychedelic Drug Use on the Canadian Pacific Coast," *International Journal of the Addictions*, 4 (Mar. 1969), 77-78.

13. Ball, Chambers, and Ball, Ref. 8, pp. 175-177.

14. Charles E. Terry and Mildred Pellens, *The Opium Problem*, New York: Bureau of Social Hygiene, 1928, seldom link opium and marihuana in this 1000-page classic reference. Nor does Michael J. Pescor, "A Statistical Analysis of the Clinical Records of Hospitalized Drug Addicts," *Public Health Reports*, Wash., D.C.: Government Printing Office, 43 (1938), 1-30.

15. Louis Harris polls, May 1969, supplied tables from this survey to the author; some data is presented in "Changing Morality: The Two Americas," *Time*, June 6, 1969, pp. 26-27.

16. Gallup International, *Gallup Opinion Index*, Report No. 53, Princeton, N.J., 1969, p. 9.

17. Robins and Murphy, Ref. 7, p. 1588. Richard Blum et al., *Students and Drugs*, San Francisco: Jossey-Bass, 1969, pp. 101-109. Erich Goode, *The Marijuana Smokers*, New York: Basic Books, 1970, pp. 183-190. *The East Village Other*, Jan. 1-15, 1968. Paul Whitehead, Reginald G. Smart, and Lucien Laforest, "Multiple Drug Use Among Marihuana Smokers in Eastern Canada," *International Journal of the Addictions* 7(1) (1972), 179-190. William McGlothlin, Kay Jamison, and Steven Rosenblatt, "Marijuana and the Use of Other Drugs," *Nature*, 228 (Dec. 19, 1970), 1227-1229.

18. Robert S. DeRopp, *Drugs and the Mind*, New York: Grove Press, 1957, pp. 152-155. Alfred Lindesmith, *Addiction and Opiates*, 2nd ed., Chicago: Aldine Press, 1968, pp. 47-96. Abraham Wikler, "Drug Addiction: Organic and Psychological Aspects," *International Encyclopedia of the Social Sciences*, IV, New York: Macmillan, 1968, 290-298.

19. See Grinspoon, Ref. 3, pp. 233-235, for early studies on this subject. Andrew T. Weil, N. E. Zinberg and J. M. Nelsen, "Clinical and Psychological Effects of Marijuana in Man," *Science*, 162 (Dec. 13, 1968), 1235-1242.

20. Robins and Murphy, Ref. 7, p. 1588.

21. Goode, Ref. 17, p. 184. Blum, Ref. 17, pp. 101-109. McGlothlin, Jamison, and Rosenblatt, Ref. 17, p. 1228. Joel Hochman and Norman Brill, "Marijuana Use and Psychosocial Adaptation" (unpublished manuscript), 1971.

22. Eric Josephson, "Adolescent Marijuana Use: Report on a National Survey," Paper presented at the First International Conferences on Student Drug Surveys, Newark, New Jersey, Sept. 14, 1971, p. 16. Similar findings in Canadian high schools are presented in Whitehead, Smart and Laforest, Ref. 17, and John Russell, *Survey of Drug Use in Selected British Columbia Schools*, Vancouver: Narcotic Addiction Foundation of British Columbia, Feb. 1970.

23. Graham B. Blaine, Jr., *Youth and the Hazards of Affluence*, New York: Harper Colophon, 1967, p. 68.

24. Goode, Ref. 17, p. 102.

25. Kaplan, Ref. 12, pp. 228-229.

26. Gene R. Haislip, "Current Issues in the Prevention and Control of Marihuana Abuse," Paper presented to the First National Conference on Student Drug Involvement, U.S. National Student Association, University of Maryland, Aug. 16, 1967, p. 3.

27. Henry L. Giordano, *The Dangers of Marihuana ... Facts You Should Know* (pamphlet), Washington,D.C.: U.S. Government Printing Office, 1968. See also "John Mitchell on Marijuana," *Newsweek*, Sept. 7, 1970, p. 22.

28. Thomas DeQuincey, *Confessions of an English Opium Eater.* See essays by Gautier, Ginsberg, and Leary in David Solomon, ed., *The Marihuana Papers,* Indianapolis: Bobbs-Merrill, 1966, pp. 121-140, 163-178, 230-248.

29. Goode, Ref. 17, pp. 82-86.

30. P. A. L. Chapple, "Cannabis, A Toxic and Dangerous Substance," *British Journal of Addiction,* 61 (Aug. 1966), 269-282. W. D. M. Paton, "Drug Dependence—A Socio-Pharmacological Assessment," *Advancement of Science,* Dec. 1968, pp. 200-212. The logic of these scientists has been adopted by BNDD spokesmen; see Haislip, Ref. 26, p. 4, and (despite the title) Henry L. Giordano, "Marijuana—A Calling Card to Narcotic Addiction," *FBI Law Enforcement Bulletin,* 37 (Nov. 1968), 5, which argues an essentially "sophisticated" position.

31. Nathan B. Eddy et al., "Drug Dependence: Its Significance and Characteristics," *Bulletin of the World Health Organization,* 32 (1965), 729.

32. BNDD, *Fact Sheets,* Washington, D.C.: U.S. Government Printing Office (no date, about 1969), pp. 7-12.

33. Erich Goode, *Drug Escalation: Marijuana Use as Related to the Use of Dangerous Drugs,* Paper prepared for the National Commission on Marijuana and Drug Abuse, Oct. 31, 1971, p. 2. It must be noted that segments of this paper depend heavily upon earlier drafts of the present book.

34. Howard S. Becker, "Becoming a Marihuana User," *American Journal of Sociology,* 59 (Nov. 1953), 235-242, and "Marihuana Use and Social Control," *Social Problems,* 3 (July 1955), 35-44.

35. Erich Goode, "Multiple Drug Use Among Marijuana Smokers," *Social Problems,* 17 (Summer 1969), 48-64. Although Goode's book *The Marijuana Smokers* contains segments from this article, the best and most condensed statements of his theory are found in the *Social Problems* article, from which the following ideas are drawn.

36. Goode, ibid., p. 54, uses the term sociogenic to apply to the social nature of drug use.

37. Ibid., pp. 55-57.

38. Ibid., pp. 57-58.

39. Ibid., p. 59.

40. Ibid., p. 60.

41. James Carey, *The College Drug Scene,* Englewood Cliffs, N.J.: Prentice Hall, 1968, p. 42.

42. Goode, Ref. 17, p. 198.

43. Kaplan, Ref. 12, p. 330.

44. Paul F. Lazarsfeld and Morris Rosenberg, "Interpretation of Statistical Relations as a Research Operation," *Language of Social Research,* New York: Free Press, 1955, pp. 115-125. Herbert H. Hyman, *Survey Design and Analysis,* New York: Free Press, 1955, pp. 242-329. (Also see Appendix A.)

45. Josephson, Ref. 22, p. 16. For other studies see footnote 17.

46. Some of these relationships may be verified in Appendix A.

47. Goode, Ref. 35, p. 59.

48. Patricia Loiselle and Paul Whitehead, "Scaling Drug Use: An Examination of the Popular Wisdom," *Canadian Journal of Behavioral Science,* 3(4) (1971), 347-356.

49. Morris Rosenberg, *The Logic of Survey Analysis,* New York: Basic Books, 1968, pp. 143-148, for a discussion of necessary conditions in sociology.

50. Federal Bureau of Narcotics, Ref. 4.

51. "Interview with John Ingersoll," Ref. 6, p. 41.

52. *Random House Dictionary of the English Language,* New York: Random House, 1966, p. 1123. Grinspoon, Ref. 3, p. 242, calls this the "fallacy of the reversed apparent equation."

53. Fred Davis and Laura Munoz, "Heads and Freaks: Patterns and Meanings of Drug Use Among Hippies," *Journal of Health and Social Behavior,* 9 (June 1968), 162.

54. Haislip, Ref. 26, p. 4. Chapple, Ref. 30, p. 270. Paton, Ref. 30, pp. 206-208. Eddy et al., Ref. 31, p. 729.

55. Goode, Ref. 35, p. 60.

56. Eddy, Ref. 31, p. 729.

57. BNDD, Ref. 32, p. 7-2 (emphasis added).

58. Carey, Ref. 41, pp. 68-71. Goode, Ref. 17, pp. 251-257.

59. Haislip, Ref. 26, p. 4. Chapple, Ref. 30, p. 270. Paton, Ref. 30, pp. 206-208.

60. Loiselle and Whitehead, Ref. 48.

61. Goode, Ref. 17, p. 254.

CHAPTER 7
Subculture Theory Extended

The stepping-stone theory has stumbled over a theory which is considerably more powerful than it may appear in the previous chapter. The present chapter, as well as the following two chapters, will present empirical evidence that further supports the importance of subculture theory.

The present chapter, assuming that many marihuana users do escalate to the use of hard drugs, asks certain questions: Which hard drugs do students begin using? How is this escalation process affected by friendships, cannabis use, and drug selling? Since the previous chapter showed that drug escalation is not an inevitable process, this will attempt to determine what factors inhibit or increase the probability of progression to various hard drugs.

In attempting to provide answers to these questions, this chapter concludes that the subculture theory best explains a wide variety of data that cannot be understood by the sophisticated stepping-stone theory. The complex argument of this chapter will attempt to show: (1) There are probably two different subcultures of drug use on college campuses in the New York metropolitan area that are structured along racial lines. (2) For both subcultures, marihuana is the drug that "introduces" persons to the subculture. (3) The hard drugs to which increasingly regular marihuana users progress are a function of the subculture in which the person participates and the depth of his involvement in the subculture. (4) Heavy involvement in one subculture, as measured by drug selling, greatly increases the probability of participating in the other subculture.

Central to the analysis is the primary question raised by subculture theory: How do students gain intimate friends who use hard drugs? Focusing upon this question means treating the question of hard-drug use as a less important problem. This lack of interest in drug use is justified by data in the previous chapter. Graphs 6.3 and 6.5 demonstrate that hard-drug use is strongly affected by having intimate friends using a particular drug; the absence of hard-drug-using friends appears to fundamentally inhibit the use of that drug. Having intimate friends using a particular drug may be seen as the precipitating factor or immediate cause in a person's use of that drug. Hence, it is important to understand how such intimate friends are gained. Even though the sophisticated stepping-stone theory may not agree that hard-drug use can be fully explained by what one's friends do,[1] it recognizes the important influence friends may have upon the respondent's use of that drug.

Indeed, the disagreement between the sophisticated stepping-stone theory and subculture theory is mainly a subtle difference in emphasis and interpretation about meaning of the Frequency of Cannabis Use Index. The sophisticated position implies that the regular use of marihuana is a major factor that "facilitates the association with social groups and sub-cultures involved with more dangerous drugs."[2] Subculture theory maintains that regular cannabis use is an indicator of involvement in the subculture;[3] the use of marihuana has little to do with gaining hard-drug-using friends when subculture involvement is held constant. Hence, one must determine whether marihuana use is an independent force leading to friendships with hard-drug users, or whether marihuana use is an indicator of subculture involvement, which in turn causes marihuana users to gain hard-drug-using intimates.

In support of the subculture theory, evidence in Graph 6.4 shows that involvement in drug selling (as a measure of subculture participation), not the frequency of marihuana use, is the crucial factor in gaining heroin-using intimates. But the relationship between cannabis and having hallucinogen-using friends is not so well explained and tends to support the sophisticated position. Graph 6.4 shows that weekly cannabis users were 50% more likely to have hallucinogen-using intimates than experimental marihuana users; this 50% difference was reduced to 31% when the Illicit Marketing Index was held constant. However, data presented in Appendix A shows that sellers of hard drugs were 44% (83%-39%) more likely to have hallucinogen-using intimates than persons who only buy cannabis; the 44% difference is reduced to 31% (APD) when cannabis use is held constant. This indicates that cannabis use and drug dealing are equally powerful (APD's of 31 and 31, respectively) and independently influence the probability of having hallucinogen-using intimates. Additional evidence which is not presented demonstrates the following conclusions: (1) To gain intimates using each drug, heavy involvement in the illicit drug market is more important than the frequency with which students use cannabis. (2) When the Illicit Marketing Index is held constant, the independent effect of marihuana use is (a) almost zero (APD = 4%) in determining exposure to heroin-using intimates; (b) minor (APD's of 10 and 11) in determining exposure to cocaine and sedatives; (c) significant (APD's of 16 and 19) in determining exposure to methedrine and amphetamines; and (d) important (APD of 31) in determining exposure to hallucinogen-using intimates.

Thus, it seems that selling drugs is not as crucial for gaining intimate friends who use hallucinogens and prescription drugs as it is for gaining intimate friends using heroin and cocaine. Students can gain friends using "soft" drugs by using cannabis. At first thought, such a finding appears to strengthen the sophisticated stepping-stone theory's ability to explain friendships with hard-drug users. But upon further reflection, the sophisticated position is weakened. If the use of marihuana was a major cause of friendships with hard-drug users, then regular marihuana users should be equally exposed to users of all drugs. This is not the case.

On the other hand, the subculture theory is strengthened. If marihuana use is an indicator of progressive subculture involvement, then the more regular the use of cannabis, the more likely persons are to be involved in groups that use subculture-approved drugs. But if a drug is not common in a subculture, even regular marihuana users should be unlikely to gain intimates using that drug and to try that drug themselves.

At this point, five questions arise that are central to the following analysis: (1) Are there different subcultures of drug use? (2) If so, in what ways are they different or similar? (3) Does the use of marihuana lead a person into both subcultures (supporting the sophisticated stepping-stone theory)? (4) Or does the use of marihuana lead a person only into a specific subculture (supporting the subculture theory)? (5) How are different subcultures related to each other?

One can begin to investigate the answers to these questions by hypothesizing that there may be different subcultures of drug use on the college campus, as well as in society at large. Although the empirical data is not conclusive, Goode; Robins and Murphy; McGlothlin; Chein; Preble; Scher; Blum; Carey; Finestone; Fiddle; and Sutter[4] provide descriptions, participant observation, and some survey data strongly suggesting that two reasonably distinct subcultures of drug use exist in the United States: the white and black drug subcultures.

The development of the white drug subculture occurred relatively recently (since 1964). In 1972, this subculture appears to be most widespread among the white college students in America and somewhat less common among high school students and working noncollege youth.[5] Although the present sample of college students is biased for reasons described in Chapter 2, the findings here are similar to trends emerging from Gallup polls and other sources, suggesting the outlines of this white drug subculture.[6] Increasingly regular participation in this white drug subculture implies experimental and regular use of cannabis, then progression to hallucinogens, amphetamines, sedatives, and methedrine. In this subculture, the use of cocaine and, to a greater extent, heroin is negatively evaluated; the hypodermic injection of heroin or other drugs is extremely rare (about 1% in the sample).

In contrast, the New York metropolitan area has, since the 1950s, had a history of heroin addiction among slum populations, especially among blacks. The black drug subculture promotes the use, by hypodermic injection, of heroin and, less frequently, heroin mixed with cocaine, barbiturates, and amphetamines (known as "speedballs," "goofballs," and "bombitas," respectively).[7] Drug users in this subculture seldom utilize "head" drugs, such as hallucinogens and methedrine.

The sample is composed of predominantly white middle-class students in the New York metropolitan area. While only 7% of the sample is black, that is a relatively high proportion of blacks for a college population in 1970. If the sample is not representative of the total black population of New York City, this is due to the underrepresentation of blacks in the educational system, not in the present sample.

The behavior of black college students is important to the present analysis. These blacks should be exposed to pressures from the predominantly white student body and drug subculture to use white drugs such as hallucinogens, pills, and methedrine and, at the same time, be exposed to pressure from blacks in their home neighborhoods to use black drugs such as cocaine and heroin. A central question of this chapter is, Do college blacks behave more like white college students or more like noncollege blacks in their patterns of drug use, and why?

The beginning point of analysis is to remember from Graph 3.1 that the marihuana use of white and black students is almost identical. Thus, 56% of the whites and 54% of the blacks had tried marihuana; 19% of the whites and 16% of the blacks were weekly users of marihuana. On the other hand, there are important racial differences in hard-drug use. About twice as many blacks as whites had tried heroin (7% to 4%) and cocaine (16% to 7%). But blacks were roughly half as likely to have tried methedrine (3% to 9%), amphetamines (6% to 16%), sedatives (10% to 14%), and hallucinogens (11% to 20%) as whites.

Even more striking racial differences in hard-drug use and exposure to hard-drug-using intimates emerge when the frequency of cannabis use is held constant. The experimental and moderate cannabis users have been combined into a category of irregular users. The regular users use cannabis weekly or more. Graph 7.1 demonstrates the following conclusions: (1) Among noncannabis users, there are no racial differences in illicit drug use and only minor racial differences in exposure to hard drugs. (2) The more frequent the use of marihuana, the greater the racial differences in hard-drug use. (3) Weekly

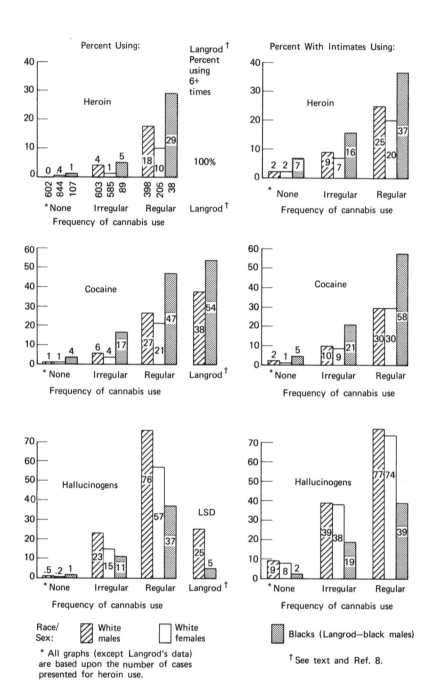

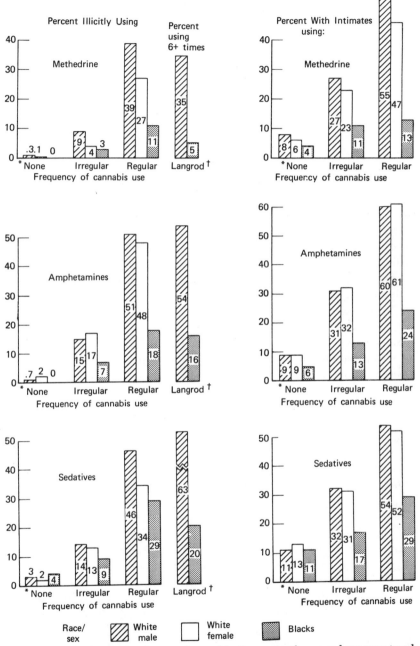

Graph 7.1. The more regular the use of cannabis, the greater the use and exposure to sub-culturally approved drugs.

cannabis-using blacks are more likely to try, and to have intimate friends using, heroin and cocaine than whites. (4) Regular cannabis-using whites are significantly more likely to use and to have intimate friends using hallucinogens, methedrine, amphetamines, and sedatives than their black counterparts. This evidence indicates that the patterns of recruitment are similar in both subcultures; a person must use marihuana with some regularity before gaining friends using, and himself actually trying, hard drugs. But the actual drugs that increasingly regular cannabis users are likely to encounter depend greatly upon race: black progress to cocaine and heroin, whites progress to hallucinogens and prescription drugs.

Such evidence demonstrates that there are probably two reasonably distinct subcultures of drug use even on the college campus. The sample of white marihuana-using students is large; most probably participate in the white drug subculture. But it is not clear that black students, although different than white students, participate in the black drug subculture, where probably the highest incidence of cocaine and heroin use and lowest incidence of hallucinogen and methedrine use occur. This study wishes to make inferences about the black drug subculture in the slums and compare the drug-use patterns of college blacks with the drug use of slum blacks (who do not make it to college). Since no slum blacks completed the questionnaire, the college blacks will be compared with institutionalized heroin addicts.

Comparison of the present data with that of John Langrod's male heroin users confined in New York City rehabilitation centers in 1968[8] will permit us to make some comparisons between college blacks and ghetto noncollege blacks, as well as similar comparisons for whites. Thus, to a limited extent, social-class (college versus institutionalized) differences in drug use, as well as racial differences, can be examined.

Langrod's sample is considerably different than the present sample of college students. All of Langrod's sample were heroin addicts, 75% had been arrested and committed for drug-related charges; less than 1% of the present sample were addicts. About 60% of the college blacks are female, but all of Langrod's sample are male. Langrod's sample is older; 50% were twenty-three or older, while about 90% of the present sample is under twenty-three. Almost all of our respondents were in college, whereas 60% of Langrod's sample were high school dropouts.[9] Despite these important differences, the data suggest that patterns of hard-drug use are influenced more by race than by class, age, sex, levels of addiction, and arrest. The white and black drug subcultures expect heavily involved participants to progress to different drugs. If both weekly cannabis use and commitment to narcotic rehabilitation centers are considered to be indicators of heavy subculture participation, then regular marihuana users in the present sample should be more similar to Langrod's heroin addicts in hard-drug use than to irregular or noncannabis users in college.

Langrod found striking ethnic differences in the use of hard drugs among heroin addicts. Although he has the data, Langrod does not report what proportion of blacks and whites have ever used these drugs; hence his data is not directly comparable to the data here. But for blacks, whites, and Puerto Ricans, he does report the use of various drugs more than six times.[10] Since all of Langrod's sample had been addicted to heroin, one cannot compare heroin use in his sample and in the present study. However, in the use of other hard drugs, there are striking similarities between Langrod's heroin addicts and regular marihuana users herein. Data on Langrod's addicts is reported in the center of Graph 7.1. One finds that 27% of this study's regular cannabis-using white males have tried cocaine, while 38% of Langrod's white male addicts have tried cocaine six or more times. Among blacks here, 47% have used cocaine, while 54% of Langrod's black males have used cocaine six or more times. Even more striking racial similarities between Langrod's sample and the present study, respectively, occur in the use of methedrine (white males, 35% and 39%; blacks, 5% and 11%) and amphetamines (white males, 54% and 51%; blacks, 16% vs. 18%).

In both Langrod's and the present sample, white males are two or three times more likely to use methedrine and amphetamines than blacks. Another striking difference comes in an examination of LSD use. Although here all hallucinogens are combined, the differences are still striking. Only 5% of Langrod's black males have used LSD six or more times, while 37% of regular cannabis-using blacks herein have tried hallucinogens. A low proportion of Langrod's white males, 25%, have used LSD, compared with 76% of regular cannabis-using white males. Perhaps there are important class differences in hallucinogen use in each racial group. Also, Langrod's data were collected about two years previous to this sample; the use of hallucinogens may have expanded greatly during that time.

The basic conclusions of Graph 7.1 are as follows: (1) White male heroin addicts have patterns of hard-drug use that more closely resemble those of regular cannabis-using white college males than of black male heroin addicts. (2) Regular cannabis-using blacks in college are more similar to black heroin addicts in hard-drug use than to their white counterparts in college. But the similarity goes even further. Langrod also asked his addicts what drugs they had tried prior to heroin. Although more than 70% of both blacks and whites had tried marihuana before using heroin, the use of other drugs prior to heroin use was different. About a third of all white heroin addicts had tried amphetamines, methedrine, sedatives, or LSD prior to heroin use; in contrast, 13% of the black addicts had tried sedatives and 5% had tried LSD, methedrine, or amphetamines prior to heroin use.[11] Langrod also found that white addicts were more likely to be multiple drug users than blacks; this finding is consistent with the present study. Except for LSD, the racial difference, not the class (college student versus institutionalized addict) difference, is the important factor in understanding which hard drugs are used by those greatly involved in drug subcultures.

Furthermore, the levels of hard-drug use among Langrod's population and regular cannabis users here are so strikingly similar that some factor other than chance must be at work. Thus, the evidence suggests that two distinctive drug subcultures do exist. The white drug subculture has legitimated hallucinogens, the illicit use of amphetamines, sedatives, and methedrine, while the black drug subculture has legitimated the use of cocaine and heroin. The implications of this interpretation will be pursued shortly.

Graph 7.1 provides two more important conclusions. First, white males are somewhat more likely at each level of cannabis use than white females to use all drugs. But sex-linked differences in exposure to hard-drug users are less pronounced. Second, at each level of cannabis use, the proportion of each race-sex group having intimate friends using a particular drug is generally higher than the proportion actually using that drug. For example, of the regular cannabis-using blacks, 37% have intimate heroin-using friends, while 29% have tried heroin. Similar findings hold for all other drugs.

Although there is not a perfect correlation between exposure to hard-drug-using friends and the actual use of drugs, these measures of drug involvement are basically interchangeable; they provide the same findings when related to the race-sex variable and frequency of cannabis use. Thus, one is justified in analyzing the central question of the subculture theory: How do students gain intimate friends who use particular hard drugs?

One can begin to answer this question by suggesting that each drug indicates different degrees of involvement in different drug subcultures. It is assumed that the least frequently used drugs indicate deep, or core, involvement in each subculture.

In the black drug subculture, regular cannabis-using blacks are likely to gain cocaine-using intimates, then heroin-using intimates. This pattern of exposure, cocaine to heroin, may be reversed among noncollege blacks; only 10% of Langrod's black heroin addicts had used cocaine prior to heroin use.[12] In the white drug subculture, increasing involvement in marihuana will bring a student in contact with hallucinogen users, then amphetamine, sedative, and methedrine users. The same conclusions emerge whether exposure to hard-drug-using intimates or the actual use of drugs is used as the criterion of subculture involvement.

Most crucial for drug subculture theory is determining how students become progressively involved in their own and the opposite subculture. Essentially, cannabis-using blacks, by virtue of attending college, are likely to be exposed to white subculture drugs. At the same time, black students bring cocaine and heroin to the campus; hence, white cannabis users are exposed to black subculture drugs. But exposure to the least popular drug in the opposite subculture will be uncommon; in Graph 7.1 regular cannabis-using blacks are less likely to have methedrine-using intimates (13%) than weekly marihuana-using white females are to have heroin-using intimates (20%).

Besides race, there are other factors affecting progressive involvement in each subculture: (1) The simple fact of being male increases the probability of involvement in drug subcultures. (2) As the sophisticated stepping-stone theory argues, the greater the frequency of cannabis use, the greater the involvement in the subculture. (3) But more importantly, as drug subculture theory suggests, drug selling greatly increases involvement in the appropriate subculture according to race, and it also increases the probability of contact with persons in the other subculture.

One can now begin to test empirically several hypotheses that have been derived from subculture theory: (1) The more widespread a hard drug is in a particular subculture, the less the importance of having to sell drugs to gain intimate friends using that drug. Thus, increasingly regular marihuana use may be sufficient to expose a neophyte drug user to a hard drug that is widely used in the subculture. (2) The less widespread a drug is in a subculture, the more necessary it is to sell drugs to gain intimates using that drug. (3) The less the predisposition to participate in a drug subculture, as indicated by sex and race, the greater the need to sell drugs to gain intimates using a particular drug. Drug selling, thus, should be a more important requirement for white females than for white males in acquiring intimate hallucinogen, amphetamine, sedative or methedrine-using friends. (4) To gain intimates using core drugs in the opposite subculture, drug selling is even more necessary. Thus, the subculture theory suggests that while whites must sell drugs to gain cocaine and heroin-using intimates, regular marihuana use may be enough to gain intimates using LSD and pills. Among noncollege blacks, drug selling would theoretically be necessary to gain intimate friends who use white drugs (hallucinogens, amphetamines, sedatives, and methedrine), but a high frequency of cannabis use would increase the probability of gaining intimates who use cocaine and/or heroin. Unfortunately, one cannot test the theories as they apply to noncollege blacks. One can only report how college blacks in the sample are exposed to white drugs.

The data presented in Tables 7-12 are exceedingly complex and cannot be simplified. Detailed data is presented for readers who wish to examine it carefully. The reader who wishes to analyze these tables is urged to understand multivariate analysis and the meaning of the average percent difference (APD) as discussed in Appendix A and the footnote on p. 61. Readers who do not wish to follow the detailed data are urged to confine their interest to the text, which will attempt to present the important conclusions.

Since this study is trying to prove several important theoretical points, it will generally confine the basic analysis in Tables 7-12 to cannabis users who have been involved in the drug market. This means that noncannabis users are seldom considered; but information about their friendships with hard-drug users is to be found in the lower right cell of each race-sex group. Likewise, cannabis users who have neither bought nor sold drugs are excluded (except for blacks) from the main part of the table because of the editing error discussed in the text near Graph 6.4. However, for whites, information about nonbuying, nonselling cannabis users is to be found in the rightmost column of Tables 7-12 and is used briefly below in the analysis of the first hypothesis. Thus, the "total" column and row in Tables 7-12 contain only cannabis users who have bought cannabis or sold drugs. A table showing the number of cases upon which Tables 7-12 are based immediately follows Table 12. In each table, percentages based upon less than 30 cases are marked with the small letter a, implying that the percentage may not be stable, and perhaps is misleading.

The sample is divided into three groups: white males, white females, and blacks. Although 60% of the blacks are female, there are too few blacks (234) to divide by sex, especially when holding constant cannabis use and drug buying or selling. In addition, regular cannabis-using blacks are lacking (38); two of these failed to indicate their involvement in drug selling and have been excluded from analysis. Since there were so few cannabis-using blacks, categories in the Illicit Marketing Index have been combined. As an indicator of noninvolvement in drug selling and in order to have a somewhat stable number of cases, cannabis buyers have been combined with those who have neither bought nor sold drugs, but even this combination does not provide a stable base ($N = 14$) among regular cannabis users who have not sold drugs. Likewise, there are too few regular (22) and irregular (22) cannabis users even when cannabis sellers and sellers of hard drugs are combined to indicate "drug sellers." Because the number of cases upon which the percentages are based is so small, findings about exposure to various hard drugs among blacks can only be suggestive. The samples of white males and females are quite stable and important generalizations may be made from them.

With the data in Tables 7-12, one can begin to verify the four hypotheses discussed above. Examining exposure to drugs that are widespread in the white drug subculture, one finds (column on far right in Tables 7-10) that whites who have tried cannabis but have not bought or sold drugs are significantly (10%-20%) more likely than noncannabis users to have intimates using hallucinogens, amphetamines, sedatives, and methedrine. But black cannabis users who have not sold drugs are no more likely (0%-3%) than noncannabis users to have intimates using methedrine, sedatives, and amphetamines (compare lower-right with cells in left column for blacks in Tables 7-10). It does appear that trying cannabis increases the probability that blacks will have intimates using hallucinogens (Table 7); but this is the only "white" drug to which cannabis-using, nonselling blacks are exposed. If Langrod's data on heroin addicts is assumed to be valid in 1970, marihuana-using, noncollege blacks should be

Tables 7-12. Percent having intimate friends using various hard drugs by frequency of cannabis use, holding constant the Illicit Marketing Index and race-sex

Table 7. Percent with intimate friends using hallucinogens

| Frequency Of Cannabis Use | Illicit Marketing Index | | | Total | % Diff. (Sell Hard- Buy Cann.) | Not Buy or Sell |
	Buy Can- nabis	Sell Can- nabis	Sell Hard Drugs			
	White males					
Irregular	33	48	70	45	37	29
Regular	56	66	90	78	34	57[a]
Total	38	62	85	61	47/36	30
% diff. (reg.-irreg.)	23	18	20	33/20		
Noncannabis user						9
	White females					
Irregular	37	61	80	49	43	27
Regular	65	71	88	76	23	50[a]
Total	43	65	85	59	42/33	29
% diff. (reg.-irreg.)	28	10	8	25/15		
Noncannabis user						8
	None + Buy Cannabis	Sell Drugs		Total	% Diff. (Sell-Buy)	
	Blacks					
Irregular	18	22[a]		19	6	
Regular	29[a]	50[a]		42	21	
Total	20	36		26	16/14	
% diff. (reg.-irreg.)	11	28		23/20		
Noncannabis user						2

[a]Percentage based upon less than 30 cases.

Table 8. Percent with intimate friends using sedatives

Frequency Of Cannabis Use	Illicit Marketing Index			Total	% Diff. (Sell Hard-Buy Cann.)	Not Buy or Sell
	Buy Cannabis	Sell Cannabis	Sell Hard Drugs			
White males						
Irregular	25	32	60	34	35	27
Regular	31	41	68	54	37	43[a]
Total	26	36	66	44	40/36	28
% diff. (reg.-irreg.)	6	9	8	20/8		
Noncannabis user						11
White females						
Irregular	34	34	59	37	25	24
Regular	33	45	68	51	35	55[a]
Total	34	38	65	43	31/30	26
% diff. (reg.-irreg.)	-1	11	9	14/6		
Noncannabis user						13

Frequency Of Cannabis Use	None + Buy Cannabis	Sell Drugs	Total	% Diff. (Sell-Buy)
Blacks				
Irregular	12	32[a]	17	20
Regular	14[a]	41[a]	31	27
Total	12	36	21	24/24
% diff. (reg.-irreg.)	2	9	14/6	
Noncannabis user				11

[a]Percentage is based upon less than 30 cases.

unlikely to gain intimates using hallucinogens.[13] Cannabis-using blacks probably gain hallucinogen-using friends because of contacts on the college campus.

Turning to black subculture drugs, one finds that among blacks, cannabis-using nondrug sellers are more likely (10%-40%) than noncannabis users to have intimates using cocaine (Table 12). However, in Table 11, 7% of the irregular cannabis-using nonselling blacks have initmates using heroin, the same level of exposure as noncannabis-using blacks. Among whites, cannabis users who have not bought or sold drugs are not significantly (1%-5%) more likely than noncannabis users to have intimates using cocaine and heroin; nor are cannabis users who only buy cannabis much more likely (3%-11%) than noncannabis users to have intimates using "black" drugs.

This evidence indicates the validity of the first hypothesis cited above and the demise of the sophisticated stepping-stone theory. Among nondrug sellers, the use of marihuana, no matter how regular, is associated with gaining friends using drugs that are widespread in one's particular subculture but not in the opposite subculture. Therefore, the simple use of marihuana increases the probability of

Table 9. *Percent with intimate friends using amphetamines*

Frequency Of Cannabis Use	Illicit Marketing Index			Total	% Diff. (Sell Hard-Buy Cann.)	Not Buy or Sell
	Buy Cannabis	Sell Cannabis	Sell Hard Drugs			
White males						
Irregular	23	32	63	34	40	26
Regular	34	41	78	60	44	43[a]
Total	25	37	73	47	48/42	27
% diff. (reg.-irreg.)	11	9	15	26/12		
Noncannabis user						9
White females						
Irregular	32	49	71	42	39	22
Regular	44	57	76	62	32	55[a]
Total	35	52	74	49	39/36	24
% diff. (reg.-irreg.)	12	8	5	20/8		
Noncannabis user						9
	None + Buy Cannabis	Sell Drugs		Total	% Diff. (Sell-Buy)	
Blacks						
Irregular	4	41[a]		13	37	
Regular	7[a]	36[a]		25	29	
Total	5	39		17	34/33	
% diff. (reg.-irreg.)	3	- 5		12/- 1		
Noncannabis user						6

[a]Percentage based upon less than 30 cases.

Table 10. *Percent with intimate friends using methedrine*

Frequency Of Cannabis Use	Illicit Marketing Index			Total	% Diff. (Sell Hard-Buy Cann.)	Not Buy or Sell
	Buy Cannabis	Sell Cannabis	Sell Hard Drugs			
White males						
Irregular	19	28	48	28	29	25
Regular	33	37	71	55	38	29[a]
Total	23	33	64	41	41/34	25
% diff. (reg.-irreg.)	14	9	23	27/15		
Noncannabis user						8
White females						
Irregular	21	29	59	28	38	17
Regular	35	39	61	48	26	40[a]
Total	24	33	60	35	36/32	19
% diff. (reg.-irreg.)	14	10	2	20/9		
Noncannabis user						6

	None + Buy Cannabis	Sell Drugs	Total	% Diff. (Sell-Buy)	
Blacks					
Irregular	6	27[a]	11	21	
Regular	0[a]	23[a]	14	23	
Total	5	25	12	20/22	
% diff. (reg.-irreg.)	- 6	- 4	3/- 5		
Noncannabis user					4

[a]Percentage based upon less than 30 cases.

whites gaining intimates using amphetamines, sedatives, and methedrine, while blacks gain intimates using cocaine and, to a lesser extent, heroin. Marihuana use, hence, is an indicator of early involvement in a racially specific subculture. The use or frequent use of marihuana, among nonsellers, does not greatly increase the probability of using drugs in the opposite subculture. The sophisticated stepping-stone theory treats the use of marihuana as a cause of subculture participation, when marihuana use is probably an indicator of participation in a racially specific subculture.

The second hypothesis is also verified; the less widespread a drug is in a particular subculture, the more necessary drug selling is in gaining intimates using that drug. In Tables 7-12, the average percent difference (APD) appears to the right of the slash (/) in the "difference" column and row. Thus, in Table 11 in the "% diff." column, "total" row for white males, "/28" indicates the independent effect of the Illicit Marketing Index upon having heroin-using intimates when marihuana use is held constant. In a similar fashion, in the "% diff." row, "total" column, "/3" indicates the independent effect of marihuana

Table 11. Percent with intimate friends using heroin

| Frequency Of Cannabis Use | Illicit Marketing Index | | | Total | % Diff. (Sell Hard-Buy Cann.) | Not Buy or Sell |
	Buy Can-nabis	Sell Can-nabis	Sell Hard Drugs			
White males						
Irregular	5	9	32	12	27	5
Regular	8	11	37	25	29	27[a]
Total	6	10	35	18	29/28	6
% diff. (reg.-irreg.)	3	2	5	13/3		
Noncannabis user						2
White females						
Irregular	7	16	20	11	13	3
Regular	4	10	34	18	30	30[a]
Total	6	14	29	14	23/22	5
% diff. (reg.-irreg.)	- 3	- 6	14	7/2		
Noncannabis user						2
	None + Buy Cannabis	Sell Drugs		Total	% Diff. (Sell-Buy)	
Blacks						
Irregular	7	41[a]		16	34	
Regular	21[a]	45[a]		36	24	
Total	10	43		22	33/29	
% diff. (reg.-irreg.)	14	4		20/9		
Noncannabis user						7

[a]Percentage based upon less than 30 cases.

use upon exposure to heroin-using intimates when holding constant drug buying and selling. Thus, the independent effect of the Illicit Marketing Index is nine times (APDs of 28 versus 3) as powerful as the independent effect of cannabis use. Among whites, similar comparisons in Tables 7-12 tend to indicate that the Illicit Marketing Index is two to four times as important as cannabis use in gaining intimates using all hard drugs.

However, for whites and blacks, the regular versus irregular use of marihuana still has an important direct effect upon having hallucinogen-using intimates

Table 12. Percent with intimate friends using Cocaine

Frequency Of Cannabis Use	Illicit Marketing Index			Total	% Diff. (Sell Hard- Buy Cann.)	Not Buy or Sell
	Buy Can- nabis	Sell Can- nabis	Sell Hard Drugs			
White male						
Irregular	7	11	29	13	22	6
Regular	13	14	42	30	29	29[a]
Total	8	13	38	21	30/26	7
% diff. (reg.-irreg.)	6	3	13	17/7		
Noncannabis user						2
White females						
Irregular	8	18	27	13	19	4
Regular	11	20	49	30	38	30[a]
Total	9	19	41	19	32/29	6
% diff. (reg.-irreg.)	3	2	22	17/9		
Noncannabis user						1
	None + Buy Cannabis	Sell Drugs		Total	% Diff. (Sell-Buy)	
Blacks						
Irregular	16	36[a]		21	20	
Regular	43[a]	68[a]		58	25	
Total	21	52		32	31/23	
% diff. (reg.-irreg.)	27	32		37/30		
Noncannabis user						5

[a]Percentage based upon less than 30 cases.

Number of cases upon which Tables 7-12 are based:

Frequency Of Cannabis Use	Illicit Marketing Index			Total	% Diff.	Not Buy or Sell
	Buy Cannabis	Sell Cannabis	Sell Hard Drugs			
White males						
Irregular	211	101	84	396	NA[a]	206
Regular	64	111	215	390	NA	7
Total	275	212	299	786	NA	213
Noncannabis users						602
White females						
Irregular	182	79	41	302	NA	281
Regular	54	51	80	185	NA	20
Total	236	130	121	487	NA	301
Noncannabis users						844
	None + Buy Cannabis	Sell Drugs	Total			
Blacks						
Irregular	67	22	89	NA		
Regular	14	22	36	NA		
Total	81	44	125	NA		
Noncannabis users			107			

[a]Not applicable.

(Table 7). For whites, the frequency of marihuana use is a minor factor (APDs of 6% to 15%) in gaining friends who use sedatives, amphetamines, methedrine (Tables 8-10), drugs that are not so widespread in the white drug subculture as hallucinogens. Likewise, among blacks, the independent effect of cannabis use is as important as drug selling in gaining cocaine-using intimates (Table 12); but drug selling is three times more important than cannabis use in determining exposure to heroin-users (Table 11). Thus, the less widespread a drug is in the subculture, the more important it is to sell drugs to gain intimates using that drug. Selling drugs takes persons deeper into their racially specific subculture than does using marihuana.

Hypothesis 4 deals with the crossing of subculture boundaries between the black and white drug subcultures. The data provide information about these boundaries and how they may be crossed. Marihuana use in college is, for blacks and whites, associated with having hallucinogen-using intimates (Table 7). Since noncollege blacks who only use marihuana would be unlikely to have hallucinogen-using intimates, marihuana-using blacks probably cross subculture boundaries by going to college, where many try hallucinogens.

With the other hard drugs, it is easier to say that they belong in one racial subculture or the other. Most important for the purposes of the subculture theory are heroin and methedrine; these two drugs probably represent relatively deep involvement in the black or white drug subcultures, respectively. Questions arise: How do whites become involved in heroin? How do blacks become involved in methedrine? Answers to these questions suggest how students cross subculture boundaries, and perhaps help in understanding how persons become heavily involved in the opposite subculture.

The answer can be seen quite clearly in the APD's of Tables 10 and 11 Marihuana use has almost nothing to do with whites gaining heroin-using intimates or blacks gaining methedrine-using intimates (APD's are less than 4%). But drug selling greatly increases exposure to intimates using drugs from the opposite subculture (APD's are greater than 20%). Among whites, about a third of those selling hard drugs have heroin-using intimates. Among blacks, only drug sellers are likely to have intimates using methedrine. Analysis of the other drugs demonstrates that involvement in selling hard drugs is crucial for whites to gain cocaine-using intimates and for blacks to gain sedative and amphetamine-using intimates. In short, persons involved in selling drugs are likely to cross subculture boundaries, and they are likely to become deeply involved in opposite subculture drugs.

There may be specific mechanisms by which this crossing of subculture boundaries occurs. The one drug common to, and most widely used and sold in, both subcultures is marihuana. Both blacks and whites who are fairly regular drug sellers are likely to engage in selling marihuana, as well as selling their own subculture's drugs. Therefore, blacks are likely to sell marihuana, cocaine, and perhaps heroin; whites sell cannabis, hallucinogens, and perhaps amphetamines, sedatives, and methedrine. For student sellers from both subcultures, marihuana sales probably constitute a majority of all drug transactions.[14] In many cases, black drug sellers may approach white sellers to obtain a supply of marihuana, and vice versa. During the course of such economically motivated transactions, both parties will smoke some of the marihuana being sold and carry on a polite conversation.[15] Such conversations open the door for friendship to develop and lay the basis for future sales. Both sellers may advertise to the other that they can supply hard drugs, mainly drugs from their own subculture, if the other party would like to obtain these drugs. If the contacts continue, more stable and intimate friendships may develop. As a result of such friendships, black drug sellers may turn on white drug sellers to cocaine and heroin. Likewise, black drug sellers may be turned on to amphetamines, sedatives, and methedrine by white drug sellers. Thus, the road by which white marihuana users escalate to heroin use appears to be no different theoretically than the process by which black marihuana users become amphetamine and methedrine users.

It is important to note that persons who only sell marihuana are relatively uninvolved in drug selling. They probably sell to close friends with minor profit and hence are not deeply involved in their respective drug subculture. Those who only sell cannabis are not much more likely than persons who only buy cannabis to have intimates using hard drugs in the opposite subculture. But hard-drug sellers may depend heavily upon marihuana sales for their profits and contact with persons who use and buy hard drugs.

Thus, marihuana selling is probably a central machanism by which marihuana users gain friends who use drugs from the opposite subculture. Since marihuana use is the major factor in cannabis sales, the illegality of marihuana may be a central factor in explaining how white college students progress to heroin and how blacks become involved in methedrine and amphetamines.

Unfortunately, these inferences about the importance of interracial friendships inspired by drug selling are unproven. It must be demonstrated empirically that sellers of one race who sell cannabis and hard drugs are more likely to have members of the other race as intimate friends than are nonsellers and that the main foundation for such friendships is drug selling. Such information was not obtained. One hopes that these findings and the exposition of the subculture theory will stimulate future researchers to explore these interesting inferences.

We can now turn to the third hypothesis: The less the predisposition to participate in drug subcultures as indicated by sex, the greater the need to sell drugs to gain intimates using a particular drug. Data supporting this hypothesis can be found in Tables 7-12, and shows that the independent effect of marihuana use in determining hard-drug-using intimates is less for white females than for white males (compare APDs in "Total" column). The idea is that marihuana use, although less important than drug selling for both sexes, is an almost unimportant factor for females but a slightly more important factor for males. Even more importantly, drug selling seems to move white females deeper into the white drug subculture than white males. At each level of drug buying and/or selling, white females are either as likely (plus or minus 4%) or somewhat more likely (5% or more) than white males to be highly exposed to users of other drugs (compare the six upper left cells (partials) for males and females). Only a few exceptions to this finding occur. Irregular cannabis-using females who have neither bought nor sold drugs are somewhat less likely (17% versus 25%) than males to have methedrine-using intimates (Table 10). Females who are irregular cannabis users and have sold hard drugs are less likely (20% versus 32%) than their male counterparts to be exposed to heroin (Table 11). Regular cannabis-using females who have sold hard drugs are less likely (61% versus 71%) than their male counterparts to have methedrine-using intimates.

What this evidence suggests is that with the exception of heroin and methedrine, white females who equal the marihuana consumption and selling activity of their male peers may be more deeply involved in the white drug subculture. However, white females are less apt to progress to successive levels of subculture participation than white males. Computations from the number of cases show that there are almost an equal number of white males (1601) and females (1632). However, females are less likely to ever use cannabis (48% = 788/1632) than males (62% = 999/1601). Among cannabis users, females are less apt (26% to 40%) to become regular marihuana users than males; among regular cannabis users, fewer (64% to 82%) females sell any drug. Among drug sellers, fewer (61% to 66%) females sell hard drugs. But the few females who do manage an equal level of participation in the drug subculture are as exposed, and frequently more exposed, to users of hard drugs than their white male peers.

Before summarizing the findings, one must briefly return to two theories developed in the previous chapter, the increased benefits theory and the euphoria theory. An attempt must be made to demonstrate that these theories and one's life style really indicate increasing involvement in the drug subculture. Thus, desiring to get high, agreeing that drugs provide certain benefits, or living a relatively "hip" life style may be values and products of participation in the drug subculture, rather than independent factors in drug use.

The previous chapter developed the Euphoria Index and the Increased Benefits Index, which were measures of different theories of drug progression. In addition, certain life styles appear to be related to drug use. What is meant by "hippie" culture seems a little vague, although it has been reasonably well described by Carey, Davis, and Pitts.[16] In an attempt to measure this lifestyle, students were asked if they agreed with two items used to form a Hip Life Style Index. About 20% of the sample agreed with both items and are high on this index. The proportion of the sample agreeing with each item is indicated in parentheses:

> Did you ever feel that other people or police would like to harass or intimidate you because of your appearance or beliefs? (35%)
>
> Try to or actually attend a rock or folk music festival like Woodstock or Newport Jazz Festival? (37%)

Of course, all three indices are significantly related to the Frequency of Cannabis Use and to the Illicit Marketing indices. The important question is, Which is more important, cannabis use or drug dealing? Graph 7.2 allows us to discover the answer.

One finds that being highly involved in the Hip Life Style Index is strongly related to cannabis use, but this relationship (%H = 25) is reduced by half when buying and selling activities are held constant. Thus, drug selling is more important than cannabis use in determining a relatively hip life style. The

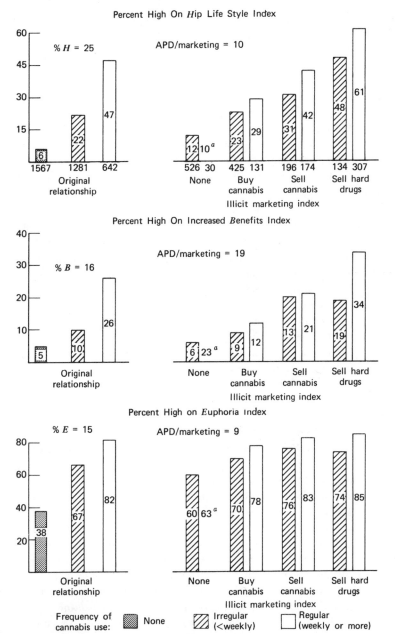

Percent High On *H*ip Life Style Index

% *H* = 25   APD/marketing = 10

Original relationship

Illicit marketing index

Percent High On Increased *B*enefits Index

% *B* = 16   APD/marketing = 19

Original relationship

Illicit marketing index

Percent High on *E*uphoria Index

% *E* = 15   APD/marketing = 9

Original relationship

Illicit marketing index

Frequency of cannabis use: ▨ None   ▨ Irregular (<weekly)   ☐ Regular (weekly or more)

Graph 7.2. Drug selling is a more important factor than cannabis use in determining a "hip" life style and agreement with prodrug values, but not in using cannabis to "get high, feel good."

143

Increased Benefits Index shows that drug selling, more than cannabis use, increases the probability of agreement with prodrug values. However, cannabis use is a somewhat more important factor than drug selling in causing persons to "get high, feel good" on cannabis.

With the exception of the Euphoria Index, this evidence tends to demonstrate that agreement with these indices is strongly related to drug buying and selling and less strongly to the use of cannabis. If drug dealing is an important measure of drug-subculture participation, increasing involvement in the drug subculture and, to a lesser extent, the use of cannabis should lead to a hip life style and agreement with drug-oriented values.

Before summarizing the findings of this chapter, one must again consider the problem of time order. Important assumptions have been made about causal relationships, but one cannot conclusively prove that one factor causes another. The most problematic causal chain in the present chapter is that drug selling causes students to gain intimates of another race who use subculturally specific drugs, which in turn leads to the use of such hard drugs. But since the sale of any particular drug probably occurs after a person is a user of that drug (Chapter 5), this chain of causality is questionable. In a similar fashion, drug selling is a more important factor than cannabis use in developing drug-oriented values and a hip life style; perhaps these preceed drug selling but come after cannabis use. But no matter what the actual direction of causality, involvement in drug selling is a more important factor than regular cannabis use in determining progressive involvement in a drug subculture or in the racially opposite subculture.

Chapter 6 carefully analyzed whether marihuana use leads to heroin and hard-drug use. It raised serious questions about, or disproved several theories of, drug escalation. Nevertheless, it found that many regular marihuana users become heroin and hard-drug users. The present chapter attempts to discuss how and why many marihuana users gain hard-drug-using friends and, hence, escalate to hard-drug use themselves.

To summarize, it has been established that the patterns of hard use among cannabis-using blacks and whites are quite different. The more regular the use of cannabis, the more pronounced racial differences in hard-drug use become. Whites are more likely than blacks to have intimates using, and to use themselves, hallucinogens, amphetamines, sedatives, and methedrine; blacks are more likely than whites to progress to cocaine and heroin. These findings indicate that there are probably two different subcultures of drug use in the New York metropolitan area. Each subculture defines marihuana use as an important indicator of early and low-level participation. But as subculture involvement increases, participants in the white drug subculture are likely to gain intimates using white drugs, while marihuana-using blacks gain intimates using black subculture drugs. Thus, nondrug selling marihuana users are likely to be exposed only to the hard drugs approved of by their own subculture but not to those drugs in the racially opposite subculture.

But as the regularity of marihuana use increases, events that are not independent of each other occur; persons become involved in drug selling and tend to gain intimates using hard drugs. Involvement in selling drugs is the important factor in explaining friendships with hard-drug users and in students becoming deeply involved in a specific (black or white) drug subculture. Drug selling, not cannabis use, is the primary factor associated with white students having amphetamine, sedative, and methedrine-using intimates and for blacks having heroin-using intimates. But most importantly, the evidence suggests that drug selling is the main mechanism by which persons are turned on to drugs in the racially opposite drug subculture. Therefore, whites have cocaine and heroin-using intimates because they sell hard drugs; their use of marihuana is a very unimportant factor. Likewise, the only blacks using sedatives, amphetamines, and methedrine are drug sellers.

Thus, the evidence supports drug subculture theory in almost all important points. The sophisticated stepping-stone theory is wrong and misleading. This position is probably wrong because it treats cannabis use as a causal factor instead of as an indicator of progressive subculture participation. More importantly, the sophisticated position is badly misleading because it ignores the crucial factor of drug selling in attempting to understand how students come to participate in social groups in which hard drugs are used.

To a certain extent, there is a good reason for the sophisticated stepping-stone theory to ignore the importance of drug selling; the present findings provide an indictment of the drug laws supported by the basic assumptions of this theory. Since cannabis use is the crucial factor in cannabis selling, and since cannabis selling is central to the sale of hard drugs (see Chapter 5), the illegality of cannabis is probably a central factor in determining patterns of drug escalation.

The present drug laws may also be involved in the development and maintenance of the two drug subcultures. The data indicate that drug selling is the major mechanism holding each drug subculture together and provides contact between the black and white subcultures. Participation in the illicit drug market, caused in part by the structure of present drug laws, increases the probability that inexperienced marihuana users will make contact with drug sellers. Such sellers are generally users of hard drugs and may have both economic and philosophical ("drugs are good") reasons for wanting to befriend and turn on less experienced users. However, the data, while not definitive, suggest that drug buyers control the interaction; they probably determine the frequency of interaction with the seller and the degree of friendship and, therefore, the probability of turning on, learning prodrug values, or living a hip life style.

The best way to unglue the subcultures of drug use may be to replace present drug laws with policies that allow cannabis users to obtain marihuana legally. Such a policy of legal cannabis would mean that students would not have to buy marihuana illegally in order to use it. Nor would students have concrete reasons to sell cannabis. The absence of cannabis sales might greatly shrink the volume and profitability of the illicit drug market. Marihuana-using students would be less apt to gain hard-drug-using intimates and perhaps less apt to turn on to hard drugs. However, the concluding chapter will develop this argument and the logic of how legal cannabis might undermine the drug subculture.

Is it possible that the present drug laws may be a cause of what they attempt to prevent—the use of hard drugs? The empirical evidence in these two chapters demonstrates that the answer is yes. But drug laws may also be a contributing factor to student involvement in unconventional behaviors and poor performance in college; these ideas will be pursued in the following two chapters.

REFERENCES

1. P. A. L. Chapple, "Cannabis, A Toxic and Dangerous Substance," *British Journal of Addiction*, 61 (Aug. 1966), 269-282. Gene R. Haislip, "Current Issues in the Prevention and Control of Marihuana Abuse," Paper presented to the First National Conference on Student Drug Involvement, U.S. National Student Association, Aug. 16, 1967. p. 4.

2. Nathan B. Eddy et al., "Drug Dependence: Its Significance and Characteristics," *Bulletin of the World Health Organization*, 32 (1965), 729.

3. Erich Goode, "Multiple Drug Use among Marijuana Smokers," *Social Problems*, 17 (Summer 1969), 56.

4. Ibid., p. 59. Lee Robins and George Murphy, "Drug Use in a Normal Population of Young Negro Men," *American Journal of Public Health*, 57 (Sept. 1967), 1580-1596. William McGlothlin, Kay Jamison, and Steven Rosenblatt, "Marijuana and the Use of Other Drugs," *Nature*, 228 (Dec 19, 1970). 1227-1229. Isidor Chein et al., *The Road to H*, New York: Basic Books, 1964. Edward Preble and John Casey, "Taking Care of Business—The Heroin User's Life on the Street," *International Journal of the Addictions*, 4 (Mar. 1969), 1-24. Jordan Scher, "Patterns and Profiles of Addiction and Drug Abuse," *Archives of General Psychiatry*, 15 (Nov. 1966), 1-20. Richard Blum et al., *Students and Drugs*, San Francisco: Jossey-Bass, 1969. James T. Carey, *The College Drug Scene*, Englewood Cliffs: Prentice Hall, 1968. Alan G. Sutter, "World of Drug Use on the Street Scene," in Donald R. Cressey and David A. Ward, *Delinquency, Crime, and Social Processes*, New York: Harper and Row, 1969, pp. 802-829. Harold Finestone, "Cats, Kicks and Color," in Howard Becker, *The Other Side*, New York: Free Press, 1964, pp. 281-297. Seymour Fiddle, *Portraits from a Shooting Gallery*, New York: Harper and Row, 1967.

5. Linda Charlton, "Gallup Finds a Continued Rise in the Use of Marijuana and LSD on Campuses," *New York Times*, Feb. 10, 1972. Boyce Rensberger, "Jobless Called Top Drug Users," ibid., Apr. 4, 1972. National Commission on Marihuana and Drug Abuse, *Marihuana—A Signal of Misunderstanding, Appendix II*, Washington, D.C.: Government Printing Office, 1972, p. 945 (henceforth the Schafer Report).

6. See Chapter 3 for a summary of trends in drug use across the college campus and other segments of the U.S. population.

7. See Casey and Preble, Ref. 4, pp. 1-24; and Fiddle, Ref. 4, for descriptions of this subculture.

8. John Langrod, "Secondary Drug Use Among Heroin Users," *International Journal of the Addictions,* 5 (Dec. 1970), 611-635.

9. Ibid., p. 613. Carl Chambers, R. Kent Hinesley, and Mary Moldestad, "Narcotic Addiction in Females: A Race Comparison," *International Journal of the Addictions,* 5 (June 1970), 257-278.

10. Langrod, Ref. 8, p. 626.

11. Ibid., p. 628.

12. Ibid.

13. Ibid., p. 626.

14. Carey, Ref. 4, pp. 36-43.

15. Erich Goode, *The Marijuana Smokers,* New York: Basic Books, 1970, p. 249. Carey, Ref. 4, p. 76.

16. Ibid., pp. 8-47. Fred Davis and Laura Munoz, "Heads and Freaks: Patterns of Drug Use Among Hippies," *Journal of Health and Social Behavior,* 9 (June 1968), 156-164. Jesse R. Pitts, "The Hippies as Contrameritocracy," *Dissent,* 1969, pp. 326-337, is particularly good.

CHAPTER 8

Delinquency, Militancy, and Sexual Permissiveness

The National Commission on Marihuana and Drug Abuse (NCM) was charged by Congress in 1970 to investigate "the relationship of marihuana use to aggressive behavior and crime." But there is a bigger question: What is the relationship between drug use and other unconventional behaviors? The basic problem is to determine whether the use of marihuana or hard drugs is a fundamental cause of aggressive behavior, crime, juvenile delinquency, political militancy, and sexual permissiveness or whether there are other social factors that may explain the relationship between drug use and these activities.

Several terms have been applied to activities that depart significantly from the expectations of appropriate behavior. Merton uses the term "deviant behavior" and Duster, "immoral behavior," but here the term "unconventional" behavior will be used.[1] The former terms presently have the connotation of evil, wrong, and badness to the layman, although Merton and Duster do not define or use these terms with such connotations. The term "unconventional" simply connotes that a behavior is incorrect when judged by wider societal and adult standards. As will be demonstrated, the drug subculture on American college campuses promote as desirable acts that are wrong when measured by the criteria of conventional expectations.

The charge to the NCM is essentially a more sophisticated version of the old-as-time argument that evil causes evil.[2] In present terminology, those who engage in one type of unconventional behavior are more likely to engage in another type of unconventional behavior.[3] Thus, marihuana use and multiple drug use are positively associated with several other unconventional behaviors. This chapter will investigate especially the relationship between drugs and crime, juvenile delinquency, aggressive behavior, political militancy, and premarital sexual permissiveness.

A brief review of the literature that connects marihuana to such unconventional behaviors is in order here. A leading proponent of antimarihuana laws and former director of the Bureau of Narcotics, Harry Anslinger, sums up nicely the view implicit in the charge by Congress to the NCM:

> In the earliest stages of [marihuana] intoxication the will power is destroyed and inhibitions and restraints are released; the moral barricades are broken down and often debauchery and sexuality results. Where mental instability is inherent, the behavior is generally violent . . . and the aggressive one often will resort to acts of violence and crime.[4]

Anslinger's supporters include the World Health Organization, the AMA, the National District Attorney's Association, and many psychologists.[5]

Support for the position that use of marihuana and hard drugs are associated with violence and crime comes generally from a limited number of studies, mostly done in other countries. Bloomquist, Giordano, Haislip, Munch, and Miller[6] cite anecdotal cases in the United States and the works of Wolff in Latin America, Gardikas in Greece, and Chopras in India[7] that link marihuana to aggressiveness and crime while ignoring evidence to the contrary.[8] Effective rebuttals of these studies can be found in Goode, Grinspoon, and Kaplan.[9]

Better evidence can be obtained to show a relationship between the use of hard drugs and crime.[10] Although heroin and barbiturate use probably decrease aggressiveness, the need to obtain funds to buy illicit heroin causes high levels of violence and crimes against property. Inciardi and Chambers found that 38 institutionalized addicts had committed more than 6000 crimes, about 6 crimes per week, with about 1% cleared by arrest.[11]

Unfortunately, the relationship between drug use and crime or aggressive behavior is somewhat muddled analytically. There are really two different issues. First, the actual use of a drug may act as a stimulant (or sedative) causing increased (decreased) activity and perhaps aggressive behavior, which may then be channeled into violence and crime. Scientific data is beginning to demonstrate that cannabis (or Tetrahydrocannabinol) works as a sedative, reducing the level of performance and inducing sleepiness when taken in large doses,[12] and perhaps reducing aggressiveness and crime.

Second, there may be a relationship between marihuana use and criminality or aggressive behavior, because "it is the kind of person, and not the drug, which is 'responsible' for criminal acts."[13] The difficulty with this theory lies in specifying what is meant by "kind of person." A psychological "kind of person" theory would hypothesize the existence of a character disorder, an alienated or aggressive personality that leads to both marihuana use and crime. A sociological "kind of person" theory would stress the nonconformist lifestyle into which persons become socialized and which induces persons both to use marihuana and to commit crime. [14]

Much of the commentary on the relationship between marihuana and crime applies also to juvenile delinquency. Important delinquent activities frequently center around the use of automobiles. The question is, Does the use of cannabis impair one's ability to drive or cause a person to use the auto in an unconventional manner? Crancer indicates that marihuana usage does not significantly impair performance on a simulated driving test, while alcohol definitely impairs such performance. [15] Waller summarizes several studies that relate drug use to crashes and traffic citations. He finds that drug users have 2.5 times more citations than control samples of nonusers in all studies, but the findings with regards to crashes are mixed. In no study is the crash rate of known drug users, whatever the drug, more than 1.5 times greater than a control group of drivers. [16] He concludes that those with "patterns of wide-ranging antisocial acts, of relatively low crash rates but extraordinarily high citations rates and of hard core recidivism suggest that many of them have sociopathic personality patterns, [17] and will continue to be problems for motor vehicle authorities. Waller does not seem too worried about "drug users who probably do not have an increased risk of crashes or citations [and] includes most teenagers and young adults who use marihuana only." [18] Similar findings emerge from analysis of the driving records of heroin addicts. [19] One can profitably try to understand the relationship between drug use and involvement in auto related unconventional activities (information on crashes is not available).

There is little question that marihuana use is strongly related to a leftist political position and active militancy. [20] However, the reasons for this relationship are not at all clear. Whatever the reason for the relationship between drugs and militancy, the public was greatly concerned about student militancy during the spring of 1970, when the present survey was conducted. [21] Indeed, the questionnaire was not administered in several classes in which arrangements had previously been made, because the student strike protesting the deaths of Kent State and Jackson State students was so effective.

Despite the fact that there is almost no enforceable law against premarital sex, student involvement in sex is an activity that concerns adults. A striking commentary on the relationship of marihuana use to premarital sex is presented in a now classic article by Kolansky and Moore and based upon thirty-eight patients that they saw in their private consultation practice:

> Thirteen female individuals, all unmarried and ranging in age from 13 to 22 [are] singled out because of the unusual degree of sexual promiscuity, which ranged from sexual relations with several individuals of the opposite sex to relations with the same sex ... individuals of both sexes, and sometimes, individuals of both sexes on the

same evening. . . . we were struck by the loss of sexual inhibitions after short period
of marihuana smoking.

In no instance was there sexual promiscuity prior to the beginning of marihuana
smoking, and in only two of the 13 cases were there histories of mild anxiety states
prior to smoking. We take these results to indicate marihuana's effect on loosening
the superego controls and altering superego ideals. [22]

Their small and highly biased sample makes the findings suspect. However,
sociologist Erich Goode, shows a strong linear relationship between marihuana
use and the number of sexual partners, which is not altered when sex and year in
school is held constant: 7% of the noncannabis users (not used in the past six
months) but 32% of the regular (three or more times per week) users had sex
with four or more persons. [23] Goode feels, but does not demonstrate, that

sexual behavior and drug use are mutual components forming parts of a particular
subculture on the college campus. . . . Thus, the student becomes socialized into the
attitudes and behavior of a sexually permissive milieu as he moves from no drug
use . . . to regular drug use. . . . The more that he smokes marijuana, the more drugs
that he has and continues to use, the greater will be his commitment to a deviant and
subterranean group and way of life, and the more sexually permissive he will
become. [24]

By using the measure of subculture participation, the Illicit Marketing Index,
one can demonstrate the validity of Goode's hypothesis.

Marihuana is not the only drug used for its aphrodisiac effect. Anslinger feels
that "if we want to take Leary literally, we should call LSD 'Let's Start
Degeneracy.' " Richard Alpert replies that "before taking LSD, I never stayed in
a state of sexual ecstasy for hours on end, but I have done this under LSD." [25]
In Sweden, intravenous Preludin (an amphetamine) users use the drug for sexual
purposes: "Their interest in sex was not only markedly stimulated, allowing
them to have intercourse repeatedly over a relatively short period of time, but in
addition on each occasion the orgasm was markedly delayed so that they could
literally fornicate for hours at a time." [26] What little evidence there is indicates
that the number of drugs used is associated with sexual permissiveness. [27]

Robins, Darvish, and Murphy have demonstrated that marihuana use is
associated with negative outcomes, even when holding other factors constant.
Using various measures of unconventional adult outcomes (illegitimate child,
extramarital affairs, divorce, arrests, heroin use, alcoholism, etc.) among 220
adult black men in St. Louis, Robins found that controlling on "high school
graduation, juvenile delinquency and alcoholism . . . failed to wipe out completely relationships between marijuana use and outcome. Failing to account
completely for the relationships found through intervening variables suggest that
the drug may have a *direct* effect on adult outcome." [28] They conclude, "Unless
some satisfactory explanation for the poorer outcome other than the direct
effect of marijuana use can be identified, it would seem foolhardy to

recommend the legalization of marijuana."[29] It is the possibility of some other explanation, namely, drug-subculture participation and peer orientation, that helps to interpret the relationship between drug use and unconventional activities, at least in the present college student sample.

Several questions in the questionnaire allow one to develop indicators of crime, aggressive behavior, juvenile delinquency, political militancy, and sexual permissiveness. (The term "sexual permissiveness" is used because it does not make the negative value judgments implied by the term "sexual promiscuity.") The indices developed below may not perfectly measure the various concepts, but they are an improvement over speculation. As each index is developed, the proportion of the total sample that agreed with each item is indicated in parentheses.

The Crime Index can also serve as an index of juvenile delinquency; questions about robbery, murder, rape, and other major crimes were not asked. However, persons who are highly involved in this index may be more likely to commit major crimes. The Crime Index is composed of four items; 11% of the students agreed with two or more of the items and are classified as "high" on the Crime Index. Respondents were asked: Did you ever?

> Take a car for a ride without the owner's permission (5.4%)
>
> Ever take things of some value (more than $10) from stores, work or school (11.7%)
>
> Purposefully destroy or damage property (break street lights, damage or move traffic signs, break into buildings and/or mess them up) (11.4%)
>
> While in high school, take things of little value (less than $10) from stores, work or school at five or more different times (12.5%)

The Aggressiveness Index may also be a measure of juvenile delinquency. Persons were classified as aggressive (13% of the total population) if they agreed with either of the following items:

> Threaten or "beat up" other persons for any reason (9%)
>
> Participate in gang fights (7.5%)

As a measure of juvenile delinquency, an Auto Deviance Index was developed. Persons agreeing with two of the following three items (20% of the sample) were classified as "high" on the Auto Deviance Index:

> Drive a car before obtaining a driver's license, but had no licensed driver with you (18%)
>
> Drive faster than 80 m.p.h. (38.5%)
>
> Participate in or attend a drag race (17%)

Students were classified on the Political Militancy Index as "militant" (11% of the population) if they agreed with two of the following items:

Sat-in or demonstrated in an office or building (21%)

Participated in a demonstration where violence occured (17%)

Been held or arrested for political activities at school or elsewhere (2.2%)

And finally, students were classified as "sexually permissive" (10% of the sample) if they admitted to having been involved in premarital sex with four or more different persons.

Two independent variables will be utilized. The Frequency of Cannabis Use Index has been used extensively in the previous two chapters. The less than monthly and the less than weekly (experimental + moderate) cannabis users have been combined; these irregular cannabis users will be compared with regular (weekly) marihuana users. In addition, as a measure of the use of all drugs, the Multiple Drug Use Index, developed in Chapter 3 will be utilized. The cannabis only category will be compared with the multiple (three or more) drug use category. To test the validity of the official position, this chapter hypothesizes that the two measures of drug use are fundamentally related to unconventional behavior. To test this hypothesis, the Illicit Marketing Index will be held constant. For this variable the category of "sell hard drugs" will be expanded into two categories; "sell 1-2 hard drugs" and "sell 3+ hard drugs" (see Chapter 5). Because percentages that may be misleading because of the small number of cases are frequently encountered, the graphs will not present a bar for such percentages. However, the number of cases and the proportion involved in the activity will be indicated.

The crucial question is whether the relationship between the use of cannabis or other drugs and unconventional activities is fundamental or caused by some other variable. It will be remembered from previous chapters that the Illicit Marketing Index was shown to be a good measure of the concept of drug-subculture participation. As Goode argues, the relationship between drug use and sexual permissiveness may be accounted for by differential participation in a distinctive subculture on the college campus.[30] It is the contention of the present chapter that participation in the drug subculture and the wider peer culture, rather than the use of marihuana or other drugs, provides a good understanding of why students become involved in these unconventional activities.

In Graphs 8.1-8.4 one can observe the original relationship between drug use indices and these five unconventional behaviors. For all activities, noncannabis (or nondrug) users (bar at far left) are the least likely to be involved, as expected. Such noncannabis users, as shown in Chapter 6, almost never buy or sell drugs or become involved in the drug subculture. Hence, the noncannabis and nondrug users will be temporarily excluded from the following analysis.

Graphs 8.1-8.4 show that both measures of drug use are significantly related to the five measures of unconventional behavior. Graph 8.1 shows the basic finding most clearly. At each level of involvement in the drug market, irregular cannabis users are almost as likely as regular users to be militant; the 10% (%M) difference in militancy due to the frequency of cannabis use is reduced to 2% (APD) when the Illicit Marketing Index is held constant. In a similar fashion, the 9% difference in aggressiveness due to cannabis use is reduced to 2% (APD) when drug market involvement is held constant.

Data not presented shows that the relationships between cannabis use and the

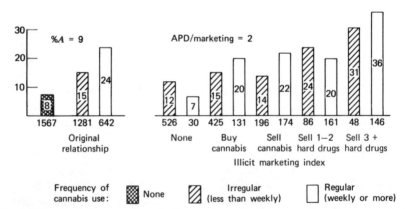

Graph 8.1. Involvement in drug dealing, and not the frequency of marihuana use, is the important factor in understanding militancy and aggressiveness.

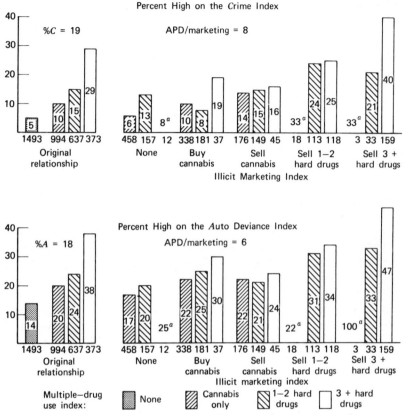

Graph 8.2. The relationship between multiple-drug use and crime or auto deviance is reduced by half when the Illicit Marketing Index is held constant.

Crime Index and Auto Deviance Index are also significantly reduced. In addition, the relationship between drug marketing (as the independent variable) and these unconventional behaviors is not affected when cannabis use is held constant. Similar findings hold for sexual permissiveness, but this will be discussed shortly. In brief, the frequency with which cannabis is used has almost no influence upon these unconventional behaviors when drug dealing is held constant.

The findings are not quite so clear when the independent variable is the Multiple Drug Use Index. Graph 8.2 shows that the number of drugs used is strongly related to unconventional behavior. For example, multiple drug users are 19% more likely than cannabis-only users to be high on the Crime Index; this relationship is reduced to about 8% (APD) when the Drug Marketing Index is held constant. A similar decrease, from 18% to 6%, occurs when the drug use-auto deviance relationship is examined. Likewise, data not presented show that the relationships between militancy and aggressiveness are reduced to about a third of their original strength when involvement in the drug market is held constant. This seems to indicate that drug use is not too strongly associated with these unconventional behaviors.

However, combining data presented in Appendix A and Graph 8.2 indicate that the strong relationships between the Illicit Marketing Index (as the independent variable) and these unconventional behaviors are reduced to about two-thirds or half when the Multiple Drug Use Index is held constant. However, the Illicit Marketing Index is somewhat more powerful than the Multiple Drug Use Index. Thus, there is a tendency for both the Multiple Drug Use Index and Illicit Drug Marketing Index to mutually explain involvement in unconventional behavior.

The basic problem with these data is that multiple drug use is highly correlated with illicit drug marketing. Only 2% of those who have only used cannabis have sold hard drugs, while 77% of those using three or more drugs have sold one or more hard drugs. As a result, there are not enough cases to provide stable percentages in theoretically crucial cells. For example, one would like to know how persons who only use cannabis and sell hard drugs behave; but information from twenty-one respondents will not provide stable percentages. Data from the twelve persons who have used three hard drugs and have not bought or sold are likely to be misleading. In Graphs 8.2 and 8.4, information from these extreme groups is presented (marked by a small letter *a*), but ignored in the analysis.

A careful examination of Graph 8.2 shows that persons who only use cannabis, even though buying or selling it, are relatively unlikely to be highly involved in any of these unconventional behaviors. For example, among those who have used cannabis, 6% of the nonbuyers or nonsellers, 10% of the cannabis buyers and 14% of the cannabis sellers are high on the Crime Index.

However, the same cannot be said for the users of multiple drugs. Of those using three or more drugs, 19% of the cannabis buyers, 16% of the cannabis sellers, 25% of sellers of one or two hard drugs and 40% of the sellers of multiple drugs were high on the Crime Index. Similar findings emerge from analysis of the other indicators of unconventional behavior; those who are multiple drug users are likely to be quite highly involved, even if they only buy or sell cannabis. Of course, the highest incidence of unconventional behavior occurs among those who use and sell three or more drugs. The implications of these findings for subculture theory will be considered after analyzing sexual permissiveness.

Graph 8.3 reveals that among noncannabis users, 5% of the males but only 1.3% of the females have engaged in sex with four or more partners. For both sexes, weekly cannabis users are more likely than irregular users (10% for males,

7% for females) to have done so. However, the differences in sexual permissiveness caused by cannabis use are reduced to 2% among males and − 1% among females when the Illicit Marketing Index is held constant. Although the number of cases for females is small (12 + 29), the most significant finding is that among those involved in selling three or more hard drugs, females are as likely (33%) as males (32%) to have had sex with four or more persons.

Percent Sexually Permissive: Have Sex With Four or More Partners

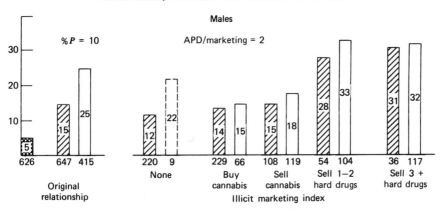

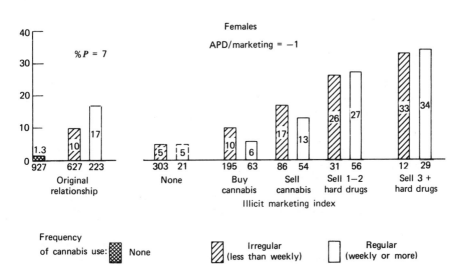

Graph 8.3. Drug selling is strongly associated with sexual permissiveness, especially for females. The frequency of marihuana use is unimportant.

However, there are fewer (41 to 153) females than males who are so highly involved in selling drugs. In addition, the level of sexual permissiveness among females who sell cannabis or one or two hard drugs is about as high as among their male counterparts. It is among those not involved in selling drugs that the sex differences in sexual permissiveness are most apparent. In addition, as will soon be shown in Graph 8.4, persons who confine their drug use to cannabis, regardless of whether they buy or sell marihuana, are relatively unlikely to be sexually permissive. One possible interpretation of these findings is that females as well as males become increasingly involved in the drug subculture via selling. As their subculture participation increases, they learn values suggesting that sex is fun and that drugs make sex better. Drug-selling friends expect them to act according to these values.

But no matter what the exact causal connection is, the frequency of marihuana use has very little to do with sexual permissiveness and a great deal to do with the associations one forms as a drug seller. Hence, Anslinger is essentially wrong: marihuana intoxication has little effect upon the sexual behavior of college students.[31] Rather, those who become highly involved in drug selling are likely to gain friends and to learn values and patterns of behavior that increase the likelihood of sexual permissiveness.

Using the same reasoning, one can understand how Kolansky and Moore come to the wrong conclusion from an observation that may be correct: "In no instance was there sexual promiscuity prior to the beginning of marijuana smoking."[32] They reach the wrong conclusions because they ignore other factors that may be very important, such as the selling activities, the friendship patterns, and the values that their thirteen marihuana-using females may have held. Such factors are of much greater importance than the simple fact of marihuana smoking. The data here show that sexual inhibitions are not lost among regular marihuana-using females who have only bought cannabis or have not bought or sold drugs (only 5%-6% are sexually permissive). It may be that Kolansky and Moore's thirteen patients were among the few females who are highly involved in the drug subculture. Their biased sample and psychological orientation bring Kolansky and Moore to incorrect conclusions. Marihuana use may precede sexual promiscuity, but so may many other social factors they fail to consider. The present evidence shows that when drug subculture participation is held constant, the use of marihuana is a minor or unimportant factor in understanding these five types of unconventional behavior.[33]

Graph 8.4 shows somewhat different results for multiple drug use. For both males and females, multiple drug users are ($\%P$ = 20% males; 22% females) more likely than cannabis-only users to be sexually permissive. In general, this relationship is reduced about in half (APD = 10%, males; 8%, females) when the Illicit Marketing Index is held constant. Unfortunately, the number of males and females who use three or more drugs and buy or sell cannabis is small (17, 28,

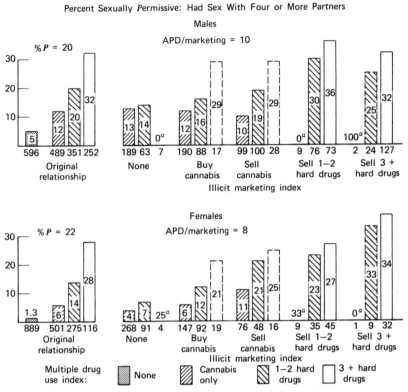

Graph 8.4. The relationship between multiple-drug use and sexual permissiveness is reduced by half when the Illicit Marketing Index is held constant.

19, 16) and may be misleading, hence, the broken line bars. If one analyzes the information provided by these respondents, one finds high levels of permissiveness among those who use multiple drugs. Among males, the level of permissiveness among multiple drug users is about 30%, regardless of drug selling. Among females, involvement in the drug market has some effect (21% to 34%) on permissiveness among the users of multiple drugs. As Graph 8.3 showed, females who are heavily involved in drug selling are as permissive as their male counterparts regardless of how many drugs they use.

At this point a crucial question arises: Is the use of noncannabis drugs a measure of drug use only or does multiple drug use also indicate heavy participation in the drug subculture? From the official point of view represented by Anslinger and Kolansky and Moore, the present findings could be used to support the contention that the use of noncannabis drugs is undesirable because it is independently related to sexual permissiveness and cannot be fully explained by involvement in the drug market. Subculture theory, however, would say that the use of multiple drugs is indicative of heavy involvement in the drug subculture regardless of drug buying or selling. This issue can only be partially resolved. It was demonstrated above (Graph 8.3) that cannabis use is not independently related to sexual permissiveness. In addition, especially among females, those who confine their drug use to cannabis and only buy (6%) or sell (11%) marihuana or neither (4%) are not a great deal more likely than nondrug users (1.2%) to be sexually permissive. Previous chapters have maintained that persons who confine their drug use and buying or selling to cannabis are relatively uninvolved in the drug subculture. If this is the case, then those who are uninvolved in the subculture are also relatively (compared to users of hard drugs) unlikely to be sexually permissive.

Thus, there are two groups that may be at opposite levels of involvement in the subculture: those who are minimally involved and confine their use to cannabis and those who are heavily involved and use three or more hard drugs. In order to clarify whether it is drug use or subculture involvement that leads to permissiveness, the important group to analyze is those who use one or two hard drugs. If the official position is correct and the use of hard drugs is an important factor in determining sexual permissiveness, then those using one or two hard drugs should be more like their peers who use multiple drugs than cannabis-only users at all levels of buying and selling. If, on the other hand, subculture theory is correct, then the level of permissiveness among users of one or two hard drugs should be dependent upon the depth of involvement in the drug market.

The data demonstrate that subculture theory is correct. Among those who neither buy nor sell drugs or only buy cannabis (low levels of subculture involvement), those using one or two hard drugs have levels of sexual permissiveness that are similar to cannabis-only users and unlike those who use three or more hard drugs. However, among those selling hard drugs (highly involved in the subculture) the users of one or two hard drugs have permissiveness levels almost identical to the users of multiple drugs. In addition, among those who sell cannabis only (intermediate level of subculture involvement), the level of sexual permissiveness among those who use one or two drugs is halfway between that of the cannabis-only and multiple drug users. In short, those using one or two hard drugs have a level of permissiveness similar to that of cannabis users when involvement in the subculture drug market is low and similar to that of multiple drug users when involvement is high. Increasing subculture participation, not drug use provides the best understanding of the evidence.

Data presented in Graph 8.4 and Appendix A indicate that both variables, the Illicit Marketing Index and the Multiple Drug Use Index, tend to mutually explain the other when related to the indicators of unconventional behavior. For example, relationships between multiple drug use and the five measures of unconventional behavior are reduced to about a third of their original strength (from about 20% to about 6%) when the Illicit Marketing Index is held constant. Likewise, the relationships between the Illicit Marketing Index and these unconventional behaviors is reduced to about half of its original strength (from about 25% to about 12%) when the Multiple Drug Use Index is held constant. Thus, our evidence shows that the independent effect of the Illicit Marketing Index is about twice (APD's, 12% to 6%) as important as that of multiple drug use; however, both variables contribute independently to involvement in unconventional behavior. The fact that they mutually explain each other indicates that they are probably measuring the same phenomena; increasing participation in a subculture of drug use.

It is possible to disagree with the interpretation that the Multiple Drug Use Index is an independent measure of drug-subculture participation but not as powerful a one as the Illicit Marketing Index. But if the use of several drugs should be of concern to society, the question of how students become involved in several different hard drugs must be answered. Chapters 6 and 7 addressed themselves to this very question and demonstrated that it is involvement in different subcultures of drug use that leads to the utilization of various drugs and not marihuana use. It is probable that the Multiple Drug Use Index is a measure of subculture participation. Hence, it is drug-subculture participation that should be of primary concern to government policy makers, not the use of drugs.

However, there is one element of the official position that the data support. Persons who do not use drugs have the lowest levels of participation in these five kinds of unconventional behavior. Could it be that the simple act of marihuana use causes students to behave in a more unconventional fashion? Or might there be some other social factor that could provide a better understanding of why nonmarihuana users do not become involved in these unconventional behaviors?

It is suggested that differential involvement in peer-culture activities may strongly affect the participation of noncannabis users in various unconventional activities. As summarized in Chapter 1, students who spend a great deal of time with friends in nonadult-controlled settings are likely to engage in a wide variety of unconventional, disapproved activities.

It will be remembered from Chapter 3 that students were asked to report whether they had dated at an early age (fourteen or younger), "hung out," or "drove around" before leaving high school and were classified on the Peer Culture Index. An examination of Tables 25A-E, presented in Appendix A, show two different outcomes for the relationship between cannabis use and nonconventional activities when holding constant the Peer Culture Index and the Illicit Marketing Index. Peer-culture involvement strongly affects the involvement of noncannabis users in crime, auto deviance, and aggressiveness.

Among the noncannabis users (similar findings hold for nondrug users), the following proportion of those "not," "some," and "high," respectively, on the Peer Culture Index were high on the Auto Deviance Index (6%, 16%, 31%), high on the Crime Index (2%, 4%, 13%), and high on the Aggressiveness Index (4%, 8%, 16%). In addition, noncannabis users who were highly involved in the peer culture had about the same level of participation on these indices as persons who were not involved in the peer culture but high in the drug subculture. Thus, of the regular marihuana users who have sold three or more hard drugs but were not involved in the peer culture, 23% were high on the Auto Deviance Index. At the logically opposite extreme, noncannabis users who were highly involved in the peer culture were somewhat higher, 31%, on the Auto Deviance Index. Similar comparisons emerge from the Crime Index (9% to 13%) and the Aggressiveness Index (18% to 16%) among these logically opposite groups. This tends to indicate that abstinence from cannabis does not prevent a person from being involved in these unconventional activities when peer-culture involvement is high.

The results, however, are fundamentally different with respect to political militancy and sexual permissiveness. Noncannabis users are significantly less likely ($p < .001$) to be involved in these activities than cannabis users, even when peer-group involvement is held constant. For example, among the noncannabis users who were not, some, and high, respectively, on the Peer Culture Index 2%, 4%, 4% were militant; 2%, 5%, 12% of the males had had sex with four or more partners; and 1%, 1%, 3% of the females were sexually permissive. In short, peer-culture involvement has a very minor effect upon the militancy and sexual behavior of noncannabis users. But the most impressive evidence of the weakness of cannabis use as an important cause of unconventional behavior is found in Table 13.

This table summarizes some very complex data presented in Table 25 of Appendix A. The information presented is confined to cannabis users because almost all noncannabis users do not buy or sell drugs. In Table 13 one can examine, in the last column, the strength of a relationship between an independent and dependent variable when the other factors are held constant. For example, in the column headed "two-way percent difference," one finds that regular cannabis users are 12% (23%-11%) more likely than irregular users to be high on the Crime Index; but when Illicit Marketing and Peer Culture Indices are held constant, there is no relationship between cannabis use and crime.

Indeed, cannabis use has virtually no direct (APD's of 2% or less) or independent effect upon any of the six unconventional behavior indices when Peer Culture and Illicit Marketing indices are held constant. However, the Peer Culture Index appears to have a substantial independent effect upon crime, auto deviance, and aggressiveness (APD of about 20%) but not upon militancy or sexual permissiveness (APDs of less than 5%), when cannabis use and illicit marketing are held constant.

Table 13. Percent differences^d (original and controlled) due to the frequency of cannabis use, Illicit Marketing Index, and Peer Culture Index for various indices of unconventional behavior

Independent Variables^a	Extreme Categories			Two-way Percent Difference	Average Percent Difference (APD) with Other Independent Variables Held Constant
A. Percent high on Crime Index					
Illicit marketing^b	37%- 7%	=		30	24
Peer culture	28%- 5%	=		23	20
Cannabis use	23%-11%	=		12	0
B. Percent high on Auto Deviance Index					
Illicit marketing	45%-18%	=		27	30
Peer culture	39%-11%	=		28	22
Cannabis use	27%-24%	=		3	- 8^c
C. Percent high on Aggressiveness Index					
Illicit marketing	34%-12%	=		22	20
Peer culture	29%- 9%	=		20	18
Cannabis use	24%-15%	=		9	0
D. Percent high on Political Militancy Index					
Illicit marketing	33%- 7%	=		26	23
Peer culture	20%-14%	=		6	1
Cannabis use	24%-14%	=		10	1
E. Percent sexually permissive: males					
Illicit marketing	32%-18%	=		20	15
Peer culture	24%-15%	=		9	5
Cannabis use	25%-15%	=		10	2
F. Percent sexually permissive: females					
Illicit marketing	33%- 5%	=		28	25
Peer culture	14%-11%	=		3	2
Cannabis use	17%-10%	=		7	- 1

aAll noncannabis users are excluded from calculation of percent differences because almost no noncannabis users buy or sell drugs.

bRead each row as in this example: Among cannabis users, 37% of those selling three or more drugs versus 7% of those not buying or selling drugs are high on the Crime Index; a two-way percent difference of 30%. When the Peer Culture Index and the regularity of cannabis use are held constant, the relationship between illicit marketing and crime is reduced to an average percent difference of 24%.

cA negative APD means that irregular cannabis users are 8% more likely than regular cannabis users to be high on the Auto Deviance Index when peer culture and illicit marketing are held constant. This may indicate that regular cannabis users either avoid cars or drive more carefully than irregular users when their life style is held constant.

dThis table is based upon data presented in Table 25 of Appendix A.

But most important, when peer culture and cannabis use are held constant, the Illicit Marketing Index strongly influences (APD's of 15% to 30%) involvement in every form of unconventional behavior. Thus, buying and selling is almost the only important variable (of these three) in understanding political militancy and sexual permissiveness. Buying and selling drugs appears to combine with peer-culture involvement to increase the probability of participating in crime, auto deviance, and aggressiveness.

It would be interesting to be able to report a similar analysis of illicit marketing, peer culture, and multiple drug use. But such an analysis cannot be reported because there are too few cases in theoretically crucial cells. As can be observed in Graph 8.2, there are thirty-seven persons who have used three or more drugs but only bought cannabis, and forty-five persons who have used three or more drugs and sold cannabis; likewise, there are only thirty-three persons who have sold three or more hard drugs but have used only one or two drugs. When peer-culture involvement is held constant, many of these cells have fifteen or fewer cases; hence, no percentage would be meaningful and computations of percent differences are not possible. Analysis of the direct effect of multiple drug use, illicit marketing, and peer culture upon unconventional behavior must wait until a larger sample can be obtained.

More than any previous chapter, this chapter has demonstrated the importance of drug subculture theory in explaining behavior that is reputed to be associated with drug use but is not a direct outcome of drug use. Involvement in the illicit drug market is an important factor determining militancy and sexual permissiveness. It is hard to understand intuitively why drug selling should be associated with these activities. If the official position's image of an adult drug seller who makes large profits from selling drugs is accepted as true, it is hard to understand why such sellers would risk involvement in political activities or sex since these activities might generate police interest. A far better explanation is subculture theory. This theory suggest that buying or selling drugs is really a good measure of participation in unconventional groups in which hard drugs are used (see Chapters 6 and 7) and political militancy and sex are expected of group members. The more involved in drug selling a student is, the greater the probability of participating in such unconventional groups and the greater the probability of learning norms, values, and patterns of conduct that promote militancy and permissiveness. In addition, participation in such groups increasingly isolate the seller from conventional friends and values.

While cannabis use is related to all unconventional behaviors, the data demonstrate that the frequency of cannabis use is a very unimportant factor when buying and selling activities are held constant. Thus, the theory of drug-subculture participation is both theoretically and empirically more adequate than the assertions that something (not specified) about the use of cannabis destroys willpower and inhibitions.

An analysis of auto deviance, aggressiveness, and crime among college students reveals that these activities are not closely tied to the use of marihuana but related to participation in the drug market and to peer-culture involvement in high school. Perhaps these activities tend to occur in high school and are given up as activities in college. It may be that patterns of unconventional behavior shift from juvenile delinquency (measured by Crime, Aggressiveness, and Auto Deviance Indices) to drug use, political militancy, and sexual permissiveness in college for large numbers of students. As with all speculations about time order, one cannot accurately determine patterns of causality with the present data.

No matter what the direction of causality actually is, this chapter has established that the frequency of marihuana use is not a very important factor in explaining several unconventional behaviors when peer-culture and drug-subculture participation is held constant. While the Multiple Drug Use Index is independently related to these unconventional behaviors, it is probable that this index is also a measure of subculture participation and not only a measure of drug use.

REFERENCES

1. Robert Merton, *Social Theory and Social Structure,* rev. ed., Glencoe, Ill.: Free Press, 1957, pp. 359-362. Robert Merton and Robert Nisbet, *Contemporary Social Problems,* 2nd ed., New York: Harcourt, Brace, and World, 1966, p. 805. Troy Duster, *The Legislation of Morality,* New York: Free Press, 1970, p. 99.

2. Travis Hirschi, *Causes of Delinquency,* Berkeley and Los Angeles: University of California Press, 1969, p. 227. Alfred Lindesmith, *Addiction and Opiates,* Chicago: Aldine, 1968, pp. 188-189.

3. Ibid. Michael J. Hindelang, "Age, Sex, and the Versatility of Delinquent Involvements," *Social Problems,* 18 (Spring 1971), 527-533. Richard Brotman, et al., "Drug Use Among Affluent High School Youth," in Erich Goode, *Marijuana,* New York: Atherton Press, 1969, pp. 128-135. Edward Suchman, "The 'Hang-Loose' Ethic and the Spirit of Drug Use," *Journal of Health and Social Behavior,* 9 (June 1968), 146-155.

4. Harry Anslinger and William Tompkins, *The Traffic in Narcotics,* New York: Funk and Wagnalls, 1953, p. 22. Nor has Anslinger changed his opinions; see Playboy Panel, "The Drug Revolution," *Playboy,* Feb. 1970, pp. 55, 58, 72, for discussions about whether marihuana, LSD, and other drugs are aphrodisiacs or cause crime. This panel discussion includes almost all viewpoints: Richard Alpert, Anslinger, Joel Fort, and others.

5. Nathan B. Eddy et al., "Drug Dependence: It's Significance and Characteristics," *Bulletin of the World Health Organization,* 32 (1965), 721-733. "Dependence on Cannabis," *Journal of the American Medical Association,* 201 (Aug. 7, 1967), 368-371; and "Marijuana and Society," ibid., 204 (June 24, 1968), 1181-1182. Jerome LaBarre, "Harms Resulting from the Use of Cannabis," *The Prosecuter,* 6 (Mar.-Apr. 1970), 91. Harold Kolansky and William Moore, "Effects of Marihuana on Adolescents and Young Adults," *Journal of the American Medical Association,* 216 (Apr. 19, 1971), 486-492.

6. Edward Bloomquist, *Marijuana,* Beverly Hills, Calif.: Glencoe Press, 1968, p. 97. Henry

L. Giordano, "Marihuana—A Calling Card to Narcotic Addiction," *FBI Law Enforcement Bulletin,* 37(11) (Nov. 1968), 2-5. Gene R. Haislip, "Current Issues in the Prevention and Control of Marihuana Abuse," Paper presented to the First National Conference on Student Drug Involvement sponsored by the U.S. National Student Association, University of Maryland, Aug. 16, 1967, pp. 4-6. Donald E. Miller, "Marihuana: The Law and Its Enforcement," *Suffolk University Law Review,* 4 (Fall 1968), 86-87. James C. Munch, "Marihuana and Crime," *U.N. Bulletin on Narcotics,* 18 (Apr.-June 1966), 15-22.

7. Pablo O. Wolff, *Marijuana in Latin America: The Threat it Constitutes,* Washington, D.C.: Linacre Press, 1949, pp. 35-55. C. G. Gardikas, "Hashish and Crime," *Enkephalos,* 2 (1950), 201-211. I. C. Chopra and R. N. Chopra, "The Use of Cannabis Drugs in India," *Bulletin on Narcotics,* Jan.-Mar. 1957, p. 25. G. S. Chopra "Man and Marijuana," *The International Journal of the Addictions,* 4 (June 1969), p. 240.

8. *Report of the Indian Hemp Drugs Commission, 1893-1894,* Smila, India, Government Central Printing House, 1894. For a more condensed and available summary, see Tod H. Mikuriya, "Physical, Mental, and Moral Effects of Marijuana: The Indian Hemp Drugs Commission Report," *International Journal of the Addictions,* 3 (Fall 1968), 268-269. New York City Mayor's Committee on Marihuana [LaGuardia Report], *The Marihuana Problem in the City of New York,* Lancaster, Pa.: Jacques Cattell, 1944; for abbreviated and available segments of this report, see David Solomon, *The Marihuana Papers,* Indianapolis: Bobbs-Merrill, 1966, pp. 296-300. W. Bromberg and T. C. Rodgers, "Marihuana and Aggressive Crime," *American Journal of Psychiatry,* 102 (May 1946), 825-827. O. M. Andrade, "The Criminogenic Action of Cannabis and Narcotics," *Bulletin on Narcotics,* 16 (1964), 23-28. T. Asuni, "Socio-Psychiatric Aspects of Cannabis in Nigeria," *Bulletin on Narcotics,* 16 (1964), 28. *Cannabis,* Report by the Advisory Committee on Drug Dependence, London: HMSO, 1969, pp. 6-14.

9. Erich Goode, *The Marijuana Smokers,* New York: Basic Books, 1970, pp. 227-235. Lester Grinspoon, *Marihuana Reconsidered,* Cambridge, Mass.: Harvard University Press, 1971, 291-312. John Kaplan, *Marijuana: The New Prohibition,* Cleveland: World Publishing Co., 1970, pp. 88-127.

10. Nils Bejerot, "Intravenous Drug Abuse in the Arrest Population in Stockholm; Frequency Studies," in Folke Sjoqvist and Malcolm Tottie, *Abuse of Central Stimulants,* Symposium for the Swedish Committee on International Health Relations, Nov. 25-27, 1968, New York: Raven Press, 1969. In the *Playboy* panel discussion, Ref. 4, pp. 64-68, almost all noncannabis drugs are implicated in crime and violence; especially methedrine and heroin.

11. James A. Inciardi and Carl D. Chambers, "Self Reported Criminal Behavior of Narcotic Addicts," Paper presented to Committee on Problems of Drug Dependence, National Research Council, Toronto, Canada, Feb. 16, 1971. Also see: Isidor Chein et al., *The Road to H,* New York: Basic Books, 1964, pp. 57-65, 138-145. Edward Preble and John J. Casey, "Taking Care of Business—The Heroin User's Life on the Street," *International Journal of the Addictions,* March 1969. In *Life,* see "The Cities Lock Up," Nov. 19, 1971, pp. 26-29; "Readers Speak Out," Jan. 14, 1972, pp. 28-31; and "A 1,000-Hit Thug Tells How He Works," Jan. 28, 1972, pp. 31-33.

12. Leo E. Hollister, "Marihuana in Man: Three Years Later," *Science,* 172 (Apr. 2, 1971), p. 23.

13. Richard Blum, "Mind Altering Drugs and Dangerous Behavior: Dangerous Drugs," in Task Force Report, *Narcotics and Drug Abuse,* President's Commission on Law

Enforcement and Administration of Justice, Washington, D.C.: Government Printing Office, 1967, p. 28.

14. Fred Davis and Laura Munoz, "Heads and Freaks: Patterns of Drug Use among Hippies," *Journal of Health and Social Behavior*, 9 (June 1968), 156-163.

15. Alfred Crancer et al., "Comparison of the Effects of Marihuana and Alcohol on Simulated Driving Performance," *Since*, 164 (May 16, 1969), 851-854.

16. Julian Waller, "Drugs and Highway Crashes," *Journal of the American Medical Association*, 215 (Mar. 1, 1971), 1480.

17. Ibid., p. 1481.

18. Ibid.

19. Dean V. Babst et al., *Driving Records of Heroin Addicts*, Research Report No. 1969-11, Albany, N.Y.: New York State Narcotics Addiction Control Commission, 1969, p. 13.

20. Erich Goode, *The Marijuana Smokers*, New York: Basic Books, 1970, pp. 43-44. Suchman, Ref. 3, pp. 150-152. "Special Report of the Attitudes of College Students," *Gallup Opinion Index*, Report No. 48, Princeton, N.J.: Gallup International, June 1969, p. 30. Richard Blum, *Students and Drugs*, San Francisco: Jossey-Bass, 1969, pp. 69-73. Lawrence Linn, "Social Identification and the Use of Marijuana," *International Journal of the Addictions*, 6 (Mar. 1971), 79-104.

21. *Newsweek*, "My God They're Killing Us," May 18, 1970, pp. 26-33, for a summary of Kent State and aftermath. See the summary of the Scranton Commission report in *Newsweek*, "The Campus: 'Bring Us Together,'" Oct. 5, 1970, pp. 24-26.

22. Kolansky and Moore, Ref. 5, p. 491.

23. Erich Goode, "Drug Use and Sexual Behavior on a College Campus," (unpublished manuscript). Much of it is published in *American Journal of Psychiatry*, 128 (Apr. 1972), 1272-1275.

24. Ibid.

25. See *Playboy* panel discussion, Ref. 4, p. 72.

26. Donald B. Louria, *The Drug Scene*, New York: McGraw-Hill, 1968, p. 82.

27. Goode, Ref. 23.

28. Lee Robins, Harriet Darvish, and George Murphy, "The Long-Term Outcome for Adolescent Drug Users: A Follow-Up Study of 76 Users and 146 Non-users," in Joseph Zubin and Alfred Freedman, eds., *The Psychopathology of Adolescence*, New York: Grune & Stratton, 1970, p. 174.

29. Ibid., p. 177.

30. Goode, Ref. 23.

31. Anslinger and Tompkins, Ref. 4, p. 22. *Playboy*, Ref. 4, p. 72.

32. Kolansky and Moore, Ref. 5, p. 491.

33. Erich Goode, "Marijuana Use and Crime," in National Commission on Marihuana and Drug Abuse, *Marihuana: A Signal of Misunderstanding, Appendix I*, Washington, D.C.: Government Printing Office, 1972, pp. 447-469, finds that among whites, marihuana users were not more likely to commit crimes than nonmarihuana users. However, among blacks, marihuana users were more likely to commit crimes than nonusers; but this difference was almost eliminated when social factors (having marihuana-using friends) were held constant. Goode's report was developed around the theoretical and methodological ideas presented in an early draft of the present chapter.

CHAPTER 9
Drugs, Grades, and Difficulties in College

Another compelling argument used against cannabis is that it instills in the highly impressionable young user an "amotivational syndrome," which produces "apathy, loss of effectiveness, and diminished capacity or willingness too . . . endure frustration, concentrate for long periods, follow routines, or successfully master new material. . . . Such individuals . . . become totally involved with the present at the expense of future goals. . . . They report a greater subjective creativity but less objective productivity."[1] A similar concern is voiced by an expert committee of the World Health Organization: "The harm to society derived from abuse of cannabis rests in the economic consequences of the *impairment* of the individual's *social functions*."[2] Such reasoning implies that cannabis use impairs a person's ability to perform his social roles. Of course, the same logic applies to the use of various hard drugs. The central question of this chapter is, Does the use of cannabis and/or multiple drugs cause students to do poorly in college?

Although the literature dealing with the association between drug use and performance in college is suggestive, it is not sufficient to determine whether school performance is affected by drug use. There are several ways to study this problem. Farnsworth, for example, indicates that the increasing use of drugs on campuses has not greatly altered the proportion of students committing suicide or dropping out of college.[3] Blum found that less than 1% of his California students had faced disciplinary action for the use of drugs; alcohol-related violations were ten times more common than violations involving the use of other drugs.[4]

Another type of study compares the ability of experimental subjects to perform some task when not under the influence of a drug with their later performance on the same or a similar task while under the influence of the drug. For example, Miller establishes that barbiturates and tranquilizers in normal prescription doses tend to impair performance. However, he finds that amphetamines used in normal doses do not have any significant effect upon performance. Amphetamines may even improve performance, especially for people who are relatively tired.[5]

Weil and Zinberg find that marihuana impairs the performance of subjects who have never used marihuana, but the performance of experienced marihuana users is not significantly impaired by the doses of marihuana given in the experiment.[6] Abel finds that marihuana has little effect upon recall of word lists.[7]

Crancer compares the effect of marihuana with that of alcohol upon simulated driving performance. He concludes that alcohol severely decreases one's ability to perform well on a simulated driving test. A person who is high on marihuana, however, performs as well on simulated driving tests as when not under the influence of any drug.[8]

Unfortunately, surveys of students have seldom attempted to measure seriously the college performance of drug users. There is a good reason for this lack of research; the concept of adequate college performance is not clear. How can one define whether a student is doing well or doing poorly? The obvious indicator of performance is grade point average; but there must be more to college performance than grades, such as the amount learned, creativity, and rewards. From the college administrators point of view, the concept of performance also implies some degree of conformity to college norms, patterns of class attendance, and steady progress toward the goal of graduation.

However, almost the only variable analyzed by drug researchers is grade point average; and the findings are mixed. Blum finds that drug users have slightly higher grades than noncannabis users but fails to indicate statistical significance.[9] Mizner and Goldstein find that drug users are somewhat over-represented among those with low grades.[10] Goode finds a slight curvilinear relationship: noncannabis and weekly users have somewhat worse grades than less than weekly cannabis users, but users of four or more drugs are quite likely to have low grades.[11] Haagen indicates that although drug users may be as intellectually capable as nonusers, they fail to perform as well in school as nondrug users.[12] However, close examination of the data indicates that if there is a statistically significant relationship between drug use and grades, it is a relatively weak one.

Although most of the above research has dealt with supposed effects of marihuana use upon grades, it is also important to know how the use of hard drugs, especially multiple drug use, affects school performance. Chapter 3 developed two main measures of drug use that will be used as independent variables: the Frequency of Cannabis Use Index and the Multiple Drug Use Index. In this analysis the association between drug use and performance in college will be compared with three dependent variables that are indicators of role performance in college. The first and most obvious indicator of difficulty in college is grade point average. This study is particularly interested in the proportion of students in the sample who receive relatively low grades (C or less), 38% of the total sample. Second, the Leave College Index is made up of three items with which the respondent could agree; the proportion of the sample agreeing with each item is indicated in parentheses:

Seriously considered dropping out of school (31%)

Taken a leave of absence or actually dropped out of school (9%)

Transferred or tried to transfer to another school (23%)

Among respondents, 14% agreed with two or more of these three items and were classified as "high" on this index. It was felt that when a student considers leaving college, for whatever reason, he has encountered some kind of difficulty. Third, the College Deviance Index measures deviance from norms governing class participation and official college rules. Students who agreed with two or more of the following items (12% of the sample) were classified as "high" on the College Deviance Index:

Taken incompletes in more than one course (7%)

Cut class frequently (25% of the time) (25%)

Changed choice of majors more than once (16%)

Refused to take a required course (9%)

Been in trouble with college officials for breaking rules (3%)

All of these indicators, of course, have their inadequacies. None of them may be said to fully measure inadequate role performance, or amotivation, in college. The Leave College Index attempts to measure how well students cope with college. The College Deviance Index attempts to measure departures from norms that college students are expected to follow. While these indices are not perfect measures of amotivation, they are better than speculation.

The use of drugs is related to each of these variables. Graph 9.1 indicates that regular cannabis users are more likely than noncannabis users and irregular users to have grades of C or less. Although the relationship between grades and cannabis use is statistically significant by the Chi Square Test ($p < .001$), such significance is probably caused by the large sample size. No one should attribute

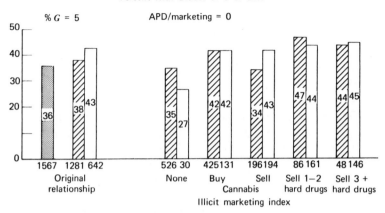

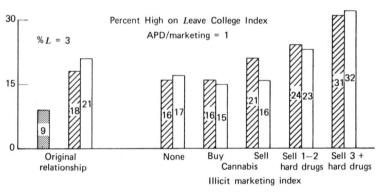

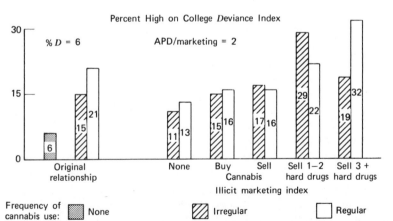

Graph 9.1. Marihuana use is an unimportant factor in determining poor grades, leaving college, and college deviance when drug selling is held constant.

too much importance to the 7% (43% − 36%) difference in grades between regular and noncannabis users. However, if the 5% difference in grades between regular and irregular cannabis users is important, the difference is eliminated (APD = 0) when drug dealing is held constant. In addition, cannabis buyers are as likely as sellers of hard drugs to have grades of C or less. Hence, one may conclude that grades are not greatly affected by the use of marihuana or by participation in the drug market or subculture.

The other two measures of school performance show that noncannabis users are less likely to be high on the Leave College Index and College Deviance Index than their cannabis-using counterparts. This finding may reflect the conventionality of noncannabis users rather than anything inherent in cannabis. The important question lies in discovering what happens to the small differences (3% on the Leave College Index and 6% on the College Deviance Index) due to the regularity of cannabis use when the measure of drug-subculture participation is held constant. The evidence is clear; the relationship between cannabis use and leaving college or being deviant is reduced (APD's of 1% and 2%, respectively). Those who sell hard drugs are more likely than cannabis buyers or sellers to consider leaving school or to have trouble in college. However, cannabis buyers or sellers are not more likely than those uninvolved in dealing to be high on these indices. Thus, it is not the "abuse" (regular use) of cannabis but involvement in selling drugs that impairs the conventional social functioning of college students.[13]

Marihuana use is not what amotivates students, but participation in the drug subculture. It is probable that subcultural values degrade the importance of working hard in school, attending classes, and other conventional patterns of college performance. Perhaps laws criminalizing marihuana are seen as a more important factor in determining poor social functioning than the use of marihuana, at least among college students in the sample.

However, the data demonstrate that there is a basis for public concern about drugs. While cannabis use does not impair social functioning, it appears that multiple drug use does so to a certain extent. Graph 9.2 shows that the Multiple Drug Use Index has a conditional effect upon social functioning. While multiple drug users are somewhat more likely (6% and 5%) to have low grades than nondrug users or cannabis-only users, the relationship is eliminated when drug dealing is held constant. Furthermore, multiple drug users who sell several drugs are as likely to have low grades as their counterparts who only buy marihuana. Thus, drug use appears to have little or no clear-cut effect upon grades independent of drug selling. Heavy drug users tend to have grades that are similar to less heavy drug users.

The same findings do not emerge from analysis of the Leave College Index and College Difficulty Index. One finds that cannabis-only users are somewhat more likely (about 6%) than nondrug users to be high on these indices, regardless

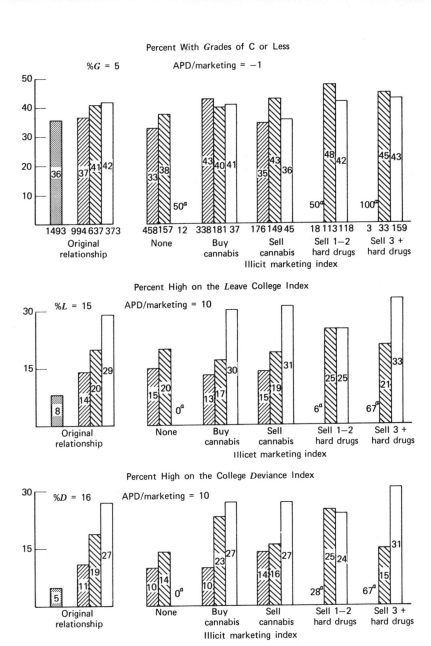

Graph 9.2. Multiple-drug use has little effect upon grades, but is strongly related to leaving college and college deviance, even when drug selling is held constant.

of drug selling activities. However, multiple drug users are about 15% more likely
to be high on both indices than cannabis-only users. This difference is not
greatly reduced (APD's of 10%) for the Leave College Index and the College
Deviance Index when Illicit Marketing is held constant.

Far more compelling evidence of the importance of multiple drug use can be
discovered with the aid of Appendix A. If one examines the relationship
between the Illicit Marketing Index and these two indices, those selling three or
more hard drugs are more likely than nonbuyers and nonsellers to be high on
these indices (15% difference on the Leave College Index, 18% on the College
Deviance Index). When holding constant the Multiple Drug Use Index, one finds
that relationships between the Illicit Marketing Index and the Leave College
Index or College Deviance Index are almost eliminated (APD's of 1% and 3%,
respectively).

Contrary to the findings in Chapters 6-8 this evidence shows that multiple
drug use, and not drug selling, is the most important factor in understanding
why students consider leaving college or engaging in college-related deviance.
Nevertheless, the data demonstrate again that marihuana use is an unimportant
factor in causing low grades, leaving college, or college deviance.

Thus, drug users have social achievement levels (grades) that are equivalent to
less heavy drug users, but they are much more likely to show signs of
amotivation that are independent of involvement of drug selling. Hence, from
the standpoint of public and college officials, multiple drug users, but not
marihuana users, show signs of impaired social functioning.

However, the problem of how persons become multiple drug users must again
be considered. The evidence in Chapters 6 and 7 demonstrates that drug-
subculture participation is probably a major factor in understanding multiple
drug use. So indirectly, drug-subculture participation, as well as the laws making
cannabis illegal, are implicated in the pattern of amotivation discovered in the
present chapter.

Nevertheless, the measure of subculture participation, the Illicit Marketing
Index, is much less important than the Multiple Drug Use Index in understanding measures of the amotivational syndrome.[14] It remains for other researchers
to replicate these findings and suggest an interpretation of what multiple drug
use means if it is not an indicator of subculture participation. It is possible that
college officials should be concerned about hard-drug use itself, perhaps more
concerned than they are at the present time.

REFERENCES

1. William McGlothlin and Louis J. West, "The Marijuana Problem: An Overview,"
   American Journal of Psychiatry, 125 (Sept. 1968), 372.

2. Nathan B. Eddy et al., "Drug Dependence: Its Significance and Characteristics," *Bulletin of the World Health Organization,* 32 (1965), p. 729 (emphasis added).

3. "No Rise Found in Student Suicide," *New York Times,* Oct. 11, 1970.

4. Richard Blum et al., *Students and Drugs,* San Francisco: Jossey-Bass, 1969, p. 154.

5. James Miller, "Objective Measurements of the Effects of Drugs on Driver Behavior," *Journal of the American Medical Association,* 179 (12) (1962). Also see Richard Blum, "Mind-Altering Drugs and Dangerous Behavior: Dangerous Drugs," in President's Commission on Law Enforcement and Administration of Justice, Task Force Report, *Narcotics and Drug Abuse,* Washington, D.C.: U.S. Government Printing Office, 1967, pp. 21-39.

6. Andrew Weil, Norman Zinberg, and Judith Nelsen, "Clinical and Psychological Effects of Marihuana in Man," *Science,* 162 (Dec. 13, 1968), 1234-1242.

7. Ernest L. Abel, "Retrieval of Information After Use of Marihuana," *Nature,* 231 (May 7, 1971), 58; "Effects of Marihuana on the Solution of Anagrams, Memory and Appetite," *Nature,* 231 (May 28, 1971), 261; "Marihuana and Memory: Acquisition or Retrieval," *Science,* 173 (Sept. 10, 1971), 1038-1040.

8. Alfred Crancer, Jr., et al., "Comparison of the Effects of Marihuana and Alcohol on Simulated Driving Performance," *Science,* 164 (May 16, 1969), 851-854. See Leo E. Hollister, "Marihuana in Man: Three Years Later," *Science,* 172 (Apr. 2, 1971), 21-28, for a good summary and critique of various experimental studies of marihuana's affect upon mental, psychological, and driving performance.

9. Blum, et al., Ref. 4, p.78.

10. George L. Mizner, James T. Barter, and Paul H. Werme, *Patterns of Drug Use Among College Students,* Denver: University of Colorado Medical School, 1969; and Joel Goldstein et al., *The Social Psychology of Student Drug Usage: Report on Phase One,* Report of the Carnegie-Mellon Drug Use Research Project, Pittsburgh, Pa., 1970, p. 21.

11. Erich Goode, "Drug Use and Grades in College," *Nature,* 234 (Nov. 26, 1971), 225-227, finds that the curvilinear relationship between drugs and grades hold up even when sex, year in college, and father's occupation is held constant.

12. C. Hess Haagen, "Social and Psychological Characteristics Associated with the Use of Marijuana by College Men," Middletown, Conn.: Wesleyan University, 1970, p. 23 (mimeographed).

13. Eddy et al., Ref. 2, p. 729.

14. McGlothlin and West, Ref. 1, p. 372.

CHAPTER 10

Police Enforcement of Drug Laws

If the present drug laws are to be meaningful, they must be enforced. To this end, the Federal Bureau of Narcotics and Dangerous Drugs (BNDD) has been given substantial power to enforce present drug laws. Most states or local governments have given similar powers to the police or special narcotics units. In the literature on the enforcement of drug laws, one is struck by the apparent contradictions between what police officials claim they do and what the arrest statistics appear to show policemen doing.

Certain claims about the enforcement of present drug laws support what can be called the "impartial theory" of police behavior. This theory holds that the police apprehend persons who are the most frequent or serious offenders of the drug laws. For example, John Ingersoll, Director of the BNDD, states:

> The most that law enforcement can do . . . is to raise its sights and apply its major efforts against the proselytizers, against the distributors, against the smugglers, and against the sources of supply both nationally and internationally. We can train our police better, improve our evidence gathering responsibilities, enforce the laws where the greatest impact will result, and strive to cut off the various sources.[1]

Ingersoll suggests that the police may not be particularly efficient in enforcing drug laws on the entire drug-using population. However, he also indicates that no factors other than the possession or sale of drugs will significantly influence police decisions of whom to apprehend on drug charges.

A contrary theory, sociological in origin,[2] may be called the "labeling theory." This theory holds that statuses (race, class, sex, and age) or social

176

behaviors (political radicalism) and lifestyles ("hippies") not directly linked to drug use play an important, if not the most important, role in determining why persons are apprehended by police for drug-related violations. Although this theory is more complex than is indicated here, the central assertion of the "labeling theory" is that some persons are unfairly subjected to police surveillance and arrested for drugs because they possess characteristics that are associated with, but not directly relevant to, drug use and sale.

How do the police really enforce drug laws? In support of the impartial theory, statistics issued by the BNDD and Customs Bureau show that their agents arrest large marihuana dealers and narcotics distributors; half of the marihuana-only seizures made by BNDD agents are for five or more kilograms.[3] But at the local level, analysis of arrest data in California and across the United States indicates that less that 15% of marihuana arrestees possess more than 30 grams (about an ounce) and less than 10% of all arrestees are charged with drug sale.[4]

In support of the labeling theory, a recent national study shows that about 70% of all marihuana arrestees have no previous arrest record and are frequently contacted in an automobile. Furthermore, almost no one over 30 years old and few persons older than 25 are ever arrested; male arrestees outnumber females by 3 or 5 to 1.[5] Also relevant is the concern of political radicals and the hippie or "street" community that police are overly eager to arrest them on drug charges when it is really their beliefs and life style that the police find objectionable. This evidence suggests that, on the state and local level, the "drug pusher" is seldom apprehended while many low-level users are being arrested for possession offenses, possibly because they have been "labeled" as drug users by police on the basis of other criteria.

Therefore, two central questions emerge: Are police "efficient" in enforcing present drug laws? Are the police "fair" in enforcing laws in the sense that they apprehend the heaviest users and/or sellers, or are they influenced by other criteria? Police officials assume that they are being fair and reasonably efficient; the labeling theory indicates that police tactics are biased.

To determine the efficiency and fairness of drug law enforcement, seven questions must be considered: (1) How many students have ever engaged in the illegal activities of drug use or sale? (2) How many persons are stopped, but not arrested, as suspects for these drug-related activities? (3) How many are actually arrested and prosecuted for such acts? (4) Are nondrug users or irregular users arrested for drug violations? (5) Are those who regularly sell and/or use drugs most likely to be arrested? (6) Are offenders arrested because they sell? Or because they possess drugs? Or for both reasons? (7) Are students stopped or arrested for drug violations because police officers have "labeled" them as potential drug users on the basis of sex, age, race, political militancy, personal beliefs, personal life style, or involvement in nondrug violations?

In order to arrive at some conclusions about the efficiency with which police stop and/or arrest students for drug violations, it is necessary to compare drug-related charges with nondrug charges. Several studies of self-reported crime in diverse populations find differing levels of delinquency or crime. Such studies also find that the more serious the crime and the more frequently a person commits it, the greater the likelihood of the person being arrested for that violation.[6] The most compelling data on crime in the United States were provided by the President's Commission on Law Enforcement in 1967. A national survey asked 10,000 Americans whether they had been victims of various crimes in the previous year. In 1965-1966, it found that for every 100,000 people about 360 had been victims of "crimes against persons," such as homicide, rape, robbery, and assault, and about 1760 had been victims of "crimes against property," such as burglary, larceny, and auto theft. This victim-reported crime was about two to three times higher than that reported by the FBI's Uniform Crime Reports (UCR), with the exception of auto theft.[7]

Compared with such information about the level of victim-reported crime, information about the victimless crimes of homosexuality, gambling, abortion, and drug use in the nation's population is less compelling.[8] The best information is about drug use; a survey conducted for the National Commission on Marihuana and Drug Abuse revealed that 15% of the nation's population had tried marihuana and a Gallup poll in November 1971 revealed that among the nation's college students, 51% have used marihuana and 18% have used hallucinogens.[9] Although the use of these drugs is generally not against the law, the basic intent of laws against possession of these substances is to prevent use; most persons have to illegally possess these drugs in order to use them.

Since the police claim to ignore drug possession and, instead, concentrate upon drug selling and since drug selling is a felony, it is important to know something about drug sales. Unfortunately, there is much less information about drug selling than about drug use. Only a few select samples have been asked about selling activities. Goode indicates that 44% of his marihuana users have sold a drug, while Blum reports that a questionnaire distributed in a college dorm in 1968 found that 4% of the women and 20% of the men have sold marihuana.[10] Although Blum has intensively studied drug sellers, his study provides no information about the proportion of sellers in the population.[11]

To the best of the author's knowledge, the data presented in Chapter 5 provide the first information about the level of selling in a relatively representative, but biased, population of college students. It will be remembered that 22% had ever sold cannabis, 13% had ever sold a hard drug, and 6% had sold three or more hard drugs as well as cannabis. Since the President's Commission found that less than 2% of the population has ever been victims of any major crime investigated,[12] surely the felonious sale of drugs in the college sample is epidemic by comparison, as is possession and use of drugs.

One central question of the present chapter is how effectively law enforcement officials are dealing with this epidemic of drug-related violations in the college student sample. Comparison of drug-related arrests among college students with arrests of minority groups is instructive. It appears that drug users in black populations are very likely to be apprehended. Among St. Louis black males, Robins, Darvish, and Murphy report that 41% of the nondrug users had a nontraffic arrest, while 66% and 91%, respectively, of the juvenile marihuana users and users of other drugs were ever arrested. Furthermore, only 3% of the nondrug users and 3% of the marihuana-only users, but 61% of the users of other drugs, had been arrested for some drug offense.[13] Glazer, Lander, and Abbott's study of a slum block in New York City indicates that 81% of the addicts, but only 5% of their nonaddict siblings, were ever arrested; while 49% of the addicts were incarcerated, only 3% of the nonaddict siblings served time in prison.[14] These two studies indicate that police are likely to arrest black males who use drugs heavily, but do not arrest nondrug users on drug charges. How effective is the enforcement of drug laws among college students? Blum finds that less than 1% of the student body, but 40% of the drug sellers, have been arrested on drug charges.[15] Goode states that 7 of his 200 selected marihuana users were arrested on drug charges. On the other hand, California and national arrest data indicate a manyfold increase in arrests for marihuana charges during the 1960s.[16] Goode summarizes these seemingly contradictory findings:

> More felons are arrested on marijuana charges than for any other felony. At the same time, a lower proportion of marijuana felonies and felons are detected and arrested than possibly for any other felony. And probably in no other crime is there so loose a relationship between seriousness and likelihood of arrest.[17]

Thus, because so many persons possess or sell cannabis, the arrest of even a small proportion constitutes a very large number of arrests.

Goode questions whether police fairly enforce the drug laws by indicating that most marihuana arrests occur for the following reasons: (1) Police stop automobiles for minor traffic violations, marihuana is observed or smelled, and the occupants are arrested on marihuana charges. (2) "Stop-and-frisk" procedures used by police to prevent crime accidently uncover drugs. (3) Police intentionally stop hippie-type youths because of their reputed involvement in marihuana.[18] Others maintain that police harass and arrest political radicals on drug charges as a way of punishing political activities that are legal but offensive to the community.[19] Thus, a majority of marihuana arrests are "accidental" in the sense that the police do not have "probable cause" to suspect a person of a marihuana charge prior to stopping the person for some other reason. As proof of the accidental nature of drug arrests, Goode (citing Morton) notes that only 9% of the Los Angeles marihuana arrests are for sale of any amount, while the majority of arrests are for simple possession of marihuana. Furthermore, only

3% of the adult arrests and 7% of the juvenile arrests are the result of systematic police and undercover agents' work based upon suspicion of selling activity. [20] Thus, the data suggest that most drug arrests are not fair because the police do not have probable cause to suspect a person of drug possession or sale. Hence, this chapter will attempt to demonstrate whether police are effective and fair in stopping and/or arresting the students in our sample.

Asking students to report their contact with the police probably overreports the level of contact, since the police seldom record informal, nonarrest contacts with suspects. [21] Indeed, contact with police is much more likely to be remembered by the student than by the policeman. However, if the names of the students could be checked against police records, then student reports of arrest and police records for arrests should be closely matched. In studies of heroin addicts, the information provided by the addict's self-report of arrest is generally more accurate than the police records. [22]

In order to measure contact with the police, the study asked respondents:

Have you ever:
(Do not include arrests
or busts for political activity)

(Mark all that apply)

0. None of these (63.0%)

Been picked up, stopped (but not arrested) for
1. a traffic violation (30%)
2. a drug related violation (4%)
3. some other violation (theft, rape, forgery, etc.) (6.9%)

Been arrested for
4. a traffic violation (given a ticket, etc.) (13.7%)
5. a drug related violation (possession, sale, instruments, etc.) (1.2%)
6. some other violation (theft, etc.) (2.1%)

Been convicted for
7. a drug related misdemeanor or felony (0.5%)
8. some other misdemeanor or felony (not a drug or traffice violation) (1.2%)
9. been committed to jail, reform school, drug treatment center, or other similar institution (0.7%)

The proportion (indicated in parentheses) of the total sample having contact with the law is greatest for traffic violations, "other" violations, and then for drugs. Only 4.1% of the total population has been stopped, arrested, or convicted for a drug violation. Slightly more students report arrest or conviction for "other" violations such as theft and property destruction (2.7%) than report arrests or convictions for drug violations (1.3%). The greatest number of arrests is for traffic violation (13.7%). Because the proportion of students arrested is so low, the terms "contact with" or "apprehended by" police will be used to refer to those who have been stopped and/or arrested by the police.

Graph 10.1 indicates that police do not randomly contact drug users. Rather, police are likely to contact students in accordance with their use of cannabis and involvement in selling drugs. Thus, less than 1% of the noncannabis users and less than 3% of the nondrug sellers have ever had any contact with police. In short, persons who are "innocent" are almost never contacted for drug-related sale or possession. However, the greater the involvement in selling, the greater the probability of having contact with police. More than a quarter (28%) of the heaviest drug sellers (three or more hard drugs) have had some contact, but less than 10% have been arrested.

Since these heavy sellers come closest to fitting the official conception of a pusher, it is important to determine whether the police are being effective in controlling such dealers. The evidence indicates that the vast majority (72%) of such heavy sellers have never been contacted, about a third (9%/28%) are ever arrested. This would seem to indicate that police are not very effective in arresting heavy drug sellers and much less effective in contacting buyers or sellers of marihuana.

However, police effectiveness is difficult to determine. The police are aware that many crimes never come to their attention and that arrests are made in less than half of the cases known to the police.[23] To further evaluate police practices, this study will develop four indices that permit the determination of the effectiveness and fairness of police practices: the Crime, Auto Deviance, Political Militancy (developed in Chapter 8), and Hip Life Style (developed in Chapter 7) indices. The Crime Index classifies persons as "high" if they have engaged in two or more of these activities:

> Taken a car for a ride without the owner's permission (5.4%)
>
> While in High School, took things of little value (less than $10) from stores, work or school at five or more different times (12.5%)
>
> Ever take things of some value (more than $10) from stores, work, or school (12%)
>
> Purposefully destroy or damage property (break street lights, damage or move traffic signs, break into buildings and/or mess them up) (11%)

The Auto Deviance Index classifies persons as "high" if they have engaged in two or more of these activities:

> Drive a car before obtaining a driver's license, but had no licensed driver with you (18%)
>
> Drive faster than 80 m.p.h. (39%)
>
> Participate in or attend a drag race (17%)

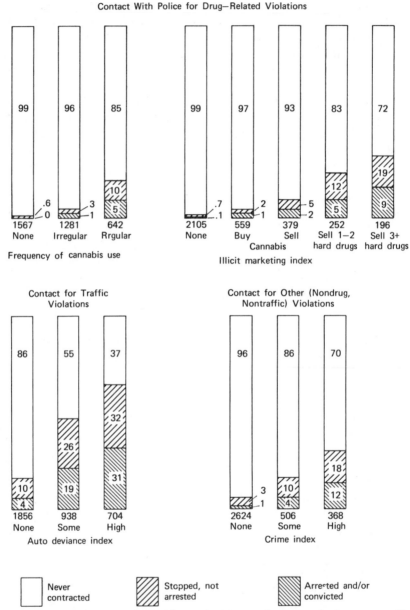

Graph 10.1. Students who are heavily involved in auto deviance and crime are more likely to be stopped and/or arrested for these violations than heavy drug users or sellers are to be contacted for drug violations.

The Political Militancy and Hip Life Style indices attempt to measure life styles that might attract police attention and can help to determine the fairness of police procedures. Students were high on the Political Militancy Index if they agreed with two or more of these items:

Been held or arrested for political activities at school or elsewhere (2.2%)

Sat-in or demonstrated in an office or building (21.0%)

Participated in a demonstration where violence occurred (17.3%)

Persons were high on the Hip Life Style Index if they agreed with both of the following items:

Did you ever feel that other people or policemen would like to harass or intimidate you because of your appearance or your beliefs (35%)

Try to or actually attend a rock or folk music festival like Woodstock or Newport Jazz Festival (37%)

The bottom half of Graph 10.1 shows that persons who are not involved in auto deviance or crime are relatively unlikely to be contacted. Police are apparently quite effective in apprehending those highly involved in speeding and drag racing. Almost two-thirds of those high on the Auto Deviance Index are contacted by police, and half (31%/63%) of those contacted were arrested or given a ticket. Police effectiveness diminishes considerably among those highly involved in "other" crimes. Of those who are high on the Crime Index, 30% have ever had police contact for these activities and 40% (12%/30%) of those ever contacted were arrested. Thus when comparing both the proportion ever contacted and the proportion of arrests among those ever contacted, the police are found to be less effective in enforcing laws against drug selling and use than traffic laws and criminal laws.

On the other hand, it could also be argued that police are relatively effective in enforcing the victimless crime of drug use and sale. The victims of crimes against property or person are likely to report such crimes to police, but the drug buyer is not likely to report a seller to the police. However, police contact with sellers is similar to police contact for criminal behavior. Although data for other victimless crimes such as fornication, homosexuality, abortion, and gambling are not available, it would seem that persons who frequently commit these "crimes" are less likely to be contacted or arrested than drug sellers.

On the basis of the above evidence, the police appear to be about as effective (or ineffective) in enforcing the drug laws as the criminal laws. The enforcement of traffic laws demonstrates clearly how effective the police can be when a violation is highly visible and amenable to public surveillance techniques. If drug laws were as effectively enforced as traffic laws, the laws against selling and drug use might make some students reconsider what they are doing. But, as demonstrated in Chapter 5, the fear of arrest does not deter students from selling marihuana.

If the police are not particularly effective in enforcing the drug laws, are they "fair" in the sense that they apprehend those who are guilty of selling drugs? The data show that police are most likely to apprehend students because they sell drugs. If one considers the Frequency of Cannabis Use and Multiple Drug Use indices as good indicators of drug possession and the Illicit Marketing Index as a measure of drug selling, one can determine whether police contact persons because they possess drugs, because they sell drugs, or for both reasons.

Graph 10.2 reveals that less than 5% of those who do not sell drugs have any contact with the police for drug charges regardless of how frequently they use

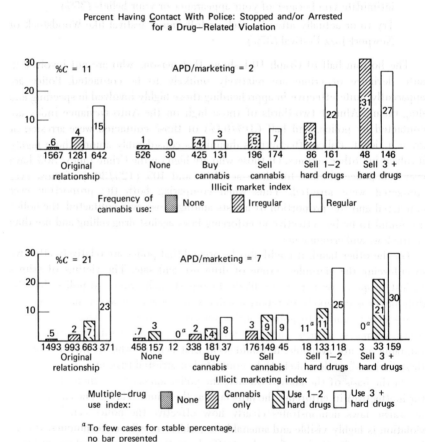

Graph 10.2. Students are contacted by police for drug violations because of selling activities and not for the use (possession) of cannabis or other drugs.

marihuana. It is among those who sell hard drugs, especially three or more drugs, who are likely (about 28%) to have contact with the police for drug charges. The frequency with which these heavy sellers use cannabis is relatively unimportant in predicting their contact with the police on drug charges. This demonstrates that police contact persons because they suspect them of selling drugs, and not because of their possession of cannabis. Even low-level sellers (sell cannabis only) are unlikely (about 6%) to be apprehended by police.

The bottom half of Graph 10.2 shows that those using three or more hard drugs are 21% more likely than cannabis-only users to have contact with police for a drug violation. However, when drug dealing is held constant, this relationship is reduced to a third (APD = 7%). In addition, persons who confine their drug use to cannabis almost never (3% or less) have contact with the police, even though involved in selling it. But among those selling hard drugs, the number of drugs used increases somewhat the probability of contact with police. Nevertheless, the major reason that students are contacted for drug violations is drug selling. Police seem to concentrate mainly on drug selling; drug possession is far less important in attracting police interest. This does not mean that drug sellers are mainly arrested for selling; it is probable that most sellers are contacted for possession charges because it is easier for police to prove drug possession than sale. However, the findings suggest that if most persons are arrested on possession charges, they are probably guilty of selling drugs at one time in their life and may have sold several different drugs. Hence, police do generally arrest drug sellers.

A second question about police fairness suggests that police "label" potential arrestees. Do police depend upon visible indicators such as sex, race, political activity, hippie appearance, and auto arrests to make drug-related contacts with students? If it can be shown that these extraneous factors are decisive in police decisions to apprehend students for drug violations, then one might say that police have unfairly labeled certain characteristics that are not relevant to drug charges.

Graph 10.3 shows that traffic violations, political militancy, and living a hip life style are weakly (%C = 9% to 13%) related to police contact. Further, when the Illicit Marketing Index is held constant these weak differences are not greatly reduced (APDs = 7%). Hence, it appears that police perceptions of students' life styles are independently related to contact with police violations. However, the strongest factor determining drug-related contact with police, the student's actual involvement in drug dealing, is not altered (APDs of 22% to 31%) when traffic arrests, political militancy, or hip life style are held constant. In addition, less than 8% of the nondrug sellers have had any drug-related contact with the police, even though they have been arrested for traffic violations or appear hip. At the other extreme, students who have sold three or more hard drugs are somewhat less (about 20%) apt to have police contact if they have

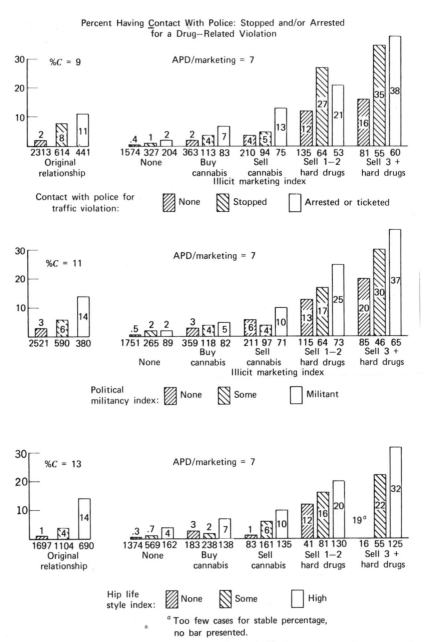

Percent Having Contact With Police: Stopped and/or Arrested for a Drug–Related Violation

Contact with police for traffic violation: None | Stopped | Arrested or ticketed

Political militancy index: None | Some | Militant

Hip life style index: None | Some | High

[a] Too few cases for stable percentage, no bar presented.

Graph 10.3. Students are generally contacted for drug violations due to drug selling, but having traffic arrests, being militant, or being hip increase the probability of contact with the police.

never been contacted on traffic charges, are relatively straight (not hip), or are nonmilitants. Goode's suggestion that police may not always have "probable cause" in the legal sense of the term to contact a person for drug violations is partially verified.[24] Among the heaviest drug sellers (3 or more hard drugs), those who have been stopped or arrested for traffic violations are likely (35%, 38%, respectively), as are the politically militant (37%), to have contact with police for drug violations.

Data presented in Table 26 (Appendix A) show that age, sex, race, and socioeconomic status (which the labeling theory suggests may be important factors in police arrest decisions) prove to be of little significance. In our college student posulation, we find almost no age or year-in-school differences in police contact or arrest; but the age range among college students is too small to make any definite conclusions. Contrary to the labeling theory, the higher the family income, the higher the probability of police contact for drug violations; those from high-income (more than $25,000 a year) families versus those from low-income (less than $7000) families are more likely (5.2% versus 2.2%) to report any contact and are more likely (1.3% versus 0.8%) to be arrested. College whites are somewhat more likely than college blacks (4.7% versus 2.8%) to report any drug-related contact, but they are slightly less likely to be arrested (1.3% versus 1.6%). We have also divided the white population according to sex. White females are somewhat less apt to be contacted (1.9%) and arrested (0.2%) for drug violations than white males (7.4% and 2.4%, respectively). In other words, white males are about four times (7.4% to 1.9%) more likely to be contacted and twelve times (2.4% to 0.2%) more likely to be arrested than white females.

As with life style variables, we have held constant involvement in drug selling. We find that heavy drug sellers are the most likely to be contacted and arrested, and that nonsellers are very unlikely to be arrested regardless of their age, year in college, or family income. However, it appears that college whites are somewhat more likely to be contacted and arrested for drug-related crimes than college blacks at each level of buying and selling drugs. Unfortunately, the number of blacks selling hard drugs (22) is so small that it makes meaningful comparisons impossible. More striking are sex differences in police contact among nonblacks. Although white females are less likely than white males to become heavily involved in drug selling, among the few females (39) who sell 3 or more hard drugs, a smaller proportion have contact with (15%) or are arrested (1.6%) by police for drug violations than their more numerous (147) male counterparts (32% contacted, 11% arrested). Sex differences emerge at all levels of drug buying and selling.

Thus, with the possible exception of male-female differences, the impartial theory better describes how police enforce drug laws on the New York college population than does the labeling theory. Although drug sellers may be the least likely to agree with this conclusion, their own behavior and report of contact with police demonstrate that the level of drug selling is the most important factor in police decisions to contact students for drug violations.

However, our data demonstrate that police do not abide completely by the impartial theory. The relationship between police contact for drug violations and sex, race, political militancy, arrests for traffic or other violations, or a "hip" life style is not completely eliminated when drug buying and selling is held constant. But the minor independent effect upon police contact of such "labeled" statuses and behaviors is due to two factors which are about equally important. First, police probably observe, with considerable accuracy, that white males, those arrested for traffic or other violations, political militants, and hippies are more likely to use and sell drugs. Perhaps police sometimes stop persons with such visible characteristics for suspicion of drug possession or sale, but if no evidence of such suspicion appears they will not arrest them. But, second, and of equal importance in understanding the relationships between these statuses and police contact, police tend to *ignore* drug sellers having characteristics associated with nondrug use and nonsale (white females, nonmilitants, nonhippie's, those not involved in traffic or other violations) until sufficient evidence is available to convince the police that such persons are indeed heavy sellers and worthy of legal sanctions. Thus, the evidence tends to suggest that the labeling theory should also be concerned with why police label some persons "innocent" until compelling evidence to the contrary is available.

Finally, labeling theory may not provide a particularly viable perspective. Certain life styles, which police could not possibly label, may, for unknown reasons, determine contact with police. For example, data in Table 26E (Appendix A) shows that the greater the number of premarital sex partners, the greater the contact with police. The strangest finding is that among those who have sold hard drugs but have never been involved in premarital sex ($N = 65$), 11% have had contact and 1.5% have been arrested for drug violations, a proportion much lower than among hard-drug sellers involved in premarital sex. Although we do not quite understand why this finding is true, it is certainly not because police "nonlabel" those abstaining from premarital sex.

Thus, our evidence indicates that decisions about whom to contact and arrest for drug violations is primarily determined by police suspicions about the person's level of drug selling and to a lesser extent by the number of drugs used, sex, and other behaviors or life styles. Despite the fact that police are relatively "fair" in enforcing drug laws among college students in New York City, the central fact is that the vast majority of heavy drug sellers and possessors never have *any* drug-related contact with the police and very small proportions are ever arrested.

Perhaps the labeling process becomes more important in determining guilt after a person is formally booked on drug-related charges, although such a hypothesis is not supported by the recent and high-quality data available.[25]

The implications of these findings are more important than they may seem at first glance. The National Commission on Marihuana and Drug Abuse is recommending that Federal Law "decriminalize" the possession of "use" amounts of marihuana.[26] While the sale of marihuana would remain illegal, penalties for small sales should be eliminated or restricted to fines. However, the present data suggest that persons who have only possessed marihuana are almost never subjected to legal sanctions and that those who sell cannabis only (small sales) are infrequently contacted by police. In the New York metropolitan area, the Schafer Commission's recommendations were the de facto drug laws in the spring of 1970.

However, the fact that persons who only possess (use or buy) cannabis are very unlikely to be contacted by police does not mean that the law criminalizing the possession of cannabis is ignored by police. It is probable that many, if not most, heavy sellers are arrested for marihuana possession rather than sale. The arrested person is generally guilty of the marihuana-possession charges pressed against him (at the minimum) and probably has been involved in several acts of selling.[27] In the sample, forty-five persons had been arrested on drug charges; of these, only one had never bought or sold drugs (he had used marihuana), 15% had only bought cannabis, 80% had sold at least one hard drug, and 38% had sold cannabis and three other drugs. Unfortunately, persons were not asked to indicate whether they were arrested for marihuana possession or for other drug-related charges (sale, instruments, etc).

Nevertheless, the small number of persons contacted by police for drug-related offenses represents a substantial number of persons when projected to the total population (about 100,000) of the twenty colleges in the New York metropolitan area. If one assumes that the data in this study fairly approximate the actual drug use and selling rates and take into account the biased nature of the sample, then probably about 40,000 or 50,000 students are guilty of possession of marihuana and about 15,000 or 20,000 have sold cannabis and/or other drugs. About 4000 have had contact with the law, about 1000 have been arrested, and less than 500 have been convicted of some drug violation. This is a relatively large number of reasonably law-abiding persons entering the court system. It appears that the court system can survive, although the costs may be very high.[28]

Does the enforcement of drug laws capture many college students who are guilty of using or selling drugs? The answer is no. This is especially true when police contact among drug users and sellers is compared to police contact and arrest of persons involved in auto violations or who have committed crimes against property. Furthermore, the heavy drug users in the college population are less likely to be subjected to drug arrests than Robin's (1970) black males in St. Louis.[29] (Of course, the students in the sample are not as old as these black men and less involved in heroin addiction, so they have not had as much opportunity to be arrested.)

Do police stop and/or arrest only whose who are guilty of drug law violations? The answer is yes. College students are stopped and/or arrested mainly because they are drug sellers; other factors such as sex, race, class, religiosity, criminality (data not presented), as well as militancy, auto violations, and hip appearance do not strongly affect this relationship. Thus, police appear to be fair in their contact with students suspected of selling drugs. If police "label" persons as likely sellers they also "nonlabel" other significant segments of the student population.

The central question generated by this chapter is, Does the ineffective, but relatively fair, enforcement of present drug laws outweigh the considerable burden that it imposes upon our overworked court system and those students who are stigmatized as felons? The answer to this question depends more upon one's values than upon empirical evidence.

REFERENCES

1. National Commission on Marihuana and Drug Abuse, *Marihuana: A Signal of Misunderstanding*, Technical Papers of the First Report of the National Commission on Marihuana and Drug Abuse, *Appendix II*, Washington, D. C., U. S. Government Printing Office, p. 729. Two papers in this appendix are a must for understanding what kinds of persons are arrested and convicted for marihuana-related crimes. One paper deals with arrest data on the local level, while a second deals with federal arrest data. (Henceforth referred to as Schafer Report, Appendix II.)

2. Howard S. Becker, *Outsiders*, New York: Free Press, 1963, pp. 8-10, 121-134; Edwin M. Schur, *Crimes Without Victims*, Englewood Cliffs, N. J.: Prentice- Hall, 1965, pp. 169-179; Harvey Marshall and Ross Purdy, "Hidden Deviance and the Labeling Approach: The Case for Drinking and Driving," *Social Problems*, 19 (Spring 1972) pp. 541-553.

3. Schafer Report, *Appendix II*, Ref. 1, p. 744.

4. Ibid., pp. 632, 656; Erich Goode, *The Marijuana Smokers*, New York: Basic Books, 1970, pp. 267-277. Goode depends heavily upon two other documents: State of California, *Drug Arrests and Dispositions in California*, 1967 (Sacramento: Department of Justice, Bureau of Criminal Statistics, 1968), and *1968 Drug Arrests in California*, *Advance Report* (April 1969), pp. 4, 6; and Allan Morton, et al., "Marijuana Laws: An Empirical Study of Enforcement and Administration in Los Angeles County," *U.C.L.A. Law Review*, 15 (Sept. 1968), pp. 1499-1585. We have examined both sources; Goode adequately summarizes the important findings and develops various statistics derived from these sources that are not presented in the original sources. Thus, we will cite from Goode.

5. Schafer Report, *Appendix II*, Ref. 1, pp. 619-636.

6. Martin Gold, "Undetected Delinquent Behavior," *Journal of Research in Crime and Delinquency* (January 1966), 13, pp. 27-46. James F. Short and Fred L. Strodbeck, *Group Process and Gang Delinquency*, Chicago: University of Chicago Press, 1965, pp. 77-101; for a good summary of this literature on self-reported crime and arrests, see Roger Hood and Richard Sparks, *Key Issues in Criminology*, New York: McGraw-Hill, 1970, pp. 11-45.

7. President's Commission on Law Enforcement and Administration of Justice, "Crime in America." *The Challenge of Crime in a Free Society,* Washington: Government Printing Office, 1967, pp. 17-46.

8. Edwin Schur, *Crimes Without Victims.* Englewood Cliffs, N. J.: Prentice-Hall, 1965, pp. 169-179.

9. Schafer Report, *Appendix II,* Ref. 1, p. 945; "Gallup Finds a Continued Rise in the Use of Marihuana and LSD on Campus," *The New York Times,* January 10, 1972, p. 16.

10. Erich Goode, Ref. 4, p. 251. Richard Blum et al., *Students and Drugs,* San Francisco: Jossey-Bass, 1969, p. 186.

11. Richard Blum, "Drug Pushers: A Collective Portrait," *Transaction,* July-Aug. 1971, pp. 18-21; *The Dream Sellers,* San Francisco, Jossey-Bass, 1972.

12. President's Commission, Ref. 7.

13. Lee N. Robins, Harriet S. Darvish, and George E. Murphy, "The Long-Term Outcome for Adolescent Drug Users" In Joseph Zubin and Alfred Freedman, eds. *The Psychopathology of Adolescence,* New York: Grune and Stratton, 1970, p. 168.

14. Daniel Glater, Bernard Lander, and William Abbott, "Opiate Addicted and Non-Addicted Siblings in a Slum Area," *Social Problems,* 18 (Spring 1971), 514.

15. Blum, et al., Ref. 10, p. 154; and Ref. 11, p. 18.

16. Goode, Ref. 4, p. 276. Shafer Report, Ref. 1, pp. 736, 754.

17. Goode, Ref. 4, p. 275.

18. Ibid., pp. 270-277. Shafer Report, Ref. 1, pp. 628-642.

19. Jerry Rubin, a "yippie" leader, was arrested on marihuana possession charges for his political activities. Jerry Rubin, "The Yippies Are Going to Chicago," *The Realist* 82 (Sept. 1968), 1. Also see *Playboy* Panel (Feb. 1970), p. 54, about Leslie Fiedler, an English professor at Buffalo, who was arrested for "maintaining a premises" where marihuana is used. Playboy has become a major publication for those who are arrested on drug charges to try and gain public support. Almost every issue of Playboy carries a letter from a person imprisoned on marihuana or drug charges.

20. Goode, Ref. 4, p. 272. Schafer Report, Ref. 1, pp. 628-642.

21. Hood and Sparks, Ref. 6, pp. 66-79, deal with the problems of reliability, concealment, and exaggeration among self-reports of crimes and arrests.

22. Lee N. Robins and George E. Murphy, "Drug Use in a Normal Population of Young Negro Men," *American Journal of Public Health,* 57 (Sept. 1967), 1584-1585. John C. Ball, "Reliability and Validity of Interview Data Obtained from 59 Narcotic Addicts," *American Journal of Sociology,* 72 (May 1967), 650-654.

23. President's Commission, Ref. 7, pp. 25-35.

24. Goode, Ref. 4, p. 273.

25. Schafer Report, Ref. 1, pp. 647-650.

26. See the preliminary report of the Commission's findings in Fred P. Graham, "National Commission to Propose Legal Private Use of Marijuana," *New York Times,* Feb. 13, 1972. Shafer Report, Ref. 1, pp. 193-194.

27. Goode, Ref. 4, p. 277, says marijuana arrestees "are almost certainly guilty of some marijuana-related crime, if not at that instance, then probably at some other time." Our findings exactly.

28. Ibid., pp. 278-282. Lester Grinspoon, *Marihuana Reconsidered,* Cambridge, Mass.: Harvard University Press, 1971, pp. 344-371. John Kaplan, *Marijuana: The New*

Prohibition, Cleveland: World Publishing, 1970, pp. 29-49. Interim Report of the Canadian Government's Commission of Inquiry, *The Non-Medical Use of Drugs,* Ottawa, Canada, Queen's Printer for Canada, 1970, pp. 378-403.

29. Robins, Darvish, and Murphy, Ref. 13, p. 168.

CHAPTER 11

The Adequacy of Subculture Theory

This study has repeatedly turned to subculture theory to interpret the basic findings. Each chapter has utilized empirical data to demonstrate the validity of this theory. But at this point, the findings are fragmented and may not seem too closely related to subculture theory. The present chapter attempts to formulate subculture theory more clearly by building upon the evidence presented in preceding chapters.

Specifically, it will show how the empirical data demonstrate the existence of several conduct norms and values in the drug subculture and will affirm that there are two distinct subcultures of drug use. In addition, it will suggest how drug subcultures articulate with the parent culture, the peer culture, and, most important, with the present drug laws.

There are certain methodological problems in demonstrating the existence of drug subcultures. This study examined the behavior of a social group (college students) and individuals who have high levels of illicit drug use. But using evidence from such groups to make inferences about the drug subculture displays some circularity of reasoning.[1] In an effort to specify and explain the dependent variable (drug use or involvement in drug-using groups), inferences are made about the independent variable (the drug subculture). Yet it is maintained that the drug subculture, which cannot be directly measured, causes persons to become involved in drug-using groups and in drug use. Another danger in the theory is making inferences about social processes that go beyond the confines of the empirical data.[2] The study progresses beyond its data by making

[handwritten annotations in margin: "Relation between different." "Danger of Theorising beyond evidence"]

193

inferences about causality that can only be supported by panel data (which it does not have). One survey in 1970 is not adequate to prove causality, but it does suggest that such causal patterns may exist. Despite the possible shortcomings of the theory, evidence, methodology, and analysis, the author is now in a much better position than in Chapter 1 to outline in detail the basic structure, conduct norms, and values of the drug subcultures.

It is necessary to remember the narrow meaning of "drug subcultures." The specific concern here is with understanding subcultures of illicit drug use. Such subcultures have well-defined boundaries. The present data demonstrate that the most important boundary and central criterion for membership in these subcultures is the use of marihuana. More than anything else, the use and willingness to use cannabis separates participation in illicit drug subcultures from other types of drug consumption. Those who medically use prescription drugs, truck drivers who use amphetamines to stay awake, medical personnel addicted to opiates, suburban matrons who alternate diet and sleeping pills, and students who use amphetamines only to help study for exams are not direct participants in the subcultures discussed here.[3] Those who use drugs for such nonmedical reasons may be more likely than their nonusing peers to become involved in illicit drug-subcultures. But such medical and nonmedical drug users do not participate in either the black or white drug subcultures if they refuse to use marihuana. Truck drivers and suburban matrons would not consider themselves, nor be considered by subculture participants, as members of the drug subcultures even though they are regular drug users.[4] Thus, there are other forms of drug use in society that may also be a problem.[5]

As indicated in Chapter 1, to understand the existence and maintenance of the drug subculture, one must attempt to describe the primary conduct norms of the subculture. The present analysis demonstrates that there are probably two relatively distinct (white and black) subcultures of drug use among college students in the New York metropolitan area. Each will be dealt with in turn.

The primary conduct norms of the white drug subculture also indicate increasing participation in this subculture. In the white drug subculture, the most fundamental conduct norms hold that a participant is expected to (1) interact with marihuana users, (2) use marihuana or hashish if offered, (3) use cannabis with some regularity (once per month or more), (4) buy from or sell cannabis to friends if one possesses a quantity of marihuana, (5) meet and befriend users of hard drugs, (6) be willing to try hard drugs, especially hallucinogens, amphetamines, sedatives, and methedrine, (7) become an increasingly regular user of these hard drugs, (8) be willing to buy and sell these hard drugs, and (9) learn beliefs and values justifying drug-using and drug-selling behavior. In addition, the drug subculture is associated with "secondary" conduct norms; these norms expect subculture participants to believe and participate in political militancy, sexual permissiveness, and plans to leave college. Such conduct norms are secondary in the sense that drug subcultures would not be disrupted if these norms were not followed. But for social and historical reasons that are not clear, these norms are presently attached to drug subcultures.

The data support the existence of each of these conduct norms. The first and second norms can be inferred from Graph 4.1, which shows that 90% of those most of whose friends use cannabis have themselves used cannabis and that a third of the sample has friends almost all or all of whom use cannabis. The third norm can be inferred from the fact that 41% of those with most friends versus 1% of those with few cannabis-using friends are regular (weekly) cannabis users. In addition, Graph 6.1 reveals that less than 10% of the experimental (less than monthly) cannabis users have used any hard drugs, while much higher rates of hard-drug use occur among moderate and regular cannabis users. The fourth conduct norm can be inferred from information presented in Chapter 5; 1% of the nonusers, 40% of the experimental users, and 95% of the regular cannabis users had bought cannabis, while 1% of the noncannabis users, but 72% of the regular cannabis users, had ever sold cannabis. Thus, the greater the use of cannabis, the greater the likelihood of buying and selling cannabis.

In Chapters 6 and 7 one finds support for the fifth and sixth conduct norms. Students without friends or with friends (but not close friends) using a particular hard drug are relatively unlikely to use that drug, while those with intimate friends using that drug are very likely to try it. Also, white college students are more likely to use and gain friends using hallucinogens, amphetamines, sedatives, and methedrine than black students. The evidence also indicates that white students frequently gain friends who use these white drugs because of involvement in cannabis-using groups and the respondent's own cannabis use. This suggests that white neophyte cannabis users are likely to particpate in groups in which these white drugs are used. The clear expectation of the subculture is that an increasingly regular cannabis user will turn on to hard drugs; the precipitating factor is having intimate friends who use that drug. Although this study has not presented evidence that increasing regular use of these white drugs occur, the reader should be assured that having intimate friends using a particular drug is crucial to the frequent (monthly or more) use of that drug (norm 7). In addition, Graph 5.2 demonstrates that among cannabis sellers the more regularly a hard drug is used, the more likely a person is to buy and to sell that hard drug (norm 8). Conduct norm 9 is demonstrated in Graph 8.2, where agreement with the Increased Benefits Index and Hip Life Style Index was seen to be strongly related to drug buying and selling.

In addition, the data demonstrate the existence of secondary conduct norms; plans to leave college, involvement in political militancy, and sexual permissiveness are highly correlated with drug selling or drug-subculture involvement. Why such secondary conduct norms are associated with subculture involvement is not clear. Perhaps in other time periods or among noncollege populations these secondary conduct norms might not be associated with drug subcultures. Such secondary conduct norms are not as essential to the existence of drug subcultures as are the primary conduct norms governing drug use, friendships with drug users, and drug purchase or sale.

The evidence suggests that there is also a second subculture of drug use. However, the data on the black drug subculture is not definitive, as it is for whites. Nevertheless, a comparison of limited data with studies of black populations[6] allows one to conclude that the conduct norms governing drug use in the black subculture are probably similar to the norms of the white drug subculture.

The major difference between these subcultures lies in the drugs that increasingly regular cannabis users are expected to use. Marihuana-using blacks are expected to use cocaine and heroin; whites use hallucinogens, amphetamines, sedatives, and methedrine. But the processes by which blacks and whites are recruited into, and maintained in, their respective drug subcultures are virtually identical. Marihuana use introduces students to each racial subculture; drug selling increases the depth of involvement in the subculture.

In addition, the data suggests how students come in contact with drugs from the racially opposite subculture. About the only whites who have a high proportion of cocaine or heroin-using intimates are those selling hard drugs. Likewise, drug selling leads blacks to gain intimates using amphetamines, sedatives, and methedrine. For both races, the use of cannabis is virtually unrelated to having intimates using drugs from the opposite subculture when involvement in the buying and selling of drugs is held constant.

From this evidence, one may infer that selling activities, especially the sale of hard drugs, tend to expand one's circle of acquaintances beyond that of close friends. Selling drugs increases the probability of meeting someone from the opposite subculture and befriending him. White college students probably become involved in cocaine and heroin because they are highly involved in drug selling, which allows them to meet and befriend black drug sellers on campus. The process works even more strongly in the reverse direction. Black drug sellers meet and befriend white drug sellers on campus and are introduced to white subculture drugs. In order to decisively prove this cross-subculture contact hypothesis, further research with a larger sample and including noncollege blacks is needed.

Thus, the evidence demonstrates the existence of conduct norms and values of two drug subcultures. How, then, are students recruited into these subcultures of drug use? It will be remembered that Chapter 1 suggested a theory of socialization into progressively more unconventional groups: from conformity to the parent culture, to participation in the peer culture and then to involvement in the drug subculture. This book has dealt with this theory of articulation between cultures or subcultures in a most cursory manner. This theory deserves far more consideration than can be given in a book analyzing illicit drug use.

The evidence shows that parent-culture expectations for college students do have a decisive impact upon the use of drugs and many other activities. Data in most chapters demonstrate that noncannabis users are generally less likely than cannabis users to engage in all forms of unconventional activities such as drug selling, hard-drug use, crime, premarital sex, auto deviance, or leaving college. Although the data is not presented, if one percentages in the opposite direction, one finds that those who are most conventional (sexual virgins, church attenders, regular class attenders, those who do not participate in delinquency or auto-related deviance) are significantly less likely to use cannabis or other drugs than their less conventional peers. Hence, conventionality inhibits drug use.

[margin note: Assumption of another trend]

The most impressive evidence for the effect of parent-culture expectations is found in Chapter 4, which found that the greater the commitment to parent-culture norms, the less the probability of having cannabis-using friends (a measure of a participation in an unconventional group) and the less likely students are to use cannabis. Thus, highly conventional persons—the very religious, noncigarette smoking, politically moderate females—were very unlikely (2%) to have most of their friends using cannabis or to ever use cannabis (4%) themselves. The few highly conventional persons with most friends using cannabis had generally tried marihuana but were much less likely than their unconventional peers (daily cigarette users, left, nonreligious males) to be weekly cannabis users. One suspects that this kind of explanation may apply to other types of unconventional behavior such as sexual activity, crime, and political activity, although this study has not investigated this possibility. Hence, the data tend to demonstrate that abiding by the norms of the parent culture does decisively reduce the probability of participation in drug-using groups, as well as the use and regular use of cannabis and other drugs.

Although not presented, data show that conventionality as measured by religiosity, cigarette smoking, political orientation, and sex is significantly related to peer-culture participation. Chapter 8 also briefly demonstrated that the Peer Culture Index is strongly associated with auto deviance, crime, and aggressiveness but not so strongly correlated with political militancy and premarital sex with four or more persons. Further, involvement in these unconventional activities has not changed much over time. Thus, about the same proportion of college freshmen, sophomores, juniors, and seniors had engaged in premarital sex, crime, and aggressiveness in high school. Since those high on the Peer Culture Index were more likely than the noninvolved to engage in these activities, it may be concluded that crime and sex have been legitimated and are relatively common among those involved in the peer culture since 1966 (the present data extend back no further).

However, cannabis use was uncommon in 1966. Chapter 3 demonstrated that the operating invention of cannabis use has been increasingly incorporated as a new and relatively legitimate behavior among those highly involved in the peer culture. As measured by our Peer Culture Index, those highly involved were more likely than those not involved to have tried cannabis prior to high school graduation in 1966 and much more likely to have done so in 1969. The greatest increase in cannabis use has occurred among those highly involved in the peer culture (Graph 3.4). Hence, the peer culture has incorporated cannabis use as a legitimate group activity in much the same manner as sex, aggressiveness, and crime have been legitimated for some time.

Unfortunately, this book is not the place to explore the details of how the peer and parent cultures are related to many different forms of deviance. The question of whether, and how, different subcultures of delinquency may emerge from the peer culture is surely a fascinating one, but it cannot be pursued in depth at present. However, the analytic scheme employed to understand drug consumption may be, to a certain degree, applicable to the analysis of other forms of unconventional behavior.

An important branch of the peer culture, the drug subculture, is directly dependent upon the peer culture's norms of spending much free time with peers in settings beyond adult social controls. This subculture also depends upon the parent culture's legitimation of alcohol use for social reasons and the use of various psychoactive drugs to get to sleep or to stay awake. Thus, the drug subculture is truly a *sub*culture because it depends upon the other two cultures for many of its basic norms. In addition, the other cultures are structured in such a way that they increase or decrease the probability of participating in drug subcultures.[7]

Having discussed the conduct norms, values, and structures of drug subcultures, as well as how students are recruited into such subcultures from the parent and peer cultures, an examination of how the present (as of 1972) drug laws articulate with drug subcultures is needed. Drug subcultures are strongly related to the present drug laws, which prohibit the possession and sale of cannabis and hard drugs. Central to this discussion is the Illicit Marketing Index. Chapter 5 asserted that this variable was a good measure of (1) participation in the illicit drug market; (2) increasing participation in the drug subculture, which is theoretically and empirically independent of the use of drugs; and (3) how present drug laws making drug possession and sale illegal influence the illicit drug market and drug subculture. This book maintains that the illegality of cannabis is central to the organization of the illegal drug market and to the maintenance of drug subcultures.

First, although there is no natural law compelling regular drug users to sell drugs, participation in the illicit drug market is closely linked to drug use. Chapter 5 demonstrated that the frequency of drug use is directly related to the illicit purchase or sale of that drug. Furthermore, the use, purchase, and sale of cannabis seems to precede the use, purchase, or sale, respectively, of hard drugs. The Illicit Marketing Index indicates different degrees of involvement in illicit drug buying or selling; all of the evidence indicates that buying cannabis is less serious than selling cannabis, while selling hard drugs indicates more serious involvement than selling cannabis only. Thus, the Illicit Marketing Index appears to be a valid indicator of increasing participation in the illicit drug market.

Even more important, the data demonstrate that the Illicit Marketing Index is probably the best indicator of drug-subculture participation. As public officials have observed, cannabis use and hard-drug use are positively related to unconventional outcomes such as political militancy, premarital sex, crime, leaving college, having hard-drug-using friends, and having contact with police for drug violations. However, the data demonstrate that officials ignore the most important factor. The Illicit Marketing Index was more strongly related to all indices of unconventionality than was the Frequency of Cannabis Use Index or, for most indices, the Multiple Drug Use Index. In most cases, when drug buying or selling was held constant, the relationship between drug use and unconventional outcomes was greatly reduced. This indicates that increasing participation in the illicit drug market is more important than the level of drug use in determining certain undesirable (from the official viewpoint) outcomes. While frequency of cannabis use, multiple drug use, and other factors may also indicate increasing subculture participation, drug selling is statistically more powerful than other factors in explaining a wide variety of phenomena associated with drug use.

Why is the Illicit Marketing Index such a important indicator of subculture participation? The following interpretation is speculative and needs further testing but is probably better than other interpretations. In both the black and white drug subcultures, those not involved in drug buying or selling and those who only buy cannabis remain, for the most part, within fairly stable peer groups in which drugs are infrequently used. Cannabis buyers probably obtain small amounts of marihuana from someone in the group who has contact with the outside drug sellers. Or if those who only buy cannabis make contact with a pusher, the relationship will probably remain instrumental; persons just buy marihuana and see no need for further interaction.

Persons who only sell cannabis probably sell a small amount of surplus cannabis on an irregular basis to close friends in order to smoke free. However, cannabis sellers have probably bought an ounce or more of marihuana and have had somewhat more opportunity to meet and befriend users of hard drugs than persons who only buy cannabis. Nevertheless, the data demonstrate that students who only sell cannabis are not a great deal more likely than cannabis buyers to have hard-drug-using intimates, be sexually permissive, and be involved in crime or delinquency. This suggest that cannabis-only sellers tend to remain in relatively cohesive peer groups and are not much more likely than cannabis buyers to gain new friends who use hard drugs.

However, those who sell hard drugs are more likely to have intimates using hard drugs than are cannabis sellers. This suggests that students who become involved in selling hard drugs are likely to leave their old peer group and, through contacts made while selling drugs, begin to participate in new peer groups in which the use of hard drugs may be a common group activity. In addition, friends in such new peer groups are likely to be highly involved in many forms of unconventional behavior. New participants in these peer groups are expected to abide by the conduct norms that govern group behavior. Acting in accordance with these primary and secondary conduct norms probably reflects, and is perhaps equivalent to, deep participation in the drug subculture. Thus, deep participation in the illicit drug market (hard-drug selling) is closely related to, and perhaps a cause of, heavy participation in drug subcultures. The data suggest that hard-drug selling and heavy subculture participation are essentially the same phenomenon.

It is also suggested that involvement in the illicit drug market is a direct function of the illegality of cannabis and hard drugs. The most compelling evidence of the direct effect of drug laws can be found in Chapter 5, in which evidence is presented that demonstrates that the more frequently cannabis is used, the more likely it is to be sold; no other factors strongly affect this use-sale relationship. In addition, evidence from Goode and Carey suggests that the illegality of cannabis is an important factor in understanding marihuana selling.[8] From the seller's point of view, the amount of work and time involved in selling an ounce or more and the risk of arrest for drug charges are about as great (or small) as for minor cannabis sales (less than $5). Thus, cannabis buyers who want to obtain a couple of marihuana cigarettes are likely to be offered an ounce or more on a "take it or leave it" basis.[9] But an ounce is more than weekly cannabis users will consume in three months, so some may be sold to friends at cost. Students quickly learn that they can smoke free and make some extra money selling to nonintimates. In short, there are very rational reasons why students become involved in drug selling: (1) Cannabis cannot be legally obtained, so the job of distribution becomes that of regular users by default. (2) An economically feasible black market that takes the threat of arrest into account sells such large quantities of cannabis that marihuana users cannot use it all and hence are likely to sell some of what they do not need. (3) Involvement in cannabis selling teaches students how to ignore the moral judgments of nonusers as well as how to avoid the legal penalties attached to selling; once the basic rules of selling are learned, it is easy for the cannabis seller to branch into selling hard drugs, especially those which he uses. (4) Since there is more money per sale to be gained from hard-drug sales, about half the cannabis sellers become involved in selling hard drugs. Thus, the data suggest strongly that present drug laws, which make the possession or sale of cannabis a criminal act, are directly

responsible for what they attempt to prevent—the illegal sale of drugs and, *VIMP*
perhaps indirectly, the illicit use of hard drugs.

If present drug laws are directly responsible for the sale of cannabis and the
illicit drug market, then such laws may indirectly support the black and white
drug subcultures. However, this is not to say that the laws against cannabis are
the historical cause of these two drug subcultures. Subcultures centered around
heroin and cocaine use appear to be an outgrowth of the enforcement of the
Harrison Act.[10] The historical reasons for the development of a subculture
emphasizing the use of hallucinogens, pills, and methedrine is even less clear,
although much more recent. It should be recognized that over time drug
subcultures may change preferences for various drugs. For example, prior to
World War I, blacks showed a preference for cocaine, while it was generally
accepted that whites were more likely to use opiates. It is not clear why
blacks began using heroin after World War I, but such a shift has definitely
occurred.[11]

The remainder of this chapter will develop arguments for making cannabis
legitimately available.[12] It will only discuss the need for a change in social
policy without discussing what policies should be pursued. Suggesting such
policy alternatives would require another full-length book and necessitate a
wide-ranging review of the literature on drug use. Such a discussion obviously is
far beyond the confines of the present, limited survey of drug use.

If the data support the theory proposed here and if the theory is generally
valid for a middle-class college population,[13] then there is a definite need for a
fundamental change in drug laws. Essentially, the author holds that illicit drug
selling and, indirectly, the drug laws, hold each drug subculture together and
provide contact between the black and white drug subcultures. Making cannabis
legitimately available might have the result of ungluing drug subcultures.

It may be objected that marihuana did not make the subculture and is only a
symbol of the youth subculture, and, further, that there are too many other
attitudes and feelings involved in the subculture for a fundamental change in
governmental action toward cannabis to have much effect upon drug use. Such
objections are serious ones and may be true; it is the job of another researcher to
disprove the present theory by defining what the other factors or explanations
of drug use may be. But a few such objections can be somewhat refuted by the
theory and evidence presented in this book.

Marihuana is a relatively new symbol among the American youth subculture,
or what has here been called the peer culture (Chapter 3). Marihuana use is
predominately symbolic within the peer culture; students use marihuana as a
symbol in much the same way as cars, parties, drinking bouts, and sexual
encounters are symbolic of independence from adult controls. But marihuana
use has consequences that are more than symbolic, just as auto accidents,

drunken fights, pregnancy, and venereal disease are the occasional, undesirable outcomes of other symbolic actions.

However, the consequences of marihuana use do not derive from any pharmacological property of cannabis. The main nonsymbolic outcome of increasingly regular cannabis use and a direct function of present drug laws is exposure to, and involvement in, cannabis purchase and sale. If there are attitudes and feelings among youth or the peer culture related to drug selling that are independent of present drug policy, they are not found in the present study. In Chapter 5, a wide variety of factors were held constant, including measures of attitudes, life style, and peer-culture involvement; none of these factors greatly affects the strong linear relationship between cannabis use and sale. If students become involved in cannabis selling, the probability of becoming hard-drug users and selling hard drugs increases. Further, the data suggest that the depth of involvement in drug selling measures involvement in drug subcultures. Thus, the crucial link between marihuana use, which is symbolic in some respects, and deep drug-subculture participation is marihuana selling. If most regular cannabis users could somehow obtain cannabis without a substantial proportion becoming sellers, it is probable that a smaller proportion of cannabis users would be recruited into new peer groups abiding by the drug-subculture conduct norms.

The author suggests that a change in cannabis policy is needed to undercut the illicit drug market and undermine drug subcultures. Making cannabis legitimately available would probably not increase, and might actually decrease, the probability of involvement in unconventional peer groups and behaviors.

There are five reasons why fundamental changes in laws controlling cannabis are needed. First, when participation in the drug market is held constant, the frequency of cannabis use is a relatively minor or unimportant factor in gaining hard-drug-using intimates and involvement in unconventional outcomes such as hard-drug use, sexual permissiveness, delinquency, militancy, leaving college, poor grades, or contact with police. In short, cannabis use does not independently cause, nor is it strongly associated with, unconventionality; rather, increasing subculture participation is a more important cause of such behavior.

Second, regardless of how frequently they use cannabis, persons who neither buy nor sell drugs and those who only buy cannabis are not much more likely than noncannabis users to be involved in unconventional behavior (graphs in Chapters 6-10). The main exception to this finding is that cannabis buyers are more likely than noncannabis users to have intimates using hard drugs that are common in the subculture of the respondent's race. Thus, the simple use of cannabis or only buying cannabis is associated with whites gaining intimates using hallucinogens, amphetamines, sedatives, and methedrine, while blacks are likely to gain intimates using cocaine or heroin. But cannabis use or purchase is not associated with having intimates using drugs in the opposite subculture.

This evidence suggests that the drug subculture's equivalent of retail customers, persons who only buy cannabis, behave much more like noncannabis users than like sellers of hard drugs. Another interpretation of this finding is that persons who are marginally involved (cannabis buyers) in the drug subculture are not much more likely to exhibit unconventional behavior than nonsubculture participants. Only those persons who are deeply involved in the subculture are likely to participate in unconventional groups and behaviors. This finding permits the suggestion that if cannabis could be legally purchased at a regulated retail store, present cannabis sellers might become buyers, and their involvement in unconventional groups and behaviors might not increase much, if at all, and might even decrease.

Third, the extensive use of cannabis among college students generates an enormous demand for the illicit drug market to meet and serve. Table 3 shows that a much larger proportion of the total population has tried cannabis (55%) than has illicitly tried hallucinogens (19%), amphetamines (15%), sedatives (14%), methedrine (9%), cocaine (7%), or heroin (4%). In a similar fashion, cannabis is much more likely to be used frequently (monthly or more) than other drugs; 34% of the total population has used cannabis monthly or more compared with 7% for sedatives, amphetamines, methedrine, and hallucinogens; 2% for methedrine; and 1% for cocaine and heroin (data not presented).

Fourth, cannabis sales are a central feature of the illicit drug market. In the sample, 22% have sold cannabis; 7%, hallucinogens and amphetamines; 5%, sedatives; 4%, methedrine; and 1%, cocaine or heroin. Almost everyone who has sold a hard drug has also sold cannabis (Table 6). In addition, although data is lacking, one suspects that among college students more than a majority of all drug sales involve cannabis. Students who only sell cannabis are very low-level sellers and probably sell small amounts for low profit to intimates within their own peer group.

However, it is only among cannabis sellers that persons are likely to sell hard drugs (Graph 5.2). Hence, selling cannabis is an important and almost necessary transitional step in becoming deeply involved in the drug subculture.

Even among hard-drug sellers, cannabis sales are probably very important. The author suspects but does not have the data to prove, that a majority of sales made by those ever selling hard drugs are for cannabis alone. It is probable that hard-drug sellers gain a large proportion of their total earnings from sales of marihuana or hashish, although they may make more money per sale from hard drugs.[14]

But regardless of how much money is made from selling cannabis, it is the enormous demand for marihuana that probably provides the hard-drug seller with a long list of potential customers for hard drugs, customers he would not meet otherwise. Without the volume of customers generated by the constant demand for cannabis, most hard-drug sellers (even the heaviest sellers) would find their earnings greatly reduced. Legal cannabis might greatly decrease the number of customers for hard-drug sellers. This could possibly undermine the very foundations of the illicit drug market existing on college campuses. As alcohol bootlegging diminished at the end of alcohol prohibition, so might the illicit drug market diminish if cannabis were legally available.

However, if cannabis were legally available but hard drugs were not, it is probable that the illicit drug market would not completely collapse but might become organized around the sale of other drugs, although on a considerably reduced scale. On the college campus, the illicit drug market would probably reorganize around hallucinogen sales. In the black ghettoes it appears that the illicit drug market is presently organized around heroin sales more than around marihuana sales. [15]

Fifth, cannabis sales and, indirectly, the illegality of cannabis are a central link between marginal and deep participation in each drug subculture. The data demonstrate that deep involvement in drug subcultures is common among persons who sell cannabis and hard drugs. Subculture theory suggests that students learn the conduct norms and values of the drug subculture through participation in drug-oriented peer groups. The central question of subculture theory is, How do students become involved in peer groups in which most of the members abide by unconventional conduct norms and values? Evidence demonstrates that students become highly involved in unconventional peer groups because of drug-selling activities. Those who sell hard drugs are more likely than cannabis-only sellers and cannabis buyers to have intimates using hard drugs, to use hard drugs themselves, to be sexually permissive, to be involved in delinquency, to leave college, and to have contact with police.

Legal cannabis might decrease the probability of progression into drug subcultures. If cannabis could be purchased on a retail basis, many cannabis-using students would no longer have a concrete reason for seeking out illicit drug sellers. Such cannabis users would not have to purchase more marihuana than they want or need. Even if regular cannabis users did meet hard-drug users and sellers, the need to maintain contacts with such sellers might decrease because cannabis could be obtained elsewhere. The opportunity of participating in new hard-drug-using peer groups might decrease. In addition, as demonstrated above, the subculture's equivalent to retail customers, cannabis buyers, are relatively less likely than hard-drug sellers to be deeply involved in subcultures and unconventional peer groups. If cannabis were available on a retail level, it is possible that a smaller proportion of college students would progress deeply into drug subcultures than do so at the present time.

In short, the findings suggest that legal cannabis might be an important ingredient in dissolving the glue that holds drug subcultures together. Legal cannabis would undermine the illicit drug market and, at the same time, undercut the social processes by which students are recruited into, and maintained in, each subculture. We can also hypothesize that fewer persons would have an opportunity to meet and befriend users and turn on to drugs from the racially opposite drug subculture.

The conclusions, inferences, and theory presented in this chapter depend upon assumptions that may not be correct. Further research with panel data is badly needed to straighten out patterns of causality between drug use, having drug-using intimates, and drug selling. In addition, much more information about patterns of illicit drug selling is needed. Information about "big" pushers is not as badly needed as information about the low-level sellers. Do low-level sellers remain with their old peer group? Or do they gain new, hard-drug-using friends and leave their old peer group? To how many different persons has a seller sold drugs? How intimate is he with his buyers? How much of his drug supply is consumed by himself, given to friends, and sold for clear profit? Does he specialize in selling certain drugs? To what extent does the seller, or the buyer, try to increase the intimacy of the interaction? To what extent are sellers seen as respected leaders in the subculture? Do sellers make most of their money from cannabis sales? Do users of hard drugs sell cannabis to support their use of hard drugs?

Answers to such questions will also allow one to test assumptions about whether cannabis selling is crucial in gaining intimates using hard drugs. Such data might demonstrate that the author's theory is incorrect. Perhaps hard-drug sellers start using hard drugs and then begin selling cannabis in order to pay for their increasing drug expenditures. Rather than one factor being predominantely causal, drug selling, gaining hard drug using friends, hard-drug use, and unconventional behavior may occur at about the same time, but still indicating increasing subculture involvement. Also needed is information about how different drugs become legitimated historically within a drug subculture, and why racial differences in drug use tend to persist in the relatively integrated atmosphere of the college. Other researchers are urged to challenge the assumptions and theory herein; empirical research can be usefully utilized to provide better understanding of crucial issues in the drug controversy. But no matter how the subculture theory is challenged, it provides a far better understanding of the empirical evidence than any theory or hypothesis propounded by supporters of the present drug laws.

Above all else, the evidence demonstrates that present drug laws play a fundamental role in structuring and organizing subcultures of drug use. It is participation in such drug subcultures, and not the use of drugs, that should be of central concern to lawmakers.

REFERENCES

1. Marvin E. Wolfgang and Franco Ferracuti, *The Subculture of Violence*, London: Tavistock, 1967, p. 155.

2. Ibid., p. 157.

3. Erich Goode, "Multiple Drug Use Among Marijuana Smokers," *Social Problems,* 17 (Summer 1969), 54.

4. Carl D. Chambers, *An Assessment of Drug Use in the General Population,* New York: Narcotic Addiction Control Commission, May 1971, pp. 60-100, shows high levels of regular pep-pill and other prescription drug use among populations that probably do not use marihuana.

5. Hugh J. Parry, "Use of Psychotoropic Drugs by U.S. Adults," *Public Health Reports,* 83 (Oct. 1968), 799-810. Glen D. Mellinger, "The Psychotherapeutic Drug Scene in San Francisco," in Paul H. Balachy, *Drug Abuse: Data and Debate,* Springfield, Ill.: Charles C. Thomas, 1970, pp. 226-240. Glen D. Mellinger, Mitchel B. Balter, and Dean I. Manheimer, "Patterns of Psychotherapeutic Drug Use Among Adults in San Francisco," *Archives of General Psychiatry,* 25 (Nov. 1971), 385-394.

6. John Langrod, "Secondary Drug Use Among Heroin Users," *International Journal of the Addictions,* 5 (Dec. 1970), 611-636. Lee N. Robins and George E. Murphy, "Drug Use in a Normal Population of Young Negro Men," *American Journal of Public Health,* 57 (Sept. 1967), 1580-1596.

7. Wolfgang and Ferracuti, Ref. 1, pp. 158-161.

8. Erich Goode, *Marijuana Smokers,* New York: Basic Books, 1970, pp. 255-259. James T. Carey, *The College Drug Scene,* Englewood, Cliffs, N.J.: Prentice-Hall, 1968, pp. 79-93.

9. Goode, Ref. 8, p. 253.

10. Alfred Lindesmith, *The Addict and the Law,* New York: Vintage, 1965, pp. 3-34.

11. David F. Musto, personal communication, June 1972.

12. We use the term "legitimately available" in preference to "legalization," which frequently is felt to mean the absence of controls. We suggest making cannabis available but severely restricting the availability of the drug. For discussion of a possible model of "legitimate availability," see John Kaplan, *Marijuana—The New Prohibition,* Cleveland, World, 1970, pp. 332-352.

13. See Chapter 3 for comparison of our sample with several other studies of college populations.

14. Carey, Ref. 8, pp. 74-81.

15. Edward Preble, "Taking Care of Business—The Heroin User's Life on the Street," *International Journal of the Addictions,* 4 (Mar. 1969), 8-12.

APPENDIX A
Statistical Appendix

In attempting to analyze sociological data, the researcher has a wide variety of statistical techniques available such as the correlation (Pearsonian r), multiple and partial correlation, and various measures of association such as gamma, tau, and chi square. Such statistics are very convenient in summarizing a great deal of data with a few numbers. Despite this advantage, the present study depends upon what sociologists call cross-tabulation or multivariate analysis techniques, which utilize percentages almost exclusively.

Percentages have one intrinsic advantage: they can be easily understood by the layman who is not acquainted with more advanced statistical techniques. In addition, cross-tabulation permits close examination of the behavior of specific subgroups. Furthermore, such data can be presented easily in graph form to help the reader visualize the important findings. The major disadvantages of multivariate analysis are that many different percentages are required and may be somewhat confusing at first and that certain theoretically crucial subgroups in a population may not contain a sufficient number of respondents (cases) to compute a percentage stable enough to be compared to another percentage. But the author feels that the advantages of clarity and understandability outweigh the disadvantages, especially since the sample obtained is quite large.

DETERMINING STATISTICAL SIGNIFICANCE

In the text, we have presented many tables and graphs without reference to statistical significance. We have generally ignored the question of significance for four basic reasons: (1) Our sample was not selected on a random basis (an important assumption of significance tests). Schools were selected for inclusion on the basis of their characteristics and cooperation (see Appendix B and Chapter 2). (2) Several groups that contained a large proportion of heavy drug users were oversampled. Yet the information from each respondent was weighted equally. (3) All too frequently, tests of significance are used as a substitute for thought and analysis of significant hypotheses.[1] Rather than analyze the "why" and "how" questions, researchers sometimes count the number of significant differences and assume that this explains something.[2] (4) The major reason for lack of concern about statistical significance lies in the fact that with a large sample, most differences between two subgroups are significant. As a rule of thumb, in the present survey, almost any two-way relationship with a 6% or greater difference is statistically significant at the .05 level.

Nevertheless, it is sometimes important to know whether a difference is significant or not. Information about significance can help to support or reject a hypothesis, especially where a relationship is relatively weak. Since our sample size is large and the true variation of a biased sample unknown, it is important that all estimates of significance be conservative; it is dangerous to accept a relationship as significant when in fact it is not. Therefore, in Table 14, instead of interpolating the percent difference needed to achieve significance, it is better to use information given for the immediately smaller number of cases. For example, if a percentage is based upon 950 cases, it is better to look in the row or column labeled "750" than the one labeled "1000"; this will increase the probability that a research finding is statistically significant.

To utilize the information in Table 14, it is necessary to understand how the data are presented in this appendix and graphs in the text. The percentages are one- or two-digit numbers that appear immediately above two- to four-digit numbers enclosed in parentheses; the latter is the number of cases upon which the percentage is based. In the graphs, the height of the bar is the percentage, with the number of cases presented immediately below the bar.

To illustrate how to use Table 14 and to show some of the possible weaknesses of significance tests, we will utilize one of the book's main findings, which casts doubt upon the assumption of the Bureau of Narcotics that marihuana use leads to heroin use. In Table 22 (also see Graph 6.3), the first row (persons with no heroin-using friends), we find ".3" over "(1422)" for noncannabis users and "5" over "(318)" for weekly or more cannabis users. This indicates that among those without heroin-using friends, 0.3% of 1422 (base number of cases) noncannabis users versus 5% of the 318 weekly cannabis users have themselves tried heroin. Thus, we may ask, among those lacking heroin-using friends, are weekly cannabis users significantly more likely than noncannabis users to use heroin? Is this 4.7% (5.0%-0.3%) difference statistically significant or does it happen by chance? Since there are 1422 noncannabis users and 318 weekly or more cannabis users, we look in Table 14 for the numbers

Table 14. Sampling errors of differences: two-tailed test for p. $<.05^a$

Size of Base Number of Cases	2000	1000	750	500	300	200	150	100	50	30
For Percentages from 30% to 70%										
2000	1									
1000	3	4								
750	4	4	5							
500	5	5	5	6						
300	6	6	6	7	7					
200	7	7	7	8	8	9				
150	8	8	8	8	9	10	11			
100	10	10	10	10	11	11	12	13		
50	13	13	13	14	14	15	15	16	18	
30	16	17	17	17	17	18	18	19	20	24
For Percentages Around 10% and 90%										
2000	1									
1000	2	3								
750	3	3	3							
500	3	3	3	4						
300	4	4	4	4	5					
200	4	5	5	5	5	6				
150	5	5	5	5	6	7	7			
100	6	6	6	7	7	8	8	9		
50	8	9	9	9	9	10	10	10	12	
30	11	11	11	11	11	12	12	12	14	16

^{a}When the percentage difference between two subgroups in the sample is equal to, or greater than, the number in the appropriate cell, there are less than 5 chances in 100 that this was due to sampling error. This table assumes that a random sample of a given population has been obtained.

immediately smaller than these numbers of cases, that is, 1000 and 300. Then reading down the column headed "1000" and across the row labeled "300" in the section "for percentages around 10% or 90%," we find the number 4. This indicates that the 4.7% difference is probably statistically significant; there are less than 5 chances in 100 that this finding occured because of sampling error or other random factors.

We have several objections to the following conclusion, which might be drawn from this finding: "Even among those without heroin-using friends, there is a slight, but significant, relationship between marihuana use and heroin use."

First, the 5% figure among weekly cannablis users is very suspect, since our research design oversampled heavy drug users, a few of whom could have ended up in that cell. Second, among those with no heroin-using friends, the 4% difference in heroin use between weekly-or-more versus weekly-or-less cannabis users is not significant according to the table: it needs to be 5%.

But, third, is this statistically significant 4.7% difference socially significant?[3] Can we assume that some pharmacological factor in marihuana use causes heroin use even among those with no heroin-using friends? Can public policy be based on such a flimsy finding? We suggest that the answer is no; at least until other factors are held constant. By isolating such a finding for discussion, we ignore the socially significant finding; persons without heroin-using friends are very unlikely to use heroin when compared with those having intimate friends. Furthermore, focusing on this one finding detracts from the pattern of findings for all hard drugs; those without friends using a hard drug are unlikely themselves to try it, even though regular cannabis users are somewhat more likely to try each drug than noncannabis users or less regular users. Thus, the reader is urged to utilize these materials on statistical significance as an aid or guide to forming judgments about the interpretations proposed in this book. Significant tests should not be substituted for theoretical thinking upon which the empirical evidence is brought to bear in a meaningful way.

READING AND INTERPRETING THREE-WAY (N-WAY) TABLES

In large samples, where small differences are frequently statistically significant, it is important to investigate what happens to a significant relationship between an independent and dependent variable when another variable is held constant. Formally, the methodology utilized in this book is called multivariate analysis. This mode of analysis is outlined in Lazarsfeld and Rosenberg, and Hyman;[4] with further elaboration and a multitude of examples of the technique provided by Rosenberg and Zeisel.[5]

In an attempt to make our reasonably complex data easier to understand, we have developed a relatively standard format for presenting the tables in this appendix. (We have discussed this methodology as it applies to graphs in the footnote of Graph 4.3). When multivariate analysis and the format of tables is understood, the data in this Appendix can be read quickly and meaningfully. In addition, these tables provide the data which may be examined in considerably greater detail than that provided in the text or graphs.

Central to understanding the tables in this appendix and the book is to ask several important questions. If asked in the correct order, these questions will help test the validity of the hypothesis in question. We will list these questions and then provide an example of how to answer them.

(1) How many variables does the author present in a given table?

(2) What is the dependent variable? What is the author trying to explain or understand?

(3) What is the independent variable? What factor has the author hypothesized might be the cause of the dependent variable? In most cases this hypothesis is discussed in the text and is a summary of the position of the Bureau of Narcotics.

(4) What other variable(s), called a test factor, does the author use to explain the relationship between the independent and dependent variable?

The answers to these questions should be clear from reading the title of the table and from discussion in the text of the book. Then the reader should locate the three variables in the column and row headings as well as the categories of each variable. Then the following questions should be answered from the numbers in the table.

(5) What is the relationship between the independent and dependent variable? (This is called the original, or two-way, relationship.) How strong, as measured by the percent difference, is the two-way relationship?

(6) What happens to the relationship between the independent and dependent variables when a third variable (test factor) is held constant? Does the percent difference due to the independent variable upon the dependent variable decrease in each or in only some of the categories of the test factor? Compute an average percent difference (APD).

(7) Does a comparison of the two-way relationship and the average percent difference with the test factor(s) held constant show that the APD is one-half to two-thirds the strength of the original relationship? If so, the independent variable is probably misleading or wrong as a cause of the dependent variable because of the confounding effect of the test factor.

(8) What is the relationship (measured by the percent difference) between the test factor (now examined as the independent variable) and the dependent variable. How strong is the relationship? Is the relationship decreased or unchanged when the original independent variable (now treated as a test factor) is held constant?

(9) Which variable the independent or test factor, has the greatest direct effect upon the dependent variable? Does a comparison of the APD's show that the independent variable is more or less important than the test factor?

With these questions in mind, the following table and explanation should be carefully examined. Table 15 contains the data upon which the top chart of Graph 8.1 is based.

Answers to the nine questions raised above can determine whether marihuana use is a fundamental cause of political militancy, the hypothesis discussed in Chapter 8. Each question is answered in turn.

Questions 1-2

The heading of Table 15 states that there are three variables involved in the table: "Percent High on Political Militancy" indicates that the dependent variable is the Political Militancy Index (developed in Chapter 8). Furthermore, the table title indicates that each cell contains information about only one category of the dependent variable: those high on the variable; excluded are those with "none" and "some" involvement in militancy. For example, excluding the percent difference (% diff.) row and column, each cell in the table should be read as in the following example: in the "buy cannabis" column and "irregular" row, "14" appears over "(425)." This means that there are 425 students who are irregular (less than weekly) cannabis users and have only purchased cannabis; of these 425, 14% are high on the Political Militancy Index, and by implication, 86% (100%-14%) of the 425 are not high on the Militancy Index. Another example: in the "total" column and "regular" row, there are 642 persons using cannabis regularly (weekly or more); 24% of these regular users are high on the Political Militancy Index (without reference to drug buying or selling).

Question 3

The title of Table 15 also identifies the independent variable with the phrase "by frequency of cannabis use." Essentially, the author is hypothesizing that

Table 15. Percent high on political militancy by frequency of cannabis use holding constant the Illicit Marketing Index

| Frequency of Cannabis Use | Illicit Marketing Index | | | | | | % diff. (Sell 3+ Hard − None) |
| | | Cannabis | | Sell Hard Drugs | | | |
	None	Buy	Sell	1-2	3+	Total	
None						3 (1567)	
Irregular	7 (626)	14 (425)	18 (196)	30 (86)	32 (48)	14 (1281)	25
Regular	10 (30)	17 (131)	20 (174)	29 (161)	34 (146)	24 (642)	24
Total	7 (556)	15 (556)	19 (370)	29 (247)	33 (194)	17 (1923)	26/25
% diff. (Reg. − irreg.)	3	3	2	−1	2	10/2	

something about marihuana use is associated with political militancy. Although sociologists hedge greatly and say that an independent variable is "significantly related to," "correlated with," or "associated with" the dependent variable, there is also an implicit assumption that the independent variable (marihuana use) is at least a partial "cause" of the dependent variable (political militancy). Given that a statistically significant association between two variables exists, the researcher must ask, "Why?" and "What other factors might possibly explain the association?"

Question 4

In the attempt to explain the association between an independent and a dependent variable, the researcher should attempt to hold constant, or take into account, other variables that might account for the link between marihuana and militancy. The phrase "holding constant the Illicit Marketing Index" identifies another variable with which the author expects to better understand the relationship between cannabis and militancy. Thus, the Illicit Marketing Index is what sociologists call the test factor or control variable.

Question 5

Having identified the appropriate variables, data in the table can be utilized to verify the hypothesis that there is an association between marihuana use and militancy. Cross-tabulating the frequency of cannabis use by the Political Militancy Index would quickly verify that there is a relationship that is statistically significant at the $< .001$ level (less than one chance in a thousand that it happened by random). In Table 15 the original, or two-way, relationship between the independent and dependent variable is found in the "Total" column: 3% of the noncannabis users, 14% of the irregular users, and 24% of the regular cannabis users are high on the Political Militancy Index. More important than the level of significance is the strength of the relationship that could be measured by such statistics as chi square or gamma. However, the present study utilizes what is probably the simplest measure of the strength of an association: the percent difference. The percent difference is abbreviated "% diff." in the tables that follow and $\%Y$ (where Y is a symbol for the dependent variable) in the graphs in the text (see footnote of Graph 4.3).

With linear variables, the percent difference is usually computed for one category of the dependent variable (high on militancy) by subtracting extreme categories of the independent variable. Thus, the militancy of regular minus noncannabis users provides a 21% (24%-3%) difference. This difference indicates that regular cannabis users are 21% more likely to be militant than noncannabis users. However, most graphs in tables for Chapters 7-10 are somewhat unusual because of the test factor, the Illicit Marketing Index. The general purpose of these tables is to demonstrate that drug buying and selling is more important than marihuana use in determining militancy and other dependent variables. But nonmarihuana users cannot be compared with users, because almost all buyers and sellers use cannabis. There were only nineteen noncannabis users who bought or sold drugs. Thus, we must compare the militancy of regular versus irregular cannabis users, and exclude from consideration all noncannabis users (eliminate the first row).

The data show that regular users are 10% (% diff. = 24%-14%) more likely than irregular cannabis users to be high on political militancy. This 10% difference is entered in the "% diff." row, "total" column (the 10 before the slash). This percent difference summarizes the strength of the two-way relationship between the independent and dependent variable.

Question 6

It is important to ask why marihuana is linked to militancy. Is it because of some inherent quality of marihuana or some other factor? Normally a researcher would hold constant several other factors such as sex, race, socioeconomic status, and political beliefs in an attempt to disprove the relationship, with only those factors having the greatest effect being reported. Having held constant such factors, we find that drug buying or selling is an important factor in marihuana-militancy association.

To show that a third factor, and not marihuana use, is responsible for militancy, we hold constant the Illicit Marketing Index. To hold constant this test variable, we separate our cannabis users into five subgroups: those who have neither bought cannabis nor sold drugs ("none"), those who have only bought cannabis ("buy cannabis"), those who have sold cannabis ("sell cannabis"), those who have sold one or two hard drugs ("1-2"), and those who have sold three or more hard drugs ("3+"). Within each subgroup, the militancy of regular versus irregular cannabis users is compared. In the first subgroup, nonbuyers and nonsellers, we find that regular cannabis users are 3% (10%-7%) more likely than irregular users to be militant. Among cannabis buyers the difference between regular and irregular users is 3% (17%-14%); among cannabis sellers, a 2% (20%-18%) difference; among sellers of one or two hard drugs, a − 1% difference (29%-30%); and among sellers of three or more drugs, a 2% difference (34%-32%). Each of these percent differences are placed in the "% diff." row and the appropriate column for each subgroup. Another observation from these data shows that regular marihuana users who are not involved in drug selling are considerably less likely to be militant (10%, 17% vs. 30%, 33%) than irregular cannabis users who sell hard drugs.

There is a simple statistic to summarize these percent differences for each of the five subgroups; this statistic is called the average percent difference (APD). This is computed by adding the percent differences from each of the subgroups and dividing by the number of subgroups. In this example, we add the five subgroup percent differences in the "% diff." row and divide by 5. Thus,

$$\text{APD/Illicit Marketing Index} = \frac{3 + 3 + 2 + (-1) + 2}{5} = 1.8 \text{ (rounded to 2)}.$$

Question 7

This APD means that the frequency of marihuana use has an effect of 2% upon militancy when holding constant (symbolized by a slash) the Illicit Marketing Index. The APD is entered after a slash to the right of the original relationship. The cell 10/2 facilitates comparison between the two-way relationship and the same relationship when a third factor is held constant. Thus, the original relationship found that regular users were 10% more likely than irregular cannabis users to be militant; but this marihuana-militancy relationship is reduced to an average of 2% when drug buying and selling are held constant. In short, the effect of cannabis use upon militancy is reduced by 80% $[(10 - 2)/10 = 8/10]$ from its original strength, when drug buying and selling is taken into account.

Another way to understand the meaning of the APD is that the independent variable (marihuana use) has an independent or direct effect of 2% upon the dependent variable (militancy) when the test factor (Illicit Marketing Index) is held constant. Hence, marihuana use has a very minor direct effect upon militancy. Generally, a reduction of half to two-thirds of the original relationship is sufficient to conclude that the effect of an independent variable upon a dependent variable is greatly diminished when the test factor is held constant.

Question 8

If marihuana use is not an important factor in political militancy, why is it strongly associated with militancy? The answer to this question is clear; there is a strong relationship between the Illicit Marketing Index and militancy. First, we change around the independent variable and test factor so that the Illicit Marketing Index becomes the independent variable and cannabis use becomes the test factor. In the "Total" row, we find the two-way relationship between the Illicit Marketing Index and political militancy. Militancy increases with each level of drug buying or selling; students selling three or more hard drugs are 26% (% diff. = 33%-7%) more likely than nonbuyers and nonsellers to be high on political militancy. This 26% difference is entered in the "% diff." column, "total" row to the left of the slash. Next we hold marihuana use constant in an attempt to affect this relationship. We divide our cannabis users into regular and irregular using groups. In the "irregular" row, we find that sellers of three or more drugs are 25% (32%-7%) more likely than nonbuyers and nonsellers to be militant; in the "regular" cannabis use row, we find that three-or-more hard-drug sellers are 24% (34%-10%) more likely than nonbuyers and nonsellers to be militant. These two percent differences are entered in the "% diff." column and the APD computed.

$$\text{APD/Marihuana Use} = \frac{25 + 24}{2} = 24.5 \text{ (rounded to 25)}$$

This APD is entered to the right of the slash. The 26/25 cell shows that the original relationship (26% difference) between illicit marketing and militancy is not affected (APD = 25) when marihuana use is held constant. Hence, the major factor affecting political militancy is drug buying or selling and not marihuana use. In addition, the reason that marihuana use is highly correlated with militancy is because cannabis use and drug selling are correlated.

Question 9

The above conclusion becomes even more clear when the direct effect of cannabis use and drug selling is compared. If the APD's are considered as pure numbers that have been computed in a similar manner, the independent effect of the Illicit Marketing Index upon militancy is about twelve times greater than the independent effect of marihuana use upon militancy (APD's of 25 versus 2).

Once results such as this have been obtained, a researcher must attempt to understand theoretically why the Illicit Marketing Index is so strongly related to political militancy. A theory of increasing drug-subculture participation is the explanation presented in the text for this intriguing result. Indeed, without this explanation the link between drug selling and a wide variety of factors appears to be almost nonsensical.

PRESENTATION OF TABLES IN THIS APPENDIX

The above example of multivariate analysis is typical of the majority of tables in this appendix; however, many tables upon which graphs in the text are based have not been presented. There are three basic reasons for not including these tables in this appendix. First, the data presented in the text may be virtually complete, as is true of two-way relationships presented in Graphs 2.1, 3.1-2, and 4.1 and tables presented in the text. Second, in Graphs 4.2, 4.4, and 7.1 our argument does not try to demonstrate that one variable is more important than another, so detailed tables have not been presented.

But most importantly, many three-way tables are not presented because they can be easily constructed from data given in the graphs combined with information given in the text (as with Graph 4.3) or with data given in Table 24 (for Chapters 7-10). The following discussion demonstrates how the interested reader can develop such three-way tables from Table 24 and graphs in Chapters 8-10). Suppose one wished to develop a three-way table examining why persons were contacted by police for drug violations: because of their marihuana use or actual involvement in selling drugs. Information in Graph 10.2 (top chart) would provide most of the information needed.

The following steps will provide sufficient information to construct Table 16. In the table each of these steps is identified in small letters.

(a) Devise a title for the table that states clearly the dependent variable, independent variable, and test factor(s).

(b) Construct the "shell" of the table; devise the row and column headings for the table and appropriate categories for the independent and test variables.

(c) In this example, from Graph 10.2 take information from the "original relationship" and place it in the "total" column of the table. In the graph, the height of each bar is the percent to be entered in the appropriate cell of the table, while the number at the bottom of the bar should be entered in parentheses underneath the percentage; this is the number of cases upon which the percentage is based.

Table 16. Percent having contact with police for drug violation by cannabis use holding constant illicit marketing[a]

| Frequency of Cannabis Use[b] | Illicit Marketing Index[b] | | | | | | % diff. (3+Hard−None) |
| | Cannabis | | Sell Hard Drugs | | | | |
	None	Buy	Sell	1-2	3+	Total	
None						0.6 [c]	[i]
						(1567)	
Irregular	1	4	5	9	31 [d]	4	30
	(526)	(425)	(196)	(86)	(48)	(1281)	
Regular	0	3	7	22	27	15	27
	(30)	(131)	(174)	(161)	(146)	(642)	
Total [e]	1	3	6	17	28	7	27/29
	(556)	(556)	(370)	(247)	(194)	(1923)	
% diff. (reg.−none)	−1	−1	2	13	−4 [g]	f_{11} [f] / 2^h [h]	

(*d*) From Graph 10.2 take the percentage and base number of cases for each combination of the independent variable and test factor and place it in the appropriate columns of the table. For example, the two rightmost bars in Graph 10.2 should go in the fifth column, second and third rows of Table 16.

(*e*) Then, from Table 24 enter the two-way relationship between the Illicit Marketing Index and the dependent variable (police contact for drug violation); the number of cases comes from the top row of Table 24. This information provides data that can be utilized to compute percentage differences and average percentage differences.

(*f*) Next, the percent difference for the two-way relationship between marihuana use and police contact is computed (15%-4% = 11%) and entered in the "total" column, "% diff." row. (Remember that the noncannabis users have been excluded because they do not buy or sell.)

(*g*) Then compute the percent differences due to the frequency of cannabis use among each of the subgroups of buyers and sellers. For example, among those selling one or two hard drugs, regular users are 13% (22%-9%) more likely than irregular cannabis users to have police contact for drugs. Enter 13 in the % diff. row.

(*h*) Compute the average percent difference:

$$\text{APD/Illicit Marketing} = \frac{-1 + (-1) + 2 + 13 + (-4)}{5} = \frac{9}{5} = 1.8 \text{ (rounded to 2)}$$

and place to the right of a slash next to the two-way relationship so that a direct comparison of the original and controlled relationship can be made.

(*i*) Next repeat steps *f-h* while treating the Illicit Marketing Index as the independent variable and marihuana use as the test factor. (Subtract numbers in the first column from those in the fifth column for each row except the noncannabis users.) Finally, interpret the results as discussed above.

Following the steps outlined in this appendix will permit the reader to utilize more fully the data presented in the following tables.

REFERENCES

1. Gerhard Lenski, *The Religious Factor*, Garden City, N.Y.: Anchor, 1961, pp. 367-376.
2. Richard Blum and Associates, *The Dream Sellers*, San Francisco: Jossey-Bass, 1972, pp. 123, 133, 149, count the number of significant differences but do not explain the theoretical usefulness of such data or findings.
3. Lenski, Ref. 1, p. 368.
4. Paul F. Lazarsfeld and Morris Rosenberg, *The Language of Social Research*, New York: Free Press, 1955, pp. 115-124. Herbert H. Hyman, *Survey Design and Analysis*, New York: Free Press, 1955, pp. 242-329.
5. Morris Rosenberg, *The Logic of Survey Analysis*, New York: Basic Books, 1968. Hans Zeisel, *Say It With Figures*, 5th ed., revd., New York: Harper & Row, 1968, pp. 118-189.

Table 17. Comparison of drug-use trends in the national college population with drug-use trends in the present study based upon student memory of drug use in high school

National College Student Samples; Percent of College Students Ever Using Various Drugs at Different Dates

Drug	Gallup[a] Spring 1967	May 1969	Newsweek[b] Nov. 1969	Groves[c] Spring 1970	Gallup[a] Dec. 1970	Schafer[d] Oct. 1971	Gallup[e] Dec. 1971
Marihuana and/or hashish	5	22	32	31	42	44	51
LSD or other hallucinogens	1	4	8	9	14		18
Amphetamines (non-medical use)			12	$-\ ^f$	14		15
Barbiturates (non-medical use)		10	14	$-\ ^f$	16		22
Cocaine							7
Heroin				0.6			1.5

Data from Present Drug Survey, Spring 1970

Percent ever using various drugs before high school graduation by present college status (indicator of year of h. s. graduation)

Present College Status: Drugs H.S. Graduate in June:	Grad. Student + Seniors 1966	Juniors 1967	Sophomores 1968	Freshmen 1969	Freshmen[g] in Spring 1970
Marihuana or Hashish	9	14	21	34	53
Hallucinogens	1	2	3	9	18
Illicit use of pre-scription drugs	4	5	9	14	19
Cocaine or heroin	0.5	1.2	1.6	3.4	9
Number of cases	(555)	(755)	(1122)	(973)	(973)

[a]*U.S. News and World Report*, "Drugs on Campus, A 'Remarkable' Increase" Feb. 1, 1971, p. 27.

[b]"The New Mood on Campus," *Newsweek*, Dec. 29, 1969, p. 44.

[c]W. E. Groves, P. H. Rossi, and D. Grafstein, "Study of Life Styles and Campus Communities," Baltimore: Johns Hopkins University, Dec. 1970, p. 4.

[d]National Commission on Marihuana and Drug Abuse (The Shafer Commission), *Marihuana—A Signal of Misunderstanding*, Washington, D.C.: Government Printing Office, 1972, p. 33.

[e]Linda Charlton, "Gallup Finds a Continued Rise in the Use of Marijuana and LSD on Campus," *New York Times*, Feb. 10, 1972.

[f]Groves reports that 33% of the nation's students have used pills for both medical and nonmedical reasons.

[g]This column reports the level of drug use among freshmen in the spring of 1970 and should be compared to their reported drug use in June 1969 as a rough indication of the growth in drug use due to attendance at college and the growing use of drugs in the whole youth population.

Table 18. Percent using cannabis before high school graduation
by year in college (as indicator of year of h.s. graduation),
holding constant Peer Culture Index and race–sex

Peer Culture Index[b]	Race/Sex	Freshman	Sophomore	Junior	Grad & Senior	Total	% diff. ('69-'66)
			Year of H.S. Graduation				
		1969	1968	1967	1966		
Total Sample:		34	21	14	9	21	25
		(970)	(1112)	(752)	(551)	(3385)[a]	
None	White	24	16	8	5	14	19
	Males	(106)	(166)	(108)	(80)	(460)	
	White	14	9	5	2	8	12
	Females	(174)	(218)	(132)	(119)	(643)	
	Blacks	15	11	20	14	15	1
		(46)	(37)	(15)	(7)	(105)	
	Total	17	12	7	3	11	14
		(326)	(421)	(255)	(206)	(1208)	
Some	White	38	25	16	12	25	26
	Males	(168)	(176)	(138)	(98)	(580)	
	White	37	17	7	7	20	30
	Females	(190)	(184)	(107)	(100)	(581)	
	Blacks	29	16	35	0	21	29
		(24)	(38)	(17)	(7)	(86)	
	Total	37	21	13	9	22	28
		(382)	(398)	(262)	(205)	(1247)	
Much	White	55	36	23	20	36	35
	Males	(134)	(173)	(140)	(84)	(531)	
	White	42	35	17	8	29	34
	Females	(118)	(110)	(87)	(52)	(367)	
	Blacks	50	50	38	75	50	-25
		(10)	(10)	(8)	(4)	(32)	
	Total	49	37	21	17	34	32
		(262)	(293)	(235)	(140)	(930)	

[a]The number of cases is considerably less than 3498 because persons who did not indicate their race, sex, or year in college, or were special students have been excluded. Graduate students have been combined with the H.S. class of 1966.

[b]See Chapter 3 for the definition of the Peer Culture Index.

*Table 19. Percent selling cannabis by frequency of cannabis use,
holding constant theoretically important variables*

Variables Held Constant	None	Less than Monthly	Less than Weekly	Weekly or more	Total	% diff. (> Wk. − None)
Total Sample:	1	10	41	72	22	71
Contact with law for drug violation						
Never	1	10	40	69	20	68 } 75
Stopped or arrested	10[a]	14[a]	65	91	72	81 }
% diff. (Stopped−None)	9	4	25	22	52/20	
Contact with law for traffic violation						
Never	1	10	33	66	17	65 }
Stopped or	1	10	50	78	31	77 } 74
arrested	3	13	56	84	38	81 }
% diff. (Stopped−None)	2	3	23	18	21/11	
Increased Benefits Index						
None	1	9	33	65	13	64 }
Some	1	10	43	70	25	69 } 71
Much	3	15	57	84	53	81 }
% diff. (Much−None)	2	6	24	19	40/13	
Exposure to hallucinogen users						
None	1	7	26	48	5	47 }
Friend	1	7	42	59	19	58 } 60
Intimate	4	20	48	78	51	74 }
% diff. (Intimate−None)	3	13	22	30	46/17	
Hip Life Style Index						
None	1	7	30	49	8	48 }
Some	2	11	37	68	25	66 } 65
Much	3	17	58	84	54	81 }
% diff. (Much−None)	2	10	28	35	46/19	

Frequency of Cannabis Use

Table 19. Percent selling cannabis by frequency of cannabis use, holding constant theoretically important variables — Continued

Variables Held Constant	None	Frequency of Cannabis Use			Total	% diff. (> Wk. − None)
		Less than Monthly	Less than Weekly	Weekly or more		
Total Sample:	1	10	41	72	22	71
Crime Index						
None	1	8	35	67	16	66 ⎫
Some	2	15	47	77	34	75 ⎬ 73
Much	3	17	64	81	48	78 ⎭
% diff. (Much−None)	2	9	29	14	32/14	
Race						
Black	1	13	43	55	18	54 ⎫ 64
White	1	10	43	74	23	73 ⎭
% diff. (White−Black)	0	−3	0	19	5/4	
Sex						
Female	1	9	34	60	14	59 ⎫ 69
Male	1	12	48	80	31	79 ⎭
% diff. (Male−Female)	0	3	14	20	17/9	

[a]The number of cases upon which percentages are based is less than thirty.

Table 20. Involvement in selling each hard drug by the use of that hard drug, holding constant the purchase or sale of cannabis

	Purchase or Sale of Cannabis			Total	% diff. (Sell − None)
	None	Buy	Sell		
Sedative use	Percent selling sedatives				
Never	.1	0	3	.4	3
	(1547)	(313)	(277)	(2137)	
Marginal	.2	2	7	2	7
	(488)	(190)	(201)	(879)	
Illicit: less than monthly	0	2	27	17	27
	(48)	(53)	(152)	(253)	
Illicit: monthly or more	3	16	61	45	58
	(31)	(38)	(153)	(222)	
Total	.1	2	20	5	20/32
	(2114)	(594)	(783)	(3491)	
% diff. (monthly or more−none)	3	16	58	45/26	
Amphetamine use	Percent selling amphetamines				
Never	0	.6	1.8	.3	1.8
	(1752)	(324)	(214)	(2290)	
Marginal	1	2	17	6	16
	(298)	(162)	(216)	(676)	
Illicit: less than monthly	0	5	38	25	38
	(38)	(66)	(183)	(287)	
Illicit: monthly or more	4	14	68	51	64
	(26)	(42)	(170)	(238)	
Total	.1	3	29	7	29/27
	(2114)	(594)	(783)	(3491)	
% diff. (monthly or more−none)	4	13	66	51/26	
Methedrine use	Percent selling methedrine				
Never	0	.2	1.6	.3	1.6
	(2063)	(506)	(433)	(3002)	
Marginal	0	0	16	9	16
	(27)	(49)	(96)	(172)	
Illicit: less than monthly	11	3	38	32	28
	(9)	(33)	(183)	(225)	
Illicit: monthly or more	0	0	65	59	65
	(3)	(3)	(68)	(74)	
Total	.1	.3	17	4	17/38
	(2114)	(594)	(783)	(3491)	
% diff. (monthly or more−none)	0	0	63	59/21	

Table 20. Involvement in selling each hard drug by the use of that hard drug, holding constant the purchase or sale of cannabis — Continued

	Purchase or Sale of Cannabis			Total	% diff. (Sell — None)
	None	Buy	Sell		
Hallucinogen use	Percent selling hallucinogens				
Never	.1	.2	8	.9	8
	(2064)	(452)	(298)	(2814)	
Less than monthly	0	5	41	28	41
	(44)	(115)	(284)	(443)	
Monthly or more	33	15	83	74	50
	(6)	(27)	(201)	(234)	
Total	.1	2	39	9	39/33
	(2114)	(594)	(783)	(3491)	
% diff. (monthly or more—none)	33	15	75	73/41	
Cocaine use	Percent selling cocaine				
Never	0	0	1	.2	1
	(2084)	(552)	(595)	(3231)	
Less than monthly	5	6	16	13	11
	(22)	(36)	(169)	(227)	
Monthly or more	0	33	53	36	53
	(8)	(6)	(19)	(33)	
Total	.1	.7	6	1	6/22
	(2114)	(594)	(783)	(3491)	
% diff. (monthly or more—none)	0	33	52	36/28	
Heroin use	Percent selling heroin				
Never	.1	0	1	.3	1
	(2101)	(578)	(666)	(3345)	
Less than monthly	0	0	16	14	16
	(6)	(11)	(92)	(109)	
Monthly or more	0	60	68	54	68
	(7)	(5)	(25)	(37)	
Total	.1	.5	5	1	5/28
	(2114)	(594)	(783)	(3491)	
% diff. (monthly or more—none)	0	60	67	53/42	

Table 21. Percent using heroin by frequency of cannabis use, holding constant indicators of the euphoria theory, increased benefits theory, and subculture theory

	Frequency of Cannabis Use					(Wk.+— None) % diff.
	None	<Monthly	<Weekly	Weekly +	Total	
Total	.3	1	5	17	4	16
	(1567)	(725)	(559)	(646)	(3497)	
Euphoria Index						
No	.4	2	5	20	3	19 ⎫
	(968)	(280)	(140)	(119)	(1507)	⎬ 17
Yes	0.0	.4	5	16	5	16 ⎭
	(599)	(445)	(419)	(527)	(1990)	
% diff. (yes—no)	-.4	-1.6	0	-4	2/-1.5	
Increased Benefits Index						
None	.4	.5	5	18	3	17 ⎫
	(901)	(350)	(196)	(164)	(1611)	
Some	.0	2	5	16	5	16 ⎬ 17
	(594)	(323)	(291)	(318)	(1526)	
Much	.0	0.0	7	17	9	17 ⎭
	(72)	(52)	(72)	(164)	(360)	
% diff. (much—none)	-.4	-.5	2	-1	6/0	
Peer-Group Cannabis Use Index						
Few	.0	.6	0	8	.2	8 ⎫
	(1050)	(154)	(29)	(12)	(1245)	
Some	.3	1	2	5	1	5 ⎬ 10
	(332)	(278)	(163)	(81)	(854)	
Most	0.0	.8	7	18	9	18 ⎭
	(129)	(257)	(348)	(509) ·	(1243)	
% diff. (most—few)	.0	.2	7	10	9/4	
Illicit Marketing Index						
Not buy/sell	.3	.9	0	10	.4	10 ⎫
	(548)	(428)	(98)	(30)	(2104)	
Buy cannabis	.0	1	1	4	2	4 ⎬ 12
	(3)	(214)	(211)	(131)	(559)	
Sell cannabis	.0	2	1	5	3	5
	(9)	(62)	(134)	(174)	(379)	
Sell hard drugs	.0	.0	24	28	25	28 ⎭
	(7)	(20)	(114)	(307)	(448)	
% diff. (sell hard drugs-/ not buy/sell)	-.3	-.2	24	18	25/10	

Table 22. Percent using various hard drugs by frequency of cannabis use, holding constant exposure to friends using hard drugs

	Frequency of Cannabis Use				Total	% diff.
	None	<Monthly	<Weekly	Weekly+		
Exposure to heroin			Percent using heroin			
None	.3	.5	1	5	1	5
	(1422)	(577)	(354)	(318)	(2671)	
Friend	.0	1.8	10	12	7	12
	(107)	(108)	(132)	(174)	(521)	
Intimate	.0	5.0	18	45	28	45
	(38)	(40)	(73)	(154)	(305)	
Total	.3	1.0	5	17	4	17/21
	(1567)	(725)	(559)	(646)	(3497)	
% diff. (intimate−none)	−.3	4.5	17	40	27/15	
Exposure to hallucinogens			Percent using hallucinogens			
None	.2	6	18	33	4	33
	(1178)	(333)	(131)	(55)	(1697)	
Friend	.0	7	20	43	13	43
	(260)	(215)	(125)	(115)	(715)	
Intimate	2.0	13	43	78	48	76
	(129)	(177)	(303)	(476)	(1085)	
Total	.3	8	32	68	19	68/51
	(1567)	(725)	(559)	(646)	(3497)	
% diff. (intimate−none)	1.8	7	25	45	44/20	
Exposure to sedatives			Percent illicitly using sedatives			
None	2	3	8	11	4	9
	(1129)	(390)	(218)	(170)	(1907)	
Friend	2	10	17	31	13	29
	(251)	(167)	(121)	(141)	(680)	
Intimate	8	11	38	60	35	52
	(187)	(168)	(220)	(335)	(910)	
Total	2	7	22	41	14	39/30
	(1567)	(725)	(559)	(646)	(3497)	
% diff. (intimate−none)	6	8	30	49	31/23	

Table 22. Percent using various hard drugs by frequency of cannabis use, holding constant exposure to friends using hard drugs — Continued

	Frequency of Cannabis Use				Total	% diff.
	None	<Monthly	<Weekly	Weekly+		
Exposure to amphetamines	Percent illicitly using amphetamines					
None	.6	4	11	19	4	18
	(1222)	(399)	(197)	(138)	(1956)	
Friend	1.0	8	14	34	13	33
	(208)	(178)	(120)	(132)	(638)	
Intimate	6.0	20	42	63	42	57
	(137)	(148)	(242)	(376)	(903)	
Total	1.0	8	25	48	15	47/36
	(1567)	(725)	(559)	(646)	(3497)	
% diff. (intimate—none)	5.4	16	31	44	38/24	
Exposure to methedrine	Percent illicitly using methedrine					
None	.2	.5	6	12	2	12
	(1267)	(417)	(224)	(181)	(2089)	
Friend	.5	3.0	9	23	8	22
	(197)	(177)	(160)	(144)	(678)	
Intimate	.0	3.0	25	50	29	50
	(103)	(131)	(175)	(321)	(730)	
Total	.2	2	13	33	9	33/26
	(1567)	(725)	(559)	(646)	(3497)	
% diff. (intimate—none)	-.2	2.5	19	38	27/15	
Exposure to cocaine	Percent using cocaine					
None	1	2	5	11	3	10
	(1455)	(587)	(364)	(286)	(2692)	
Friend	2	4	12	17	11	15
	(89)	(89)	(111)	(156)	(445)	
Intimate	0	6	33	54	39	54
	(23)	(49)	(84)	(204)	(360)	
Total	1	2	11	26	7	26/26
	(1567)	(725)	(559)	(646)	(3497)	
% diff. (intimate—none)	-1	4	28	43	37/25	

Table 23. *Percent having intimates using heroin or hallucinogens by the frequency of cannabis use, holding constant the illicit marketing index*

Frequency of Cannabis Use	Illicit Marketing Index				% diff. (Hard − Buy)	Not Buy or Sell[b]
	Cannabis		Sell Hard Drugs	Total[c]		
	Buy	Sell				
Percent with heroin-using intimates						
Less than monthly	4	16	25	8	21	4
	(214)	(62)	(20)	(296)		(428)
Less than weekly	8	12	31	15	23	6
	(211)	(134)	(114)	(459)		(98)
Weekly and more	8	13	36	24	28	27
	(131)	(174)	(307)	(612)		(30)
Total (all cannabis users in drug market)	7	13	34	17	28/24	5
	(556)	(370)	(441)	(1367)		(556)
% diff. (weekly+−monthly)	4	−3	11	16/4		
Noncannabis users	0	0	14	5		2.4
	(3)	(9)	(7)	(19)		(1548)
Percent with hallucinogen-using intimates[a]						
Less than monthly	21	44	55	28	34	22
Less than weekly	46	53	75	55	29	50
Weekly and more	58	66	88	75	30	47
Total (all cannabis users in drug market)	39	57	83	58	44/31	28
% diff. (weekly+−monthly)	37	22	33	47/31		
Noncannabis users	0	33	29	26		9

[a]Number of cases upon which these percentages are based are the same as for heroin-using intimates.

[b]Persons who have not purchased or sold drugs have been eliminated from computations of percentage differences because of an editing error that mistakenly classified respondents who left blank the questions on drug purchase or sale as never buying or selling.

[c]In Graph 6.4, the "original relationship" combines the information given in the "Total" and the "Not Buy or Sell" column of this table. Thus, the two way relationship between cannabis use and having intimates using hard drugs is somewhat greater in the graph than in this table (percent differences: 18 versus 16 for heroin, 50 versus 47 for hallucinogens).

Table 24. Relationship between the Illicit Marketing Index and various dependent variables used in Chapters 7-10

Various Dependent Variables	Illicit Marketing Index					Total	% diff. (Sell 3+ Hard − None)
	None	Cannabis		Sell Hard Drugs			
		Buy	Sell	1-2	3+		
Number of Cases[a]	556	556	370	247	194	1923	
Dependent variables from Chapter 7							
Percent high on Hip Life Style Index	12	25	36	52	64	31	52
Percent high on Increased Benefits Index	7	10	17	28	31	15	24
Percent high on Euphoria Index	65	72	79	82	82	72	17
Dependent variables from Chapter 8							
Percent high on Political Militancy Index	7	15	19	29	33	17	26
Percent high on Aggressiveness Index	12	16	18	21	34	18	22
Percent high on Auto Deviance Index	18	24	22	32	45	25	27
Percent high on Crime Index	7	10	15	25	37	15	30
Percent sexually permissive Males	12	14	16	31	32	19	20
	(220)	(295)	(227)	(158)	(153)	(1062)	
Females	5	9	16	27	33	12	28
	(324)	(258)	(140)	(87)	(41)	(850)	
Dependent variables from Chapter 9							
Percent with Grades of C or less	35	42	38	45	45	39	10
Percent high on the Leave College Index	16	16	18	23	31	19	15
Percent high on the College Deviance Index	11	15	16	24	29	17	18

Table 24. Relationship between the Illicit Marketing Index and various dependent variables used in Chapters 7-10 — Continued

| Various Dependent Variables | Illicit Marketing Index | | | | | Total | % diff. (Sell 3+ Hard — None) |
| | Cannabis | | | Sell Hard Drugs | | | |
	None	Buy	Sell	1-2	3+		
Dependent variable from Chapter 10							
Percent stopped or arrested by police for drug violation	1	3	6	17	28	7	27
Number of cases[b]	627	556	370	249	195	1997	
Total number of cases[c]	2104	559	379	252	196	3490	

[a]The information in this table can be used to construct three-way tables as suggested earlier in this appendix. There are basically three different sets of tables that can be developed. This number of cases should be used to construct three-way tables when the independent variable is the frequency of cannabis use. This excludes 19 noncannabis users who have bought or sold drugs plus 1548 noncannabis users who have not bought or sold. Thus, the percentages in this table should be entered in the "total" row with the base number of cases given at the top of this table. This data should be used in conjunction with Graphs 7.2, 8.1, 8.3, and 9.1 and the top chart of Graph 10.2.

[b]This number of cases should be used to construct three-way tables when the independent variable is the Multiple Drug Use Index. Excluded are 16 nondrug users who have bought or sold drugs plus 1477 nondrug users who have not bought or sold. The difference between this information and footnote *a* is that there are 74 noncannabis users who have illicitly used some other hard drug (mainly pills); only 3 of these persons have sold drugs. Thus, 71 additional cases have been added to the "not buy/sell" category of the Illicit Marketing Index. Inclusion of these additional cases does not alter the percentages in the "none" column by more than 2%. This number of cases should be entered in the "total" row in conjunction with data in Graphs 8.2, 8.4, and 9.2, and the bottom chart of Graph 10.2.

[c]This number of cases includes all persons in the sample, with the exception of the 7 excluded in Chapter 5. Included are all noncannabis and nondrug users. This information should be used to construct three-way tables when the independent variable is not the Frequency of Cannabis Use Index or the Multiple Drug Use Index such as the data presented in Graph 10.3.

Table 25. *Percent high on various measures of unconventional behavior by Frequency of Cannabis Use, holding constant the Illicit Marketing Index and the Peer Culture Index*

| Peer Culture Index | Frequency of Cannabis Use | Illicit Marketing Index | | | | | Total | % diff. (Sell 3+ Hard − None) |
| | | None | Cannabis | | Sell Hard Drugs | | | |
			Buy	Sell	1-2	3+		
A. Percent high on Crime Index (sample = 11%)								
None	None	2	$(50)^a$				3	--
Some	None	4	$(9)^a$				4	--
High	None	13	$(17)^a$				13	--
Total	None	5	$(16)^a$				5	--
	Irregular	1	4	6	0^a	9^a	3	8
None	Regular	9^a	11	10	13	9^a	11	0
	Total	1	6	8	9	9	5	8/4
	% diff.	8	7	4	13	0	8/6	
	Irregular	6	5	9	21^a	57^a	8	51
Some	Regular	0^a	5	16	15	28	15	28
	Total	6	5	12	16	35	10	29/39
	% diff.	–6	0	7	–6	–29	7/–7	
	Irregular	18	20	16	48^a	39^a	23	21
High	Regular	11^a	28	27	37	48	35	37
	Total	17	23	22	41	46	28	32/29
	% diff.	–7	8	11	–11	7	12/2	
% diff. (due to Peer Culture Index; high–none)	Irregular	17	17	10	48	30	20/24	
	Regular	2	17	17	22	20	24/18	
B. Percent high on Auto Deviance Index (sample = 20%)								
None	None	6	0^a				6	--
Some	None	16	27^a				16	--
High	None	31	33^a				31	--
Total	None	14	26^a				14	--

Table 25. *Percent high on various measures of unconventional behavior by Frequency of Cannabis Use, holding constant the Illicit Marketing Index and the Peer Culture Index* — Continued

Peer Culture Index	Frequency of Cannabis Use	Illicit Marketing Index					Total	% diff. (Sell 3+ Hard − None)
			Cannabis		Sell Hard Drugs			
		None	Buy	Sell	1-2	3+		
None	Irregular	8	12	2	13^a	55^a	10	47
	Regular	0^a	19	10	10	23	14	23
	Total	8	14	5	11	33	11	25/35
	% diff.	−8	7	8	−3	−31	4/-5	
Some	Irregular	20	22	28	34^a	29^a	23	9
	Regular	10^a	5	23	20	38	21	28
	Total	20	18	25	25	36	22	16/19
	% diff.	−10	−17	−5	−14	9	-2/-7	
High	Irregular	32	43	35	52^a	57^a	40	25
	Regular	0^a	38	21	46	52	39	52
	Total	30	41	28	48	53	39	23/38
	% diff.	−32	−5	−14	−6	−5	-1/-12	
% diff. (due to Peer Culture Index; high−none)	Irregular	24	31	33	39	2	30/26	
	Regular	0	19	11	36	29	25/19	

C. Percent high on Aggressiveness Index (sample = 13%)

None	None	4	50^a				4	- -
Some	None	8	18^a				9	- -
Much	None	16	17^a				16	- -
Total	None	8	21^a				8	- -
None	Irregular	6	8	9	7^a	18^a	7	12
	Regular	9	14	7	13	18^a	13	9
	Total	6	10	8	11	18	9	12/11
	% diff.	3	6	−2	6	0	6/3	

Table 25. *Percent high on various measures of unconventional behavior by Frequency of Cannabis Use, holding constant the Illicit Marketing Index and the Peer Culture Index — Continued*

| Peer Culture Index | Frequency of Cannabis Use | Illicit Marketing Index | | | | | Total | % diff. (Sell 3+ Hard − None) |
| | | | Cannabis | | Sell Hard Drugs | | | |
		None	Buy	Sell	1-2	3+		
Some	Irregular	11	13	9	31^a	29^a	13	18
	Regular	0^a	5	25	17	26	18	26
	Total	11	11	17	21	26	14	15/22
	% diff.	−11	−8	16	−14	−3	5/-4	
Much	Irregular	20	26	26	26	39	25	19
	Regular	11^a	36	27	29	45	34	34
	Total	20	29	26	27	44	29	24/26
	% diff.	−9	10	1	3	6	9/2	
% diff. (due to Peer Culture Index; high−none)	Irregular	14	18	17	19	21	18/18	
	Regular	2	22	20	16	27	21/17	

D. Percent high on Political Militancy Index (sample = 11%)

Peer Culture Index	Frequency of Cannabis Use	None	Buy	Sell	1-2	3+	Total	% diff.
None	None	2	0^a				2	- -
Some	None	4	0^a				4	- -
High	None	4	17^a				5	- -
Total	None	3	5^a				3	- -
None	Irregular	5	14	11	33^a	27^a	11	22
	Regular	18^a	11	33	28	18^a	22	0
	Total	5	13	19	30	21	14	16/11
	% diff.	13	-3	22	-5	-9	11/4	
Some	Irregular	8	15	22	41^a	36^a	15	28
	Regular	10^a	12	17	24	31	21	21
	Total	8	14	19	29	31	17	23/25
	% diff.	2	-3	-5	-17	-5	6/-5	

Table 25. Percent high on various measures of unconventional behavior by Frequency of Cannabis Use, holding constant the Illicit Marketing Index and the Peer Culture Index — Continued

Peer Culture Index	Frequency of Cannabis Use	Illicit Marketing Index					Total	% diff. (Sell 3+ Hard − None)
		None	Cannabis		Sell Hard Drugs			
			Buy	Sell	1-2	3+		
High	Irregular	8	14	18	21	35[a]	15	27
	Regular	0[a]	25	17	35	39	28	39
	Total	8	17	18	29	38	20	30/33
	% diff.	-8	11	-1	14	4	13/4	
% diff. (due to Peer Culture Index; high−none)	Irregular	3	0	7	-12	8	4/1	
	Regular	-18	14	-16	7	21	6/2	

Number of cases upon which Tables 25 A-D are based

		None		Buy	Sell	1-2	3+	Total
None	None	728	(2)[a]	2	0	0	0	730
Some	None	530	(11)[a]	1	5	3	2	541
Much	None	290	(6)[a]	0	4	2	0	296
Total	None	1548	(19)[a]	3	9	5	2	1567
	Irregular	170		138	47	15	11	381
None	Regular	11		37	30	39	22	139
	Total	181		175	77	54	33	520
	Irregular	220		172	87	29	14	522
Some	Regular	10		41	69	59	39	218
	Total	230		213	156	88	53	740
	Irregular	136		115	62	42	23	378
Much	Regular	9		53	75	63	85	285
	Total	145		168	137	105	108	663

[a]This column is composed of noncannabis users who have bought or sold, and is presented for the reader's information. For example, the 11 cases equals the sum of 1 + 5 + 3 + 2. In Tables 25 A-D, the percent "high" on each index is indicated in a similar bracket column.

Table 25. *Percent high on various measures of unconventional behavior by Frequency of Cannabis Use, holding constant the Illicit Marketing Index and the Peer Culture Index — Continued*

Peer Culture Index	Frequency of Cannabis Use	Illicit Marketing Index				Total	% diff. (Sell Hard-Buy Cannabis)
		None	Cannabis		Sell Hard Drugs[c]		
			Buy	Sell			

E. Percent sexually permissive:
  Males = 14%

Peer Culture Index	Frequency of Cannabis Use	None	Buy	Sell	Sell Hard Drugs[c]	Total	% diff.
None	None	2 (252)	0[a] (2)			2 (254)	- -
Some	None	5 (224)	33[a] (6)			5 (230)	- -
High	None	12 (139)	0[a] (3)			12 (142)	- -
Total	None	5 (615)	18[a] (11)			5 (626)	- -
	Irregular	11 (55)	9 (68)	17 (24)	23[a] (13)	12 (160)	14
None	Regular	20[a] (5)[b]	10[a] (20)	8[a] (24)	34 (41)	21 (90)	24
	Total	12 (60)	9 (88)	13 (48)	31 (54)	15 (250)	22/19
	% diff.	b	1	-9	11	9/1	
	Irregular	7 (94)	12 (90)	16 (50)	40 (30)	14 (264)	28
Some	Regular	0[a] (2)[b]	24[a] (17)	21 (47)	23 (65)	22 (131)	-1
	Total	7 (96)	14 (107)	19 (97)	28 (95)	17 (395)	14/13
	% diff.	b	12	5	-17	8/0	
	Irregular	20 (71)	20 (71)	12 (34)	23 (47)	20 (223)	3
High	Regular	50[a] (2)[b]	14[a] (29)	19 (48)	37 (115)	29 (194)	23
	Total	21 (73)	18 (100)	15 (82)	33 (162)	24 (417)	15/13
	% diff.	b	-6	7	14	9/5	

Table 25. *Percent high on various measures of unconventional behavior by Frequency of Cannabis Use, holding constant the Illicit Marketing Index and the Peer Culture Index — Continued*

| Peer Culture Index | Frequency of Cannabis Use | Illicit Marketing Index | | | Sell Hard Drugs[c] | Total | % diff. (Sell Hard — None) |
| | | None | Cannabis | | | | |
			Buy	Sell			
% diff. (due to Peer Culture Index; high—none)	Irregular	9	11	-5	0	8/4	
	Regular	b	4	11	3	8/6	

F. Percent sexually permissive:
  Females = 6%

Peer Culture Index	Frequency of Cannabis Use	None	Buy	Sell	Sell Hard Drugs[c]	Total	% diff. (Sell Hard — None)
None	None	1	0[a]			1	- -
		(465)	(0)			(465)	
Some	None	1	0[a]			1	- -
		(304)	(5)			(309)	
High	None	3	0[a]			3	- -
		(150)	(3)			(153)	
Total	None	1	0[a]			1	- -
		(919)	(8)			(927)	
	Irregular	3	12	14[a]	31[a]	9	28
		(115)	(69)	(22)	(13)	(219)	
None	Regular	0[a]	6[a]	17[a]	35[a]	19	35
		(6)	(16)	(6)	(20)	(48)	
	Total	3	11	14[a]	33	11	30/31
		(121)	(85)	(28)	(33)	(267)	
	% diff.	-3	-6	3	4	10/0	
	Irregular	6	10	14	38[a]	10	32
		(125)	(82)	(36)	(13)	(256)	
Some	Regular	0[a]	4[a]	9[a]	28	14	28
		(8)	(24)	(22)	(32)	(86)	
	Total	6	8	12	31	11	25/30
		(133)	(106)	(58)	(45)	(342)	
	% diff.	6	-6	-5	-10	4/-4	

Table 25. *Percent high on various measures of unconventional behavior by Frequency of Cannabis Use, holding constant the Illicit Marketing Index and the Peer Culture Index — Continued*

Peer Culture Index	Frequency of Cannabis Use	Illicit Marketing Index			Sell Hard Drugs[c]	Total	% diff. (Sell Hard − None)
			Cannabis				
		None	Buy	Sell			
	Irregular	6	9	25^a	18^a	12	12
		(63)	(44)	(28)	(17)	(152)	
High	Regular	14^a	9^a	15^a	27	18	13
		(7)	(23)	(26)	(33)	(89)	
	Total	7	9	20	24	14	17/12
		(70)	(67)	(54)	(50)	(241)	
	% diff.	8	0	-10	9	6/2	
% diff. (due to Peer Culture Index; high−none)	Irregular	3	-3	11	-13	3/1	
	Regular	14	3	12	-8	-1/2	

[a]Number of cases based upon less than 30 cases.

[b]The extremely small (*N*=2) number of cases among regular cannabis using males who don't buy or sell drugs prevents stable percentages. Thus the "not buy/sell" column is excluded from computation of percent differences. Since the *N*'s among females are somewhat higher (6-8) this column is not excluded from percent differences there. (Table 25F)

[c]Because of the small number of cases, those respondents who sold 1-2 hard drugs have been combined with sellers of 3+ drugs into the category of "Sell Hard Drugs."

Table 26. Percent having contact with police for drug violations by illicit marketing index holding constant factors indicating police "labeling"

Variables Held Constant	Illicit Marketing Index						% diff. (Sell 3+ Hard − None)
	None	Cannabis		Sell Hard Drugs			
		Buy	Sell	1-2	3+	Total	
Total Sample	1	3	7	17	28	5	27
	(2105)	(559)	(379)	(252)	(196)	(3490)[b]	
A. Year in college							
Freshmen	1	4	8	24	25	5	24 ⎫
	(587)	(149)	(111)	(71)	(53)	(971)	
Sophomore	1	4	8	13	34	5	33 ⎪
	(683)	(181)	(116)	(79)	(62)	(1121)	⎬27
Junior	1	2	3	12	23	3	22 ⎪
	(451)	(123)	(90)	(44)	(44)	(752)	
Senior	1	2	6	18	31[a]	4	30 ⎭
	(334)	(91)	(54)	(49)	(26)	(554)	
% difference (senior-freshman)	0	−2	−2	−6	6	−1/-1	
B. Family income							
<$7,000	.4	2	3	6[a]	31[a]	2	30 ⎫
	(250)	(46)	(33)	(16)	(13)	(358)	
$7,000-$12,500	1	4	10	18	33	5	32 ⎪
	(728)	(172)	(104)	(73)	(61)	(1138)	⎬26
$12,500-$25,000	1	3	5	14	27	4	26 ⎪
	(652)	(203)	(146)	(94)	(62)	(1157)	
>$25,000	1	3	6	23	18	5	17 ⎭
	(284)	(95)	(72)	(53)	(39)	(543)	
% difference (>$25,000-<$7,000)	0	1	3	17	−13	3/2	
C. Race							
Black	1	5	0[a]	9[a]	20[a]	3	19 ⎫
	(150)	(44)	(27)	(12)	(10)	(243)	⎬24
Whites	1	3	7	18	29	5	28 ⎭
	(1852)	(498)	(341)	(236)	(184)	(3111)	
% difference (whites−blacks)	0	−2	7	9	9	2/5	

Table 26. *Percent having contact with police for drug violations by illicit marketing index holding constant factors indicating police "labeling" — Continued*

| Variables Held Constant | Illicit Marketing Index | | | | | | % diff. (Sell 3+ Hard − None) |
| | None | Cannabis | | Sell Hard Drugs | | Total | |
		Buy	Sell	1-2	3+		
D. Nonblacks by sex							
(White) Females	.3	2	5	14	15	2	14 ⎫
	(1139)	(237)	(133)	(84)	(39)	(1632)	⎬23
(White) Males	1	5	8	20	32	7	31 ⎭
	(806)	(277)	(217)	(155)	(147)	(1602)	
% difference (males−females)	0	3	3	6	17	5/6	
E. No. of premarital sex partners							
None	.5	.6	8	10	12[a]	1.3	11 ⎫
	(1252)	(179)	(88)	(48)	(17)	(1548)	
One	1	6	6	18	26	6	25 ⎬24
	(440)	(189)	(108)	(65)	(57)	(859)	
2-3	3	5	6	26	27	9	24 ⎬
	(176)	(73)	(88)	(57)	(45)	(439)	
4 and more	1	3	5	15	36	11	35 ⎭
	(91)	(66)	(60)	(73)	(64)	(354)	
% difference (4 + − None)	0	3	-3	5	24	10/6	

[a]Percentage based upon less than 30 cases.

[b]The number of cases may not add to this total because persons who did not know or left the questions on sex, race, year in college, unanswered have been excluded.

APPENDIX B
Data Collection Problems

OBTAINING COOPERATION FROM THE SCHOOLS

One of the most important problems in this study was gaining the cooperation of an official at each college who would give permission for the study to proceed. Since the random sample was only of the Ethics Department (pseudonym for a social science department), the researcher first contacted the department chairman who either gave his approval, requested further information (letter from thesis advisor and copies of the questionnaire) or referred the decision to the dean of students.

Table 27 presents the outcome of contacts with the twenty-nine colleges that were ever part of the sampling frame.

Table 27 shows that twenty-one of twenty-five, or 84%, of the contacted colleges participated in the study. Permission was usually obtained easily and quickly from the department chairman (fifteen of seventeen, or 88%) with the deans of students somewhat less willing to cooperate (five of seven, or 71%).

Chairmen who refused did so for the following reasons: One Ethics department chairman at a college in New York City refused because "there is too much use of students as guinea pigs for Ph.D. students who need some data for their thesis." That statement came at the end of a very brief telephone conversation in which the chairman told the researcher to make contact with one member of the department who was doing research on drug use, but that a random sample of classes in the Ethics Department was out of the question. Perhaps contact with the instructor mentioned might have provided access to the department at a later time, but since a very similar college was part of the sample, it was not felt to be crucial that this college be sampled. Another

Table 27. Participation and nonparticipation of colleges that were ever part of sampling frame

	Number of Colleges
Participation	
Department chairman approved study on basis of telephone call	6
Department chairman approved study after obtaining further information	9
Dean of students approved study after obtaining information	5
No official approval obtained; instructors were contacted directly	1
Total colleges participating in study	21
Nonparticipation	
Department chairman refused cooperation	2
Dean of students refused cooperation	2
Total refusals	4
Part of sampling frame, but researcher did not have time to make contact	4
Total colleges not participating	8
Total colleges ever part of sampling frame	29

department chairman at a college outside New York City, after considering the questionnaire with department members and the dean of students, denied cooperation, because the college was planning its own briefer study of drug use on the campus and felt that there would be too much overlap.

The two deans who refused to permit the cooperation of their colleges did so because it was university policy not to allow surveys to take up class time, and this rule applied to their own faculty members as well. The researcher could have distributed questionnaires in classes and had the students return the answer sheets by mail, but this was not done.

At one college permission to conduct the study had been obtained and three classes had completed the questionnaire when a student strike was called to protest the extension of the Vietnam war into Cambodia and the killing of students at Kent State University. This prevented the inclusion of additional classes at the college. There were five other colleges included in the sample, but lack of time to make contact and administer the questionnaire prevented the researcher from ever contacting these schools. Thus, obtaining cooperation from most of the colleges in the sampling frame was relatively easy, and the few refusals did not greatly harm the study.

OBTAINING COOPERATION FROM CLASSROOM INSTRUCTORS

Once the department chairman and/or dean had given his permission to contact instructors, the problem of obtaining access to the college classes themselves arose. Each instructor was contacted by a letter that indicated which class was included in the sample, a suggested date, and a postcard for the teacher to indicate his cooperation or refusal. (The letter and postcard are reproduced on pp. 248 and 249.) Table 28 indicates the rate of refusals and cooperation of all classes that were ever part of the random sample (not including non-Ethics Department classes that were not part of the random sample, where the refusal rate was much higher).

Table 28 shows that cooperation was the most common response. Over 70% of all instructors contacted in the Ethics Department were willing or actually cooperated in the study. Most teachers who refused to cooperate did so on the grounds that they could not spare a whole class hour in the class chosen. Three of the professors who refused suggested one of their other classes as a substitute. The most interesting fact about teacher refusals is that 75% of them occurred after the first six weeks of class. Only 3% of the teachers who were contacted before that time refused. The vast majority of refusals came either during the midterm-exam time or afterwards, when teachers realized how far behind they were in their classes.

Table 28.   Cooperation and noncooperation of randomly sampled classes

	Number of Classes	%
Complete cooperation—allowed questionnaire to be given during a regular class hour	120	71
Partial cooperation—allowed questionnaire to be distributed in class; students completed and returned the answer sheets to researcher	11	6
Teacher refusal—would not allow questionnaire to be given during class hour	15	9
Student (class) refusals—students in the class voted not to take the questionnaire (though the instructor was willing)	3	2
Teacher never replied to letter requesting cooperation of his class	8	5
Instructor not asked for the cooperation of his class even though part of the random sample	7	4
Instructor promised cooperation of class, but the questionnaire was not given because of student strike in May 1970	5	3
Total	169	100

Many of those instructors who refused to set aside a whole hour would have allowed the researcher to distribute the questionnaires to be completed by the students at home. However, at the beginning of the semester the researcher did not permit students to take the questionnaires home because it would have meant lost questionnaires (which were valuable at the time) and a departure from the original research design. Toward the end of the semester, the only way any cooperation from some instructors could be obtained was by distributing the questionnaire in class. Students completed it at home, and returned the answer sheets to the instructor, who sent them to the researcher.

There was a greater tendency for instructors at upper-status (or quality) colleges to refuse either to set aside an hour of class time or to request that students be allowed to take the questionnaires home to complete. But cooperation was still the most frequent response even at these schools.

OBTAINING COOPERATION FROM STUDENTS IN THE CLASSES

The cooperation of students, however, was the most important factor in the success of the study. Most of the classes had been informed ahead of the actual administration of the questionnaire, and many instructors had let the students vote on taking the questionnaire. In some classes an undercurrent of hostility was evident when the class had not been informed beforehand. It would appear that the best way to obtain student consent is to have the instructor inform the students ahead of time and perhaps let the class vote on whether or not to take the questionnaire; in only three classes did the students vote not to take the questionnaire, while probably 30-50 classes voted to take it. However, it is not a good idea for the instructor to announce the exact date for the administration of the questionnaire. It appeared to the instructors that more of the conservative students and also radical students tended to be absent when they knew the questionnaire would be given on a particular day. But in terms of actual response rates and the rate of drug use in various classes, it did not make much difference whether the instructor announced the questionnaire ahead of time or on the day it was administered. The problem of students who stay away from class only to avoid the questionnaire appears to be a relatively minor problem.

A much more serious problem (far more serious than originally anticipated) is the low rate of class attendance at almost all colleges. It appears that a significant number of students either do not attend class at all or do so very irregularly. It is probable that many heavy drug users are among this group of nonattenders, although there are no good statistics to prove or disprove this hypothesis. At the beginning of the study it was anticipated that the rate of nonattendance would be from 15% to 30% on any given day. Experience tends to indicate, however, that the rate of nonattenance in college classes runs from about 20% to 50% with the average class being in the 24%-45% nonattendance range. Further, attendance slips toward the end of the semester. This high rate of nonattendance is the major unknown bias in the study. Almost all classes and colleges in this sample have similar problems of nonattendance but upper-quality colleges appear to have better attendance than medium- and low-quality colleges. Unfortunately, accurate statistics on the number of students registered in each class were not obtained, although it was available from the instructor, so that no accurate estimate of nonparticipation in this study can be made. Nonattendance was probably the most serious defect in the use of college classes as the basic sampling unit.

The main advantage of classroom administration lies in the low rate of direct refusals by students in the class. Of the students attending class on the day that the questionnaire was administered, only 3% either walked out after hearing about the questionnaire, failed to complete the questions on drug use, or handed in a blank answer sheet. Thus 97% of the students present actually completed the questionnaire, or enough of it for their responses to be included in our analysis.

On the whole the present study was reasonably successful in obtaining comparable data for a representative sample of students in the Ethics Department at each of the colleges included in the sample design. The best evidence that the sample was accurate is the small range of differences between colleges on selected variables such as sex, religiosity, sexual activities, drug use, etc. Colleges that are similar in quality or type of control have similar drug-use rates, etc. (Table 2).

NONCOOPERATION OF CLASSES OUTSIDE THE ETHICS DEPARTMENT

Although most of the researcher's time was spent obtaining cooperation from the randomly selected classes in the Ethics Department, he also tried to give the questionnaire in other departments but had little success. The amount of effort required to make and sustain contacts with department chairmen was considerable. In one low-quality college where the dean's permission had been obtained, a serious effort was made to obtain cooperation of nonethics classes. The researcher made contact with department chairmen in mathematics, arts, English, physical education, and business, by telephone or in person. The chairman of the Math Department called and talked to the dean about the study but finally refused to cooperate, because he felt that instructors could not justify setting aside one hour of class for the questionnaire. The Art Department chairman refused to cooperate. The English, physical education, and accounting chairmen took the study under consideration, but none replied positively or

negatively to repeated phone calls. The only cooperation obtained was in the
Data Processing Department. At two other schools, the Physical Education
Department was formally approached. The chairman at one school refused
almost immediately. The chairman at the other college felt that approval from
the dean was necessary. Such permission was eventually obtained and a couple
of physical education classes were sampled. In short, the lack of cooperation in
nonethics classes was great and the little cooperation that did occur was the
result of considerable work; it is doubtful that it was worth the effort. Perhaps
cooperation outside of the Ethics Department might have been higher at the
beginning of the semester and particularly if the questionnaire had been shorter
(five or ten minutes).

OBTAINING A SUBSAMPLE OF HEAVY-DRUG-USING FRIENDS

The original sample design called for a greater proportion of heavy drug users
than would be obtained in the Ethics Department sample. The major technique
for obtaining such heavy drug users was to ask students in all classes surveyed to
take questionnaires to their drug-using friends. While the students were
completing the questionnaire, the researcher would hold up a brown manila
envelope, containing a copy of the questionnaire, three answer sheets, a pencil,
and a stamped self-addressed envelope to be returned to the researcher, and say
to the class, "If you have a friend who has used more than six times either
methedrine, cocaine, LSD, other hallucinogens, or heroin, and you feel quite
certain that he would complete this questionnaire, would you please pick up one
of these brown envelopes which contain all the materials he needs to complete
the questionnaire and return the answer sheet to me." This proved to be both a
beneficial strategy for increasing the number of heavy drug users and a waste of
resources. About 5%-15% of each class picked up the brown envelopes, which
resulted in a total distribution of 400-500 questionnaires. Since there were three
answer sheets in each packet, up to 1500 persons could have responded to the
questionnaire. However, only 165 answer sheets from less than 100 questionnaire packets were received, and so, putting multiple answer sheets in the
packets proved to be a good idea. However, the response rate (25% or less) from
the 400-500 packets handed out was very low. It is not clear why the response
rate was so low, but it is probable that many persons from the classes failed to
get the questionnaire into the hands of drug-using friends. Although the response
rate from all the questionnaires handed out was very unsatisfactory, the persons
who did return the questionnaires were very heavy drug users when compared to
the random sample. Thus, this strategy significantly increased the size of the
heavy-drug-using sample.

CODING AND CHECKING OF RESPONDENT'S ANSWER SHEETS

The respondents marked their answers on a specially printed answer sheet that could be read by an Optical Scanning Machine 100 (at the Teacher's College Computer Center, Columbia University). This machine is very accurate in its sensing of marks; it picks up the slightest mark in the sensing area and converts it into a punch. It does the mark-to-punch conversion with more than 99.5% accuracy. However, it is so sensitive that it will convert well-erased marks into punches; it is almost impossible to erase a mark well enough so that it will not be converted into a punch by the Optical Scanner. Thus, it was necessary for the researcher to eliminate such erasures with Snopake (a white liquid used by typists). At the same time, the researcher examined each answer sheet for obvious lying, extremely inconsistent answers, and for inaccurate answers to single item questions.

From the more than 3500 answer sheets obtained, only 9 had to be eliminated from the active sample. Of these answer sheets 5 were refusals of persons who answered very few questions, or failed to answer the questions on drug use, or several other important questions such as SES, age, sex, etc. Four answer sheets had to be eliminated because of extremely inconsistent answers or what appeared to be random marking of answers. For example, one respondent claimed to be black, male, a conservative jew, sixteen years of age, but had started smoking pot at age eighteen. Another respondent marked that he had used almost every drug with considerable regularity, but at other points in the questionnaire where check questions were asked, he claimed never to have used any drugs. One respondent in an all-male class claimed to be female, fifteen years of age, but had started to use drugs at ages eighteen and nineteen. When a questionnaire was eliminated from the sample because of lying, therefore, the contradictions were obvious ones.

Actually, though, the rate of lying as measured by multiple checks on drug questions appears to have been very low. Contradictions were found in less than 2% of the questionnaires; this could have easily occurred if a few students mistakenly marked the wrong question. The answer sheets discarded from the sample made up less than 0.3% of the number of questionnaires returned, a very low rate of nonusable questionnaires in a self-administered interview.

A more difficult problem was that students did not always mark the questions correctly, and some of the marks they made had to be eliminated in order for the question to be answered properly. For example, the students were asked at what age they had first been involved in certain activities (see questionnaire, questions 42-49). Some students marked several ages for each activity. The researcher eliminated all answers but the youngest age at which a respondent said he had been involved in the activity. Questions on the recency and frequency of drug use (questions 81-87) were supposed to have one answer, but many respondents marked two answers (one for each time period, before and after July 1, 1969), so the researcher kept the most recent use of the drug and eliminated the answer for the period before July 1, 1969.

Thus, the sample actually obtained suffered from several problems that had to be dealt with as efficiently as the limited time and resources available to the researcher permitted. With more resources it might have been possible to adhere more closely to the original sample design. The sample appears to be adequate, however, to measure the intercorrelation of variables. In sum, the sample actually obtained was essentially what was sought.

Dear Professor John Doe,

I am presently involved in research which deals with the use of legal and illegal drugs among students attending several colleges in the New York City area. I would like to obtain your cooperation and the cooperation of your students in aiding me in this important research.

In February or March 1970, I will be administering precoded questionnaires in several classes in your college. The classes have been selected by using a table of random numbers. One of these randomly selected classes is your class of Soc. 50.1B meeting TThF 10 in 207 A.

Since your class was chosen as part of a scientific random sample, it is hoped that you will be able to cooperate. Most students have found participation to be an interesting experience and have willingly cooperated. The questionnaire takes about 40 - 50 minutes to complete.

Since drug use is a controversial issue, I realize that you are concerned about anonymity and confidentiality. I have carefully considered this problem and have devised means of assuring the complete anonymity of all respondents. The accompanying letter will be attached to the questionnaire to assure students of their anonymity.

Your cooperation and that of your students is requested. Would you please indicate on the enclosed card whether you would be able to cooperate in this research and the time which you would prefer. I have indicated a date which would be most convenient for me; if you are unable to cooperate at that date, please indicate a time which would be most convenient for you.

If you have any questions or wish to obtain more information, please make a note on the enclosed card. I will be most happy to supply such information. I have discussed this study with your Department Chairman and have obtained his cooperation. His secretary has copies of the questionnaire if you wish to see it.

Sincerely yours,

Bruce Johnson
Lecturer
Department of Sociology
Barnard College

Phone
   Days   - 280 - 2159.

This card was sent to each professor suggesting a date for sampling his class. He was to indicate his willingness (or not) to cooperate, sign, and return the card to the researcher.

Dear Mr. Johnson,

You may___ may not___ administer your questionnaire in my class.
_____ I would be able to cooperate at the time you have indicated.

_____ I would prefer that you attended my class at the time I have indicated. (Please give two different dates.)

	Course	Date	Hour	Building & Room #	Approximate # of Students
John Doe	Ethics 1C	Thursday	10 AM	207A	35
First Choice					
Second Choice					

Date _____   Signature _____

College & Department _____

Phone No. _____

APPENDIX C

Questionnaire and Sample Answer Sheet

ANSWER SHEET

USE NO. 2 PENCIL ONLY
ERASE MISTAKES COMPLETELY

BUREAU OF APPLIED SOCIAL RESEARCH   605 West 115th Street

Spring 1970

Dear Student,

This study will investigate some of the issues affecting American
college students. It is especially concerned with patterns of
drug use and changing values. The study is being conducted at
many colleges in the New York City area.

Your opinions and experiences will contribute greatly to a better
understanding of drug use and non-use, a subject of growing interest and controversy in our society. Student opinion, as provided
by the students themselves, is essential to any reconsideration of
drug policy to be made by officials in colleges and society.

Some of the questions deal with behavior that is considered private,
wrong, or even illegal. In order to encourage free response, the
study has taken several steps to ensure your complete anonymity.

1. You are requested not to put your name or other identification
    on either the questionnaire or the ANSWER SHEET.

2. All answers will be marked on an ANSWER SHEET. An optical
    scanning machine will convert your answers into punched cards.
    The data will be used only for statistical purposes.

3. You are asked to fill out the questionnaire voluntarily. You
    may choose not to participate and hand in a blank ANSWER SHEET.

4. In the final report, there will be no identification of the
    classes, individual teachers, administrators, or the institu-
    tions (colleges, organizations, etc.) which take part in this
    study.

It is hoped that you will enjoy filling out the questionnaire and
that the results will prove useful to college students.

Thank you for your cooperation.

Bruce Johnson
Lecturer
Barnard College

254

INSTRUCTIONS FOR COMPLETING THE QUESTIONNAIRE

Please answer all questions by marking the correct blank on the ANSWER SHEET.

In the questionnaire, the question number is always in the parentheses (#) on the Left side of the page. Each question has a set of codes which are always on the Right side of the page.

For each question, mark the ANSWER SHEET with the code (or codes) which you feel is most correct. Use a #2 pencil for marking answers. Please study the following examples before beginning.

        Questionnaire   ANSWER SHEET

Example A

(17) What year are you 1. Freshman
      in college: 2. Sophomore
                   3. Junior   **17** ██②③④⑤⑥⑦⑧⑨
      (Choose one)   4. Senior
           0.& 1. Graduate student (This indicates that the
                                     person is a graduate
                                     student)

Example B

(81) Which of these   0. NONE
      substances have   1. Cigarettes
      you ever used: 2. Alcohol
                  3. Methedrine   **81** ⓪①██④⑤██⑨
      (Mark all that   4. Other Amphetamines
      apply)   5. Barbiturates   (This indicates that the
                  6. Marijuana   person has used alcohol,
                  7. L.S.D.   methedrine, marijuana,
                  8. Cocaine   and cocaine)
                  9. Heroin

Please do not leave any questions blank. If you do not wish to answer a question, please mark an X through the question number on the ANSWER SHEET. Feel free to write any comments you might have on the back of the ANSWER SHEET.

Please begin to answer the questionnaire now!

(1) How much education do you
want to get:

(Choose one)

(2) How much education did your
father receive:

(Choose one)

0. Less than 8 grades
1. 8th grade completed
2. Some high school
3. High school graduate
4. Some job-related (vocational)
   training
5. Some college (1-2 years)
6. 2 years of college completed
   (but less than 4)
7. College graduate (B.A., B.S., etc.)
8. Master's Degree
9. Ph.D.
0.& 1. M.D. degree
0.& 2. Law degree

Indicate your opinion of
and exposure to each of the
following substances:

(3) Cigarettes

(4) Alcohol

(5) Methedrine, Desoxyn

(6) Other Amphetamines

(7) Barbiturates or Tranquilizers

(8) Marijuana or Hashish

(9) L.S.D. or other Hallucinogens

(10) Heroin or Cocaine

Opinions about the substance
(Mark all that apply)

0. No one should be allowed to use
   this substance
1. No one should be allowed to use
   this substance unless prescribed
   by a doctor
2. A person should be allowed to use
   this substance if he wishes
3. I would encourage my friends or
   family to use this substance

Exposure to the substance
(Mark all that apply)

4. I have never been offered this
   substance
5. I have been offered this substance, but have never used and
   don't intend to use it
6. I have been offered this substance, but never used it; I
   might like to use it now if an
   offer were made
7. I have been offered this substance,
   and used it the first or second
   time it was offered
8. I have used this substance, and
   might or will use it in the
   future
9. I have used this substance in
   the past, but have little
   interest in it now, and would
   refuse a free offer

----

(11) Which of these substances have you had prescribed for you by a physician or received during medical treatments:

(Mark all that apply)

(12) Which of these substances have you had prescribed for you by a physician, but you used in larger doses or more frequently than directed:

(Mark all that apply)

0. None of these (to my knowledge)
1. Methedrine, Desoxyn
2. Other Amphetamines (Benzedrine, Biphetamine, Dexamyl, Dexedrine, Preludin, etc.)
3. Barbiturates (Amytal, Chloral Hydrate, Doriden, Nembutal, Seconal, Tuinal, Veronal)
4. Tranquilizers (Compazine, Equanil, Librium, Mellaril, Meprospan, Miltown, Reserpine, Thorazine, Valium, etc.)
5. Cough Medicines with Codeine
6. Darvon
7. Opiates (Morphine, Dilaudid, Demerol, Methadone, Dolophine-"Dollies," Talwin, etc.)
8. Opium, Laudanum, or Paregoric
9. I may have had some of the above drugs prescribed for me, but I do not know what they were

----

Please indicate the greatest frequency (at any time) with which you have ever used each of the following substances:

(Do not include the use of medically prescribed drugs)

(13) Cigarettes

(14) Alcohol (beer, wine, hard liquor)
(Do not consider use with your parents or in religious rituals)

(15) Methedrine, Desoxyn

(16) Other Amphetamines (Pep pills, diet pills, "ups," Benzedrine, Biphetamine, Dexamyl, Dexedrine, Preludin, etc.)

(17) Barbiturates (Sleeping pills, "downs," "goofers," Amytal, Chloral Hydrate, Doriden, Nembutal, Paraldehyde, Phenobarbital, Seconal, Tuinal, Veronal, etc.)

(Choose one answer per substance)

0. I have never used this substance

1. Only once

2. 2 - 6 times

3. More than 6 times in my life, BUT less than 6 times per year

4. 6 times or more per year, to about monthly

5. 1 - 3 times per month

6. 1 - 2 times per week

7. 3 - 6 times per week

8. Once per day

9. More than once per day

257

(18) Tranquilizers (Compazine,
Equanil, Librium, Mellaril,
Meprospan, Miltown, Reserpine,
Stelazine, Thorazine, Valium,
etc.)

(19) Marijuana (Pot)

(20) Hashish

(21) L.S.D. or other Hallucinogens
(D.E.T., D.M.T., Mescaline,
Peyote, Psilocybin, S.T.P., etc.)

(22) Cocaine

(23) Heroin

(24) Opiates (Opium, Codeine, Demerol,
Dilaudid, Dolophine, Laudanum,
Methadone, Morphine, Paregoric,
Talwin)

(25) Other substances to get high
(glue, Carbona, Freon, banana
peels, morning glory seeds, etc.)

(Choose one answer per substance)

0. I have never used this substance

1. Only once

2. 2 - 6 times

3. More than 6 times in my life,
    BUT less than 6 times per year

4. 6 times or more per year, to
    about monthly

5. 1 - 3 times per month

6. 1 - 2 times per week

7. 3 - 6 times per week

8. Once per day

9. More than once per day

----

(26) Which of these substances have
you used with the specific
intention of getting "high":

(27) Which substances have you purchased from friends, acquaintances, or illegal drug sellers:

(28) Which substances have you sold
to other persons (or acted as
an intermediary):

(29) Which of these substances did
you use before graduation from
high school (not including
medical use):

(Mark all that apply)

0. None of these

1. Methedrine, Desoxyn

2. Other Amphetamines

3. Barbiturates or Tranquilizers

4. Marijuana or Hashish

5. L.S.D.

6. Mescaline or Peyote

7. Psilocybin, DMT, DET, STP

8. Cocaine

9. Heroin

----

(30) Did you ever:
       (Mark all that apply)

0. None of these
1. "Go steady" more than once while in high school
2. Participate in petting at age 16 or younger
3. Feel that other people or policemen would like to harass or intimidate you because of your beliefs
4. Try to or actually attend a rock or folk music festival like Woodstock or Newport Jazz Festivals
5. Drive a car before obtaining a driver's license, but had no licensed driver with you.
6. Drive faster than 80 m.p.h.
7. Participate in or attend a drag race
8. Take a car for a ride without the owner's permission
9. Know anyone who earned his living by burglary, theft, mugging, prostitution, forgery, pimping, or other criminal means, but not only selling drugs illegally

---

(31) In your family are you:
       (Choose one)

0. An adopted or foster child
1. An only child
2. First child (implies two or more children)
3. Second child
4. Third child   6. Fifth
5. Fourth   7. Sixth
                 8. Seventh
                 9. Eighth born or later

In what religion

(32) were you raised?

    (choose one)

(33) are you presently?

    (choose one)

0. None
1. Roman Catholic
2. Congregational
3. Episcopal
4. Presbyterian
5. Methodist
6. Lutheran
7. Baptist
8. Quaker, Unitarian
9. Any other Protestant church (A.M.E., Pentecostal Sects, etc.)
0.& 1. General Protestant (none of above preferred)
0.& 2. Greek or Russian Orthodox
0.& 3. Orthodox Jewish
0.& 4. Conservative Jewish
0.& 5. Reform Jewish
0.& 6. Jewish (one of the above preferred)
0.& 7. Oriental Religion (Hinduism, Buddhism, etc.)
0.& 8. Black Muslim
0.& 9. Other religious preference (please write the name of the religion on the back of the ANSWER SHEET)

How frequently did (do) you attend church or synagogue

0. Never
1. Hardly at all
2. Religious holidays only or 2 - 3 times per year

(34) your senior (or last) year in high school?

3. Occasionally (more than 3 times per year but less than once per month)

(Choose one)

4. Once per month

(35) at the present time?

5. More than once per month, but not weekly

(Choose one)

6. Once per week
7. More than once per week

----

(36) Approximately what is your family's income before taxes?

0. Under $3,000
1. $3,000 - $4,999
2. $5,000 - $6,999

(Please make as close a guess as possible if you don't know)

3. $7,000 - $8,499
4. $8,500 - $9,999
5. $10,000 - $12,499

(Choose one)

6. $12,500 - $14,999
7. $15,000 - $24,999

(If your father is dead or retired, how much was the family income in his last year of work?)

8. $25,000 - $34,999
9. $35,000 - $49,999
0.& 1. $50,000 and up
0.& 2. I really have absolutely no idea

----

(37) When you use or have used drugs illegally are (were) you alone or with someone else?

0. I have never used drugs illegally
1. Always take alone
2. Usually take alone
3. As likely to take with others as alone

(Choose one)

4. Usually take with others
5. Always take with others

----

(38) Are you:

(Choose one)

1. Not dating
2. Dating several persons
3. Dating one person
4. Going steady
5. Engaged
6. Married
7. Separated from spouse
8. Divorced
9. Widowed
0. Other

---

(39) While you were in high school, did you ever:

(Mark all that apply)

(40) While you were in high school, which of these things did you do <u>five</u> or more times:

(Mark all that apply)

0. None of these
1. Skip a whole day of school without any excuse from your parents or doctor
2. Intentionally try to give the teacher a bad time; "cut up" in class
3. Drive around with friends
4. Spend time around a local "hang out" (a store, drive-in, or the street)
5. Bought or sold liquor or cigarettes before reaching age 18
6. Attend a party where there were no adults present and where minors used alcohol
7. Take things of little value (less than $10) from stores, work, or school
8. Refuse to come home at hour set by your parents
9. Hold (or attend) parties where the parents were away and hadn't given their permission for a party to be held

---

(41) Did you ever:

(Mark all that apply)

0. None of these
1. Ask or beg money from strangers (panhandle)
2. Threaten or "beat up" other persons for any reason
3. Participate in gang fights
4. Run away from home or stay out all night without your parents knowing where you were (this applies only to the time when you were living with your parents)
5. Chalk or paint buildings or walls
6. Hang around pool halls or bars
7. Gamble for money (play cards, pitch pennies, shoot diec, etc., for money)
8. Take things of some value (more than $10) from stores, work, or school
9. Purposely destroy or damage property (break street lights or windows in school, damage or move traffic signs, break into buildings and/or mess them up)

At what age did you first do each of the following:

(Choose one age for each activity)

(42) Participate in any of the activities listed in the three previous questions (Questions 39 - 41)

(43) Use cigarettes

(44) Use alcohol (do not include drinking with parents or in religious rituals)

(45) Use Amphetamines, Barbiturates, or Tranquilizers (please include medical use of these drugs)

(46) Use Marijuana or Hashish

(47) Use L.S.D., or other Hallucinogens, or Heroin or Cocaine

(48) First arrested on a non-traffic charge

(49) Participated in premarital sexual intercourse

0.	Never did this
0.& 1.	6 years old and younger
0.& 2.	7 - 9 years old
0.& 3.	10 - 11 years old
0.& 4.	12
1.	13
2.	14
3.	15
4.	16
5.	17
6.	18
7.	19
8.	20
9.	21
0.& 5.	22
0.& 6.	23
0.& 7.	24
0.& 8.	25
0.& 9.	26 and older

----

(50) Which of these substances did you use before using marijuana: (Include medically prescribed use)

(51) Have you ever had problems trying to stop or reduce your use of any of these substances?

(Mark all that apply)

0. Never used pot OR none of these
1. Cigarettes
2. Alcohol
3. Methedrine, Desoxyn
4. Other Amphetamines
5. Barbiturates or Tranquilizers
6. Hashish
7. L.S.D. or other Hallucinogens
8. Cocaine
9. Heroin

To the best of your knowledge, which substance(s) do any of the following persons use: (Include medically prescribed use)

(52) Your parents (either one)

(53) Brother(s) and Sister(s)

(54) Close friends

(55) Friends and acquaintances (but not considered close friends)

(Mark all that apply)

0. This (these) person(s) do not use any of these substances
1. Cigarettes (uses weekly or more often)
2. Alcohol (uses weekly or more often)
3. Methedrine, Desoxyn
4. Other Amphetamines
5. Barbiturates or Tranquilizers
6. Marijuana or Hashish
7. L.S.D. or other Hallucinogens
8. Cocaine
9. Heroin

----

(56) What is your major in college, or what will it probably be?

(Choose one)

0. Business (Accounting, etc.)
1. Education (Elem. or Secondary)
2. English, Comparative Literature
3. Chemistry, Physics, Math, Biology, and other physical or natural sciences
4. Humanities (Philosophy, Religion, Art, Art History, Dramatics, Music, etc.)
5. Languages (Spanish, German, French, Latin, Linguistics)
6. Engineering
7. Sociology
8. Psychology, Social Psychology
9. Other Social Sciences (Economics, Political Science, History, Architecture, Urban Studies, Black Studies, etc.)
0.& 1. Other fields (Nursing, Pharmacy, etc.)
0.& 2. Completely undecided

----

(57) What year are you in college?

(Choose one)

1. First Semester Freshman
2. Second Semester Freshman
3. First Semester Sophomore
4. Second Semester Sophomore
5. First Semester Junior
6. Second Semester Junior
7. First Semester Senior
8. Second Semester Senior
9. Graduate student
0. Special status (non-matriculated, conditional status)
0.& 1. Just taking course for my interest
0.& 2. Other

----

(58) Where do you live while going to college?

(Choose one)

1. At home with my parents
2. At a University dormitory
3. At a University-approved group living quarters (fraternity, sorority, etc.)
4. In a room in someone else's home or apartment
5. In an apartment or home with my wife (husband) and children
6. Live alone in a room or off-campus apartment
7. Live in an apartment off-campus with a roommate
8. Live with relatives (not parents)
9. Other

----

(59) Which of these is true about your family:

(Mark all that apply)

0. None of these
1. My parents' marriage has been somewhat better than average
2. My father has lived separately from my mother for more than a month
3. I strongly disagree with my parents about some topics such as sex, drugs, politics, or religion
4. While I was a teenager, my father was at work most of the time; I saw little of him during the week
5. Every member of my family participated in important family decisions such as money, vacations, etc.
6. I feel more affection for my mother than for my father
7. My family has occasionally experienced severe financial difficulties
8. One or both of my parents expect me to do very well in school
9. When I came home from school as a teenager, my mother was frequently not at home because she worked or was involved in other activities (clubs, church, etc.)

----

(60) Mark all statements with which you agree:

0. I agree with none of the following statements
1. Marijuana should be legalized on the same basis as alcohol
2. Most drug users in college are among the more independent, thoughtful, and creative students
3. The regular use of marijuana might lead to the use of other drugs such as L.S.D., "Speed," Heroin, or Cocaine

Mark all statements
with which you agree:

4. Apart from the legal issues involved,
   it is wrong for a student to give or
   share his drugs with another student
5. The general public is too worried about
   the use of drugs among college students
6. The possession of Heroin and Cocaine
   should be controlled by strong laws
7. When a student finds evidence of illicit
   drug use on campus, he should report
   it to authorities
8. A person who uses illicit drugs should
   encourage non-users to try these drugs
9. A college administration should issue a
   clear statement of policy on the use
   of drugs on campus, including the
   disciplinary procedures (if any) for
   violations of the policy

----

(61) What is your race and sex;

(Choose one)

0. None of these
1. White, male
2. White, female
3. Black, male
4. Black, female
5. Oriental, male
6. Oriental, female
7. Other, male
8. Other, female

----

(62) Where did your parents
live when you were a
high school senior?

0. Foreign country
1. Manhattan
2. Brooklyn
3. Bronx
4. Queens
5. Staten Island or Long Island
6. Westchester County
7. New York State (north of
   Westchester County)
8. New England
9. New Jersey
0.& 1. Penn., Del., Maryland, Washington, D.C.
0.& 2. Midwest States (Ohio, W. Vir., Mich.,
   Ind., Ill., Wisc., Minn., Iowa,
   Mo., Kans., Nebr., S.D., N.D.)
0.& 3. Southern States (Vir., Ky., Tenn.,
   N.C., S.C., Ga., Fla., Ala., Miss.,
   Ark., La., Okla., Texas)
0.& 4. Western States (Mont., Wyo., Colo., N.M.,
   Ariz., Utah, Idaho, Wash., Ore., Nev.,
   Calif., Hawaii, Alaska)
0.& 5. Puerto Rico

265

(63) In what size community did your family live when you were a high school senior?

(Choose one)

0. Rural farm
1. Rural non-farm or small unincorporated village
2. Small town (under 10,000) not near large city
3. Small city (10,000 to 50,000) not near large city
4. Inside medium size city (50,000 to 250,000)
5. Suburb of medium size city
6. Inside large city (250,000 to 1 million)
7. Suburb of large city
8. Inside large metropolis (over 1 million)
9. Suburb of large metropolis

----

(64) What kind of high school did you graduate from?

1. Public high school
2. Parochial high school
3. Private day school
4. Private boarding school
5. High school equivalency (or never graduated from high school)
0. Other high school (foreign)

----

(65) What grade point average would you like to have when you finish college?

(Choose one)

(66) What is your cumulatige grade point average now? (Make best approximation)

(Choose one)

(Where straight A = 4.0, or an equivalent scholastic index)

1. A+ (3.75 and up)
2. A (3.50 - 3.74)
3. A- (3.35 - 3.49)
4. B+ (3.20 - 3.34)
5. B (3.00 - 3.19)
6. B- (2.75 - 2.99)
7. C+ (2.50 - 2.74)
8. C (2.00 - 2.49)
9. C- (Less than 2.00)
0. No grade point yet (or I don't care about grades)

----

(67) While you were in high school, in which of the following activities were you a member or did you participate?

(68) In which activities were you considered (or elected) a leader while in high school?

(69) While in college, in which activities did (do) you participate or were a member?

(70) In which of these activities were (are) you considered a leader in college?

(Mark all that apply)

0. None of these
1. An organized school team (Basketball, track, etc.)
2. Non-school sponsored athletic team
3. Play any sport casually about once per week (basketball, football, etc.)
4. School sponsored activities (Band, clubs, newspapers, etc.)
5. Organizations in the community (Scouts, political clubs, etc.)
6. Church or synagogue sponsored activities (fellowships, recreation centers)
7. Work at part-time job during the school year
8. Engage in volunteer work (summer work, tutoring, settlement house, etc.)
9. Participate in a social fraternity, sorority, or eating club

---

(71) Since beginning college, have you ever:

(Mark all that apply)

0. None of the following
1. Seriously considered dropping out of school
2. Taken incompletes in more than one course
3. Taken a leave of absence or dropped out of school
4. Cut classes frequently (25% of the time)
5. Transferred or tried to transfer schools
6. Changed choice of majors more than once
7. Been in trouble with college officials for breaking school rules
8. Had psychotherapy, psychoanalysis, or psychological counseling
9. Visited the school counseling service

For each of the following activities, (dating, petting, intercourse).please indicate the

A. Frequency
B. Number of persons with which involved

(If never involved in the activity, mark code 0 (zero))
(If ever involved in the activity, mark an answer in part A and B respectively - make two marks for the activity)

(MARRIED PERSONS): Before you were married, while single)

(72) Dating

(73) Petting

(74) Sexual Intercourse

---

0. I have never been involved in this

A. Greatest frequency of participation

1. 10 times or less
2. More than 10 times BUT less than once per week
3. 1 - 2 times per week
4. 3 or more times per week

B. Number of persons with which you were involved

5. Only one person
6. 2 - 3 persons
7. 4 - 10 persons
8. 11 - 25 persons
9. More than 25 persons

---

(75) Regardless of your use or non-use of pot, what are (or might be) the most important reasons for your using pot (or beginning marijuana use):

(Mark all that apply)

0. None of these
1. General curiosity
2. Feel good, get high
3. Relieve tension, sadness, depression
4. Aid in socialization or communication with others
5. Pot has no bad after effects like alcohol, no hangover, not addicting, etc.
6. The "in thing" to do
7. Improve my creativity or performance, to better understand people or my inner self
8. My friends offer or urge me to try it
9. To have a new and different experience

----

(76) What reasons do you have for NOT using pot OR why have you stopped or greatly reduced your use of pot:

(Mark all that apply)

0. I use pot; this doesn't apply to me
1. Risk of being caught for legal violation
2. No access to pot OR no good quality pot
3. Influence of parents
4. Influence of friends
5. Risk of possible physical and mental harm
6. No interest or curiosity about pot, or my curiosity about pot is satisfied
7. Pot doesn't (or might not) live up to some of its claims such as increasing sexual pleasure or creativity
8. Might lead to the use of other more dangerous drugs such as L.S.D., Cocaine, Heroin, Methedrine
9. Don't smoke tobacco, so difficult for me to use pot because it is usually smoked

----

(77) Have you ever:

(Mark all that apply)

0. None of these
1. Been held or arrested for political activities at school or elsewhere
2. Sat-in or demonstrated in an office or building
3. Participated in a demonstration where violence occurred
4. Participated (physically present) in a demonstration of any kind
5. Actively supported a demonstration (but not physically present) by any means (letters, money, etc.)

Have you ever:
6. Agreed with the goals and tactics
   of a demonstration, but did not
   actively support it
7. Agreed with the goals of a demonstration, but opposed the tactics
8. Opposed a demonstration in principle
   by disagreeing with its demands
9. Actively opposed a demonstration of
   any kind (by participating in a
   counter-demonstration, money to
   opposing parties, letters, etc.)

How many close friends did (do) you have

(78) when you were a senior (or last
     year) in high school:

     (Choose one)

(79) at the present time:

     (Choose one)

(80) How many of your present friends
     (in #79) are the same as the friends
     you had when a high school senior
     (in #78):

     (Choose one)

0. None
1. 1
2. 2
3. 3
4. 4
5. 5
6. 6 - 7
7. 8 - 10
8. 11-15
9. 16 or more

How recently and how often do (did)
you usually use each of the following substances:

(Choose one answer per substance)

(81) Cigarettes

(82) Alcohol (consider only use away
     from your parents)

(83) Amphetamines or Methedrine

(84) Barbiturates or Tranquilizers

(85) Cocaine or Heroin

(86) L.S.D. or other Hallucinogens

(87) Marijuana or Hashish

0. Never used this substance

The last time I used this substance
was before June 30, 1969. During
this time, I usually used the
substance:
1. Less often than monthly
2. 1 - 3 times per week
3. 1 - 6 times per week
4. Just about daily

I have used this drug since July 1,
1969 (to the present time). I
currently use the substance:
5. Less often than monthly
6. 1 - 3 times per month
7. 1 - 2 times per week
8. 3 - 6 times per week
9. Daily

269

(88) Have you ever:

(Do not include arrests or busts for political activity)

(Mark all that apply)

0. None of these

Been picked up, stopped (but not arrested) for

1. a traffic violation
2. a drug-related violation
3. some other violation (theft, shop-lifting, rape, forgery, etc.)

Been arrested for

4. a traffic violation (given a ticket, etc.)
5. a drug-related violation (possession sale, instruments, etc.)

Been convicted for

7. a drug-related misdemeanor or felony
8. some other misdemeanor or felony (not a drug or traffic violation)

9. Been committed to jail, reform school, drug treatment center, or other similar institution

----

(89) What kind of job has your father (or head of the household) usually held:

(Choose one)

(If he has only held short-term jobs, give his most recent job) (If your father is dead or retired, what job did he hold when actively employed)

(90) When you finish college, what kind of job would you like to have:

(Choose one)

1. Elementary or secondary school teacher or administrator
2. College teacher, researcher, or administrator
3. Self-employed professional (Architect, Artist, Author, Dentist, Doctor, Entertainer, Lawyer, Musician, Pharmacist
4. Employed Professional (Clergyman, Engineer, Government official or administrator, Librarian, Journalist, Judge, Pilot, Officer in Armed Forces, Researcher, Scientist, Social Worker)
5. Big Business (Banker; Business executive; Owner, Manager, or Supervisor of depart-ment store with 25 or more employees; Accountant; Computer Programmer
6. Small Business (Farm owner or operator; Owner, Manager, or supervisor of department or store with fewer than 25 employees; Insurance agent, Salesman, Undertaker)
7. Protective Services (Fireman, Guard, Mailman, Non-commissioned officer in Armed Forces, Nurse, Policeman, Detective)

(Responses continued on next page)

8. White Collar (Clerk in store of office;
Bookkeeper, Office worker, Secretary,
Typist)

9. Skilled Labor (Carpenter, Electrician,
Foreman, Machinist, Plasterer, Plumber
Printer, Union Official, Repairman,
Tailor, Bricklayer)

0. Semi-skilled labor (Bus driver, Clothes
presser, Garbage Collector, Grinder,
Filling station Attendant, Fisherman,
Longshoreman, Taxi driver, Truck driver,
toll collector)

0. & 1. Service Worker (Barber, Bartender, Cook,
Gardener, Janitor, Maid, Milk route man,
Servant, Shoe Shiner, Railway Conductor,
Waiter)

0. & 2. Any other occupation (Write the occupation
at the bottom of the Answer Sheet.)

----

(91) In what year were you born:

0.	1955 or more recently		
1.	1954	0. & 1.	1945
2.	1953	0. & 2.	1944
3.	1952	0. & 3.	1943
4.	1951	0. & 4.	1942
5.	1950	0. & 5.	1941
6.	1949	0. & 6.	1940
7.	1948	0. & 7.	1939-1930
8.	1947	0. & 8.	1929-1920
9.	1946	0. & 9.	1919 & earlier

----

(92) In what month were you
born:

1.	January	7.	July
2.	February	8.	August
3.	March	9.	September
4.	April	0.	October
5.	May	0. & 1.	November
6.	June	0. & 2.	December

----

(93) Did (or do) you ever:

(Mark all that apply)

0. None of these
1. Have a driver's license
2. Have your own car (not your parents')
3. Serve in the armed forces
4. Work at a job during the summer
5. Work more than 10 hours per week
   while going to college full-time
6. Live with a person of the opposite
   sex, for a week or more, but were
   not married or engaged to them
7. Work at full-time job (or jobs) for
   more than a year
8. Date at an early age (14 or younger)
9. Use hypodermic needle as a means of
   taking any drug (not including
   injections given for medical reasons)

----

(94) Indicate the birthplace   1. Italy
of your grandparents (or 2. Ireland
parents if they are   3. Central Europe (Austria, Czechoslovakia,
foreign born):   Hungary)
                          4. Western Europe (France, Belgium, Holland,
(Mark two or less)   Switzerland)
                        5. Northern Europe (Germany, Scandinavia)
                        6. Eastern Europe (Russia, Poland, Baltic
                             countries, Yugoslavia)
                        7. Great Britain, Canada, Australia, New
                             Zealand, South Africa
                        8. Mediterranean (Greece, Turkey, Israel
                             Lebanon, etc.),and Africa
                        9. Asia (China, India, Japan, etc.)
                        0. U.S.A. (3 or more grandparents born
                             in U.S.)
              0.& 1. Puerto Rico
              0.& 2. Spain, Latin America, Caribbean Islands
                          (other than Puerto Rico)

----

(95) Which two of these goals 1. Have a lot of money
do you consider to be   2. Have a secure job
most important in your   3. Have a good education
life: 4. Have a pleasant personality
                        5. Have a job that allows the pursuit of
(Mark two or less)   individual interests and self-expression
                        6. Have a successful family life
                        7. Make a large improvement in the life of
                           the community
                        8. None of these goals are worth while

----

(96) Do you consider yourself to be: 0. Don't know
                            1. Very conservative
(Choose one)   2. Moderately conservative
                            3. Moderate
                            4. Moderately liberal
                            5. Very liberal
                            6. Radical
                            7. Indifferent

----

(97) When you were a senior (or   0. None to my knowledge
last year) in high school,   1. Only one
about how many of your   2. Less than a quarter
friends had tried marijuana?   3. About half
                        4. More than half

(98) Among your present friends,   5. About 3/4
about how many have tried   6. Almost all
marijuana?   7. All

     (Choose one)

----

(99) Please indicate those statements with which you _agree_.

(Leave blank the statements with which you _disagree_ or are _not certain_

(Mark all that apply)

0. None of these
1. There's little use in writing to public officials because often they aren't interested in the problems of the average man.
2. Most people can still be depended on to come through in a pinch.
3. These days a person doesn't really know who he can count on.
4. It's hardly fair to bring children into the world with the way things look for the future.
5. Next to health, money is the most important thing in life.
6. In spite of what they say, the lot of the average man is getting worse.
7. Nowadays a person has to live for today and let tomorrow take care of itself.
8. Most of our social problems would be solved if we could somehow get rid of immoral, crooked, and feeble-minded people.

----

(100) Please indicate those statements with which you _agree_.

(Leave blank the statements with which you _disagree_ or are _not certain_

(Mark all that apply)

0. None of these
1. There are legitimate channels for reform which must be exhausted before attempting disruption.
2. U. S. involvement in Vietnam is morally wrong.
3. Real participatory democracy should be the basis for a new society.
4. In general, I would consider myself alienated from the society.
5. Although men are basically good, they have developed institutions which force them to act in opposition to this basic nature.
6. Disruption is preferable to dialogue for changing society.
7. You can't blame a person for wanting to commit suicide.
8. Emotional commitments to others are usually a prelude to disappointment.
9. Parents often expect too much of their children.

273

For each of the substances, indicate those effects which which you have experienced.

If you have never used the substance, indicate what effects you believe might occur from using the substance.

(101) Alcohol

(102) Amphetamines or Methedrine

(103) Barbiturates or Tranquilizers

(104) Heroin, Opium, Codeine, or Cocaine

(105) L.S.D. or other Hallucinogens

(106) Marijuana or Hashish

(Mark all that apply)

0. None of these

1. Excessive sleepiness, sluggishness

2. Distortion of vision or hearing

3. Inability to concentrate on studies

4. Prolonged nervousness or anxiety

5. Difficulty in controlling impulses

6. More creativity in school work or other activities
7. Better understanding of your or others' personality
8. More sociable, can relate better to others
9. Relaxation, reduction of tension

----

(107) Which substances do your parents know or think (even if they are wrong) you use:

(108) With which substance have you ever had a bad trip;

(109) Which substances have provided generally satisfying experiences:

(110) Which substances have provided really good and rewarding trips;

(Mark all that apply)

0. None of these OR never used these
1. Alcohol
2. Amphetamines or Methedrine
3. Barbiturates or Tranquilizers
4. Marijuana
5. Hashish
6. L.S.D.
7. Mescaline or Peyote
8. Cocaine
9. Heroin

(If other substances, not on the above list, would answer the question, please list these substances (and the question number) on the back of the ANSWER SHEET.)

At last, the questionnaire has come to an end. Please feel free to make any specific or general comments you might have on the back of the ANSWER SHEET.

THANK YOU VERY MUCH FOR YOUR TIME AND COOPERATION

One last request: Do you have a friend or friends who have used more than 6 times either L.S.D., or Methedrine, or Cocaine, or Heroin? If you have such friend(s), do you think they would complete this questionnaire? If so, please pick up a manila (brown) envelope when you leave. Then ask the friend to complete the questionnaire (just like you did now) and mail the ANSWER SHEET to the address which is indicated.

Index of Authors and Organizations

Subject Index

279